the ultimate first book guide

Editors: Leonie Flynn,
Daniel Hahn & Susan Reuben

For L.M.H. (because), for A.G.F. (no cheese here!) and for all the A.H.
boys who prove, day after day, that life with books can never be boring.
Leonie Flynn

For my parents, who started me reading, and whose fault this all is...
Daniel Hahn

To Benjamin, Isaac, Joshua, Molly, Sasha, Talia and Thomas –
this guide is for you.
Susan Reuben

First published 2008 by
A & C Black Publishers Ltd
38 Soho Square, London, W1D 3HB

www.acblack.com
www.ultimatebookguide.com

Text copyright © 2008 Leonie Flynn, Daniel Hahn and Susan Reuben
Introduction copyright © 2008 Julia Donaldson
Pages 309–315 constitute an extension of this copyright page

The rights of Leonie Flynn, Daniel Hahn and Susan Reuben to be identified
as the authors of this work have been asserted by them in accordance
with the Copyrights, Designs and Patents Act 1988.

ISBN 978-0-7136-7331-9

A CIP catalogue for this book is available from the British Library.

This book is produced using paper that is made from wood grown in
managed, sustainable forests. It is natural, renewable and recyclable.
The logging and manufacturing processes conform to the
environmental regulations of the country of origin.

Printed and bound in Singapore by Tien Wah Press (Pte) Ltd

Contents

INTRODUCTION
by Julia Donaldson

I have to confess to a horror of the 'I' word. Not 'I' as in 'me', but as in 'Important'. I hate being asked, as I often am, 'Is it Important to Read to Your Child?' (The capital letters are always there in the tone of the journalist's voice.) Yes, shared reading doubtless does confer all sorts of benefits but, as I hope most of you with this book in your hands will agree, that's not why we do it. We do it because we love it. Also, sometimes, because it's miraculously easy – take one parent, one child and one pile of books; result: total pleasure.

My own love affair with picture books started, at the age of two or three, with some endpapers. I'm sure I liked sitting on my mother's knee, too, and that I enjoyed the story about a duckling who went in search of rain, but I absolutely adored the book as an object, and in particular the endpapers, which had a diamond pattern with alternating pictures of jolly suns and slanting rainfall.

In those days (the early 50s) there probably weren't a lot of books specifically for sevens and under, and we moved quite quickly on to the gory Grimms and heartbreaking Hans Andersen. By the time I had children myself all that had changed, and my love affair could continue. I discovered what a huge variety of stories and styles there were, and how a picture book can be or do almost anything. One night we would be wiping a tear over the realistic Shirley Hughes story *Dogger*, about a little boy with a battered soft toy and a noble older sister; then we would be roaring with laughter over Arnold Lobel's wonderful **Frog and Toad** fables (not so good for bedtime, as my kids had hysterics every time Toad said 'Blah!'); another night we might agonise together over the questions posed by John Burningham's *Would you Rather...* (well, it *is* hard to decide if you'd rather eat spider stew or mashed worms, or if you'd rather an elephant drank your bathwater or a pig tried on your clothes). There were rhyming texts, quickly memorised; there were factual texts imparting fascinating knowledge about the planets or how wood is made into paper, and some books – like Raymond Briggs' *The Snowman* – had no text at all!

Two more decades have passed since then, and the array is even vaster. It can be quite perplexing to walk into a bookshop where there are vast stacks of a few 'three for two' titles, and scores of other titles of which there is only one copy, spine out, on the shelves. How do you decide? One way is to arm yourself with this book. The thoughtful and varied recommendations are made by people who know what's out there and have read countless books to countless children. The descriptions of the books are lively and tempting, and the selections for each age group are interspersed with lots of tips about choosing books, discussing books and reading books aloud. There's also an excellent section for children who are beginning to read themselves and making that transition from picture books to 'chapter books' – though of course that doesn't mean you should stop reading aloud to them. I still read Richmal Crompton's **William** stories to my sons who are in their twenties.

And don't worry – although the contributors are all experts, they are never earnest. Not once did I come across the dreaded 'I' word.

Julia Donaldson

Julia Donaldson

ABOUT THE EDITORS

LEONIE FLYNN is the librarian at a prep school in north London. She combines her work there with editing *The Ultimate Book Guide* (*UBG*) and writing, and sadly finds that there are not enough hours in the day for either of the above. Since the teen *UBG* she has managed to get married and also to find herself collecting cookery books – though there is apparently no correlation between the two.

Since completing *The Ultimate Teen Book Guide* with Leonie and Susan, **DANIEL HAHN** has spent a year and a half as editorial director of ICONS, a website commissioned by the Department for Culture, Media and Sport (a real job!); he has also translated a second Angolan novel and the autobiography of Brazilian footballer Pelé, co-edited a new reference book for Oxford University Press and written a history of north London's Roundhouse. He has continued to work regularly with Shakespeare's Globe and Human Rights Watch, and started making plans to write a new history book, but, umm… hasn't got very far with that just yet.

SUSAN REUBEN co-owns Baobab Editorial and Design Limited (www.baobabltd.com), a company that carries out freelance work for children's publishers. Her recent commissions have covered wizardry, the Bible, and tips for entering the financial sector. Her leisure activities have included clambering around a soft play area in pursuit of a small child and learning to make good chocolate cake. She has a husband called Anthony and a son called Isaac, both of whom are very nice, if a handful at times.

ABOUT THE CONSULTANTS

WENDY COOLING works as a consultant to a range of children's publishers. She was the creator of Bookstart, a national project which aims to encourage parents and carers to read to their children from a very early age and which provides three packs of books to all pre-school children. She has also been chair of the British Section of IBBY (International Board on Books for Young People). In 2006, Wendy was given the Eleanor Farjeon Award for distinguished service to the world of children's books.

LINDSEY FRASER was a children's bookseller in Cambridge before becoming executive director of Scottish Book Trust. She is now a partner in Fraser Ross Associates, an Edinburgh-based literary agency and consultancy. She and Kathryn Ross are also the national co-ordinators of Read Together (www.readtogether.co.uk), the Scottish Executive's initiative to encourage parents and carers to share books with their children.

NICOLA MORGAN is an award-winning children's author, writing mainly for (and about) teenagers. A former English teacher and then literacy / dyslexia specialist, she has also written best-selling home learning books for three-to-nine-year-olds, including Egmont's **I Can Learn** series, with her constant aim being to help parents help their children. She founded and runs The Child Literacy Centre (www.childliteracy.com), giving free advice to parents about all aspects of reading and writing development.

KATHRYN ROSS is a former English teacher, independent children's bookseller and deputy director of Scottish Book Trust. Since 2002, she has been a partner in Fraser Ross Associates, an Edinburgh-based literary agency and consultancy. She and Lindsey Fraser are also the national co-ordinators of Read Together (www.readtogether.co.uk), the Scottish Executive's initiative to encourage parents and carers to share books with their children.

0–2 years

Can there be anything more exciting than the arrival of a new baby? And along with the excitement comes worry, and a wish to do the very best possible for the new child. There's so much to think about at first, but do try to find time for reading, talking and singing, as these contribute so much to your child's growing view of the world. Books for babies today are more wonderful and varied than ever before. They offer pleasure to both baby and adult as they're shared, and very soon become an important part of family life. So check out some of the titles recommended in the following pages, and involve everyone in the book sharing – not just Mum and Dad, but grandparents, too, and of course older siblings, who love the grown-up feel of reading to a smaller child.

Don't see reading as quiet time – soon your baby will gurgle and point and try to join in with lifting flaps and turning pages. Later, as language develops, baby will try out the rhyming words at the end of pages, or the animal sounds in the story, and a favourite book will be demanded again and again and again… You may be fed up with it but your child won't be – there are

Special Features

so many new things for babies to take in that they will love and respond to something safe and known.

Be comfortable with early book sharing; try a mix of voices if you feel like it and remember that five minutes is sometimes enough for a baby. The time will grow as baby learns to listen and concentrate and to take some part in the experience.

Very young babies will try to turn pages – they're already learning how books work – and this, along with the growing ability to listen and talk, will be valuable later when it's time for school. Learning to read is important eventually, but not for your baby! For now, relax and have fun with books to touch and feel, books full of noises and animal sounds; these can give your child a love of books that will last for ever. The early years pass by all too quickly: enjoy them as you share the wonder of stories, pictures and rhymes with your baby.

Wendy Cooling

AMAZING BABY series

This award-winning series reflects how babies learn and develop in their first two years – from starting to focus on individual objects to imitating sounds and actions and enjoying picture books. If that makes them sound too 'educational', one look at these bright, attractive and robust board, activity and bath books, with their jolly photos of babies, mirrors and foil, textures and shapes, will banish all thoughts of worthiness. The rhyming texts, eye-catching images and novelties have great baby appeal and will intrigue the adults who share them, too.

Kathryn Ross

* * * * * * *

BABIES Ros Asquith

This first book for babies is just as good for those toddlers who like to shout 'baby!' at every child they see. As the book says, there are big babies and little babies, and all the others in between, including the 'I'll-show-you-who's-boss' baby and the 'Oh-no-not-the-honey!' baby. And, of course, the very best baby appears in a mirror, on the last page.

   A lovely, warm book, full of teddies and tickles, and perfect for sharing with a cuddle, it will remind you of all the wonderful things babies do. It's also great for restoring a sense of sanity in an overwrought parent!

Yzanne Mackay

Board Books

Elmer's Colours by David McKee
Baby Touch Playbook (*UFBG* 12)
Bear in a Square by Stella Blackstone (*UFBG* 13)
Boo Barney by Alex Ayliffe (*UFBG* 15)
Five in the Bed, **DK Baby Fun** series (*UFBG* 26)
Head, Shoulders, Knees and Toes by Annie Kubler (*UFBG* 32)
Maisy's Favourite Clothes by Lucy Cousins
What's at the Zoo, Miffy? by Dick Bruna
Number One, Tickle Your Tum by John Prater (*UFBG* 43)

BABY EINSTEIN series

Baby Einstein books are just one part of the **Baby Einstein** empire, which includes DVDs and CDs and a book for interested adults reminding us that Great Minds Start Little. Galileo, Wordsworth, Da Vinci and Mozart are all drafted in to enforce the truth of the motto upon the reader. As the babies and toddlers enjoy the brightly coloured pictures and features such as mirrors and lift-up flaps, adults are given prompts about how to maximise the educational potential. Whether they promote genius or not is debatable but, either way, the books are portable, durable and fun to share.

Antonia Honeywell

■ Among the many **Baby Einstein** titles available are *Colours*; *Shapes*; *See and Spy Counting*; *Neighbourhood Animals*; *Wild Animals*; and *Wheels, Wings and Moving Things*.

* * * * * * *

BABY FACES Sandra Lousada

Baby Faces is a book for the very young, with its focus clearly on babies and early language. 'Is it a book or is it a toy?' you may ask, and the answer is that it really doesn't matter, as what it does is associate reading, the voice of someone who loves you, with pleasure and fun. The tough, circular pages are securely joined by a braid, which also holds a rattle. Sandra Lousada's stunning black and white photographs – there's a baby on every right-hand page – are a joy to look at, for of course babies like nothing more than seeing other babies. The short text – just 13 words in total – works perfectly, and the whole is a brilliant first book that is quite at home in the toy box.

Wendy Cooling

■ Look out for other books by the same author, such as the **I Love Baby** series, including *Noisy Baby*; *Happy Baby*; *Bath Baby*; *This Little Baby* (the mirror at the end makes every baby giggle!) and *My Nose, My Toes*.

BABY GOES Verna Wilkins, illustrated by Derek Brazell

This book of opposites for the very young features babies of various ethnic origins, all beautifully illustrated in bold colours. The rhyming text is one to read again and again, and will ease tiny children into the world of language, and black and white vignettes on every spread support the main, full-colour picture. There's plenty to chat about as you share this book, packed as it is with the normal events of a baby's day.

Wendy Cooling

■ This is one of a series of four small board books that really do reflect the early lives of all our babies. Look out for *Baby Noises*; *Baby Plays* and *Baby Finds*, too.

* * * * * * *

THE BABY'S CATALOGUE
Allan Ahlberg, illustrated by Janet Ahlberg

A favourite to give as a present to new parents, this is a catalogue of six babies, and the people, objects and activities that make up their daily routine. There's no story, but the cosy, comic-book inspired pictures, grouped under such headings as Mums and Dads, Dinners, Bedtimes and even Accidents (nothing serious!), provide an absorbing source of familiar things to point at, discuss and laugh about. A simple idea, executed with peerless humour, warmth and quirky observation.

Kathryn Ross

* * * * * * *

BABY TOUCH PLAYBOOK

This large board book offers hours of fun to one- and two-year-olds. It's packed with bright pictures, intriguing textures, good words – and, yes, a bit of learning, too. Early concepts are introduced in a very relaxed way – I particularly love a page inviting children to feel the rainbow. The language will really help children to know the wonder of words as they move from the fast 'Brrrm! Brrrm!' of the car to the snail creeping 'Slowly, slowly, very slowly' through the garden. There are shapes to touch and explore, and introductions to rhymes and games, animals and more in this friendly, interactive book.

Wendy Cooling

BEAR IN A SQUARE Stella Blackstone

Bear in a Square teaches about shapes in a friendly, storybook way. Each double-page spread focuses on a different shape, with some of the more unusual ones included, such as hearts, zigzags and ovals. As Bear (who is rather dignified, yet charming) takes us through the story, the reader is asked to spot the shapes in each richly coloured scene. The book also acts as a counting exercise from one to ten, with one square to find, then two hearts, three circles and so on. It's ideal for children who know the basic shapes and are ready for something a bit more challenging.

Susan Reuben

■ This is one of a series of books about Bear, which are available in both paperback and board book format. Look out for *Bear About Town*; *Bear on a Bike*; *Bear at Home*; *Bear's Busy Family* and *Bear in Sunshine*.

* * * * * * *

THE BIG BOOK OF BEAUTIFUL BABIES
David Ellwand

Babies fill the pages of this book of black and white photographs, and they really do live up to the title. The good, rhyming text is based on simple opposites and teaches something about feelings and faces. Sometimes people are upset by the idea of a 'bad baby', but the photograph chosen to represent this reflects happiness – and mess – and the word is introduced with a very light touch.

Ideal for the very young – research has shown that babies are able to focus on black and white before they can focus on colours – this is a book to be enjoyed by babies and adults alike.

Wendy Cooling

Talk to Your Baby

It's never too soon to start talking to your new baby,
as **Liz Attenborough** explains.

Talking and listening to babies from the moment they are born helps them develop good language and communication skills, which in turn enables them to listen and express themselves. It also helps them to learn and to develop good relationships.

Most brain development occurs from birth to the age of two, so babies and toddlers need stimulation as much as they need nourishing food. The best way to stimulate babies' brains is to talk to them, listen to them, sing to them, play with them and share books together.

People don't talk to their babies enough these days. Talk to Your Baby (www.talktoyourbaby.org.uk), the early language campaign of the National Literacy Trust, was established to encourage parents and carers to talk more to children aged 0–3. It was started in response to growing concerns from head teachers that too many children are starting school ill equipped in basic communication skills, and are therefore disadvantaged in the classroom. The ability to communicate forms the basis of learning, and is also vital for social and emotional development.

Babies love to communicate. They are born to be sociable, but they can't do that on their own. They need an adult to be sociable with them, to look at them and speak gently to them, touching them and responding to their sounds. Babies need to be able to gurgle and babble back – a dummy should be kept just for sleeping.

A language-rich home helps a child develop in many ways. Talking to babies helps them learn to listen, and gives them the chance to respond and be listened to. Over time, their coos, babbles and smiles will move on to first words and sentences, as they learn to control and use their tongue, soft palate, lips and voice. Interaction helps this natural process along.

Storytelling and reading books aloud are easy ways to have regular, valuable talking time. Storytelling introduces structure and language patterns that help form the building blocks for reading and writing skills. Reading aloud combines the benefits of talking, listening and storytelling within a single activity, and gets parents and carers talking regularly to young children.

Singing, too, helps develop language skills, as it is often easier to string words together when they are part of a tune or a rhyme. Watching television with your baby occasionally is fine, as it gives you the opportunity to talk about it while watching. But the television should always be turned off if no one is watching, as it is a distraction to your baby and might get in the way of communication.

Communication is the basis of your relationship with each other, and will help the two of you form a close bond. Talk to your baby whenever you can – it really will make a difference. ●

BING BUNNY series
Ted Dewan

Bing – a button-bright bunny with attitude – is the engaging star of a stylishly retro series of little hardbacks all about the everyday challenges of being a toddler. From getting dressed to playing, eating and going to bed, Bing tackles the familiar rituals with great aplomb,

calmly assisted by his soft toy, Flop. The easy-going, conversational text encourages each success, and when things go wrong – damp dungarees or a tomato-induced temper tantrum – it's 'no big thing'. Excellent for gently reinforcing new accomplishments, and done with humour and style. It's a Bing thing!

Kathryn Ross

■ Bing Bunny also appears in *Go Picnic*; *Get Dressed*; *Paint Day*; *Make Music*; *Bed Time* and *Something for Daddy*.

* * * * * * *

BOO BARNEY
Alex Ayliffe

A big, well-designed board book that celebrates all the things Barney the toddler can do, and encourages your baby to show off his / her emerging skills as he / she listens and looks. There's real movement in the pictures that makes it impossible not to turn the pages, and the rhyming text works for readers and listeners alike. Barney fills every bit of space as he demonstrates that he can crawl, throw his ball and do noisy things like bash a saucepan lid and stomp in a puddle.

There are pages to initiate a game of 'peepo', as well as a very positive image of sharing books; in fact, real life with all its excitement and warmth is to be found in this book.

Wendy Cooling

■ Look out for the other three titles in the series: *Yum Yum Molly*; *Tickle Tickle Tom* and *Ruby Loves*.

BROWN BEAR, BROWN BEAR, WHAT DO YOU SEE?

Bill Martin Jr, illustrated by Eric Carle

In this treasured favourite about colour, Brown Bear is the first in a succession of animals to answer the repeated question of the title. Readers, too, are invited to look and guess which creature is coming next as, one by one, a menagerie parades across the pages, from familiar Brown Bear and Green Frog to startling Blue Horse and Purple Cat. Pattern, rhyme, rhythm and repetition entrance both eye and ear, inspiring a singsong response. In this, his first book, Carle plays with the possibilities of illustrating with collage – juxtaposing textures, colour and strong visual patterning to bring his cast to lustrous life.

Green Frog,
Green Frog,
What do you see?

I see a purple cat looking at me.

Elizabeth Hammill

* * * * * * *

BUGGY BUDDIES series

Ever played the 'buggy game'? You know the one. A toddler forcibly ejects the contents of the buggy, confident that you'll pick it all up and return it... only to have those same items relaunched into the surrounding car park / supermarket / doctor's surgery with ever-increasing whoops of delight and velocity. Whoever devised the basic premise of **Buggy Buddies** knows it well. A bright, appealing board book is attached to a plastic strap, so that even when thrown with the force of a future cricketer for England, the book will bounce right back. Some have interactive content, such as a rattle, 'touch and feel' pages or buttons to push that make sounds; others are simply brightly coloured books with simple, baby-friendly illustrations. **Buggy Buddies** are both a technological triumph and a sanity saver.

Lindsey Fraser

CAN YOU CHOO CHOO TOO?
David Wojtowycz

Do not take this book to a quiet restaurant. It's LOUD! Exploding with sound and colour from the first page, you'll find police cars dashing, planes zippety-zooming, buses beeping and rockets blasting. Meanwhile, the words and in-your-face illustrations encourage you to shout out the noises – *nee-nar! choo-choo! whoosh fizz!*

It does rhyme if you read it in order, but your child is more likely to flick backwards and forwards, enjoying the revelation that it's not just plastic toys that produce noisy sounds. And, of course, it won't ever run out of batteries…

Yzanne Mackay

■ There is a sequel, *Can You Moo Too?* (likewise unsuitable for restaurants).

* * * * * * *

CHIMP AND ZEE
Laurence Anholt, illustrated by Catherine Anholt

These bold, bright, beautiful picture books have all the makings of modern classics.

With a refrain of 'Ha ha ha, Hee hee hee' that even a young toddler can imitate, twins Chimp and Zee monkey their way around Jungletown and its surroundings, getting into no end of trouble.

The large format of the storybooks and their primary colours are reminiscent of *Babar*, and the series is imbued with a joyful energy that transfers itself to the reader, making this a bouncy daytime read.

Susan Reuben

■ Picture book titles include *Chimp and Zee and the Big Storm*; *Happy Birthday, Chimp and Zee*; *Monkey About with Chimp and Zee* and *Chimp and Zee's Noisy Book*. Board books dealing with early concepts are also available.

17

CHOCOLATE MOOSE FOR GREEDY GOOSE
Julia Donaldson, illustrated by Nick Sharratt

An engaging, beautiful picture book that is simply a romp of a read. Donaldson's funny, rhyming text is very short and combines well with Sharratt's wild and hilarious illustrations. The characters fill the pages and are easy to focus on, and the text really will help children develop an ear for language. This book is certainly not about good manners, although some animals do try to be civilising!

The message here, for those of 18 months and over, is that reading is fun – enjoy this today and there will be more tomorrow.
Wendy Cooling

* * * * * * *

CLACKETY-CLACKS series
Luana Rinaldo

These curvy, friendly books are great for even the smallest baby. The thick, foam-filled pages are hinged in such a way that the book can be shaken so they clack softly together. The cover is entirely taken up with a smiley picture of the creature in question – bee, fish, ladybird or butterfly – and inside is a simple story with vividly coloured pictures.

These books can be sucked, chewed, banged and shaken, and there's even a special finger hole to hold them with as you go 'clackety-clack'!
Susan Reuben

COCK-A-MOO-MOO
Juliet Dallas Conte

Cockerel has forgotten how to crow. 'Cock-a-moo-moo!' he tries. 'Cock-a-quack-quack!' and so on, through the toddler's much-loved repertoire of farmyard noises.

Young children find this hilarious. They know just how it feels to get words wrong, and love messing around with language (expect renditions of 'Cock-a-oink-oink!' for hours afterwards…).

In the end, of course, cockerel remembers the right sound, after saving the farmyard from disaster and showing that he isn't quite so silly after all.

Yzanne Mackay

* * * * * * *

COME ON, DAISY
Jane Simmons

Daisy the baby duckling may be cute, but she's always getting into bother. Especially when there are so many exciting new things to discover on her walk with Mama duck. 'Come on, Daisy' is Mama's constant cry, as Daisy chases dragonflies, plays with frogs, spies on fishes and bounces on the lily pads. But then Daisy realises she's all alone and that 'something big' is rustling in the reeds, getting closer and closer all the time…

Bright, bold brushstrokes bring Daisy to life in a deceptively simple yet ultimately reassuring story, which is great to read aloud. Simmons' skilful use of page space and jewel-like colours create real atmosphere.

Eileen Armstrong

■ **Daisy** books are available in a wide range of formats including board books, mini books and a stunning carousel book that opens up into five scenes showing Daisy and Pip's day (*Goodnight Daisy, Goodnight Pip*). Picture book titles include: *Daisy and the Beastie*; *Daisy and the Egg*; *Daisy and the Moon*; *Daisy to the Rescue* and *Go to Sleep, Daisy*.

Everybody's Favourite...

DEAR ZOO Rod Campbell

Dear Zoo really has stood the test of time and become a classic. It sits alongside *Where's Spot?* (*UFBG* 63) as a perfect lift-the-flap book that children will enjoy from age one well into school.

The story is about writing to the zoo to send for a pet, but the animals that arrive are too big, too tall, too fierce... until the final page when the perfect pet arrives and there's no more sending back to be done. Campbell's design and illustration work like a dream, and all adults must be prepared to read the book again, and again, and again!

The popularity of *Dear Zoo* has never waned; it is now not only available as a board book and a picture book, but it is published in 17 dual-language editions from Arabic to Vietnamese.

Wendy Cooling

Rod Campbell knows just how to invite the youngest listeners to participate in the telling of a story and how to delight them with a simple, repetitive tale that is both a guessing and a predicting game.

'I wrote to the zoo to send me a pet...'

The zoo's responses arrive in packing cases made of flaps shaped like crates, a basket, and boxes for the reader to open to discover what animal is inside. Some are unsuitable: an elephant – 'too big'; a giraffe – 'too tall'; a lion – 'too fierce'; but one is 'perfect'.

And *Dear Zoo* is perfectly irresistible!

Elizabeth Hammill

DIG DIG DIGGING
Margaret Mayo, illustrated by Alex Ayliffe

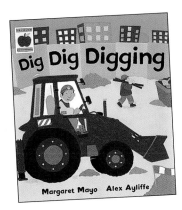

Got a child who loves trucks, diggers and lorries? Can't think of the right words for all the different types? Then this is the book for you! It's got cranes, rubbish trucks, dump trucks, car transporters, road rollers – the works.

Appealing to a child's mechanical side, each page has a wealth of real, active detail – hard hats, site visits, bins and pipes – and should add a new dimension to playing with trucks at home.

A good, fast rhythm and interesting typeface help keep the adult reader's attention. Whether your child will stop *vroom-vrooming* when the machines do is another matter!

Yzanne Mackay

* * * * * * *

DINOSAUR ROAR!
Henrietta Stickland, illustrated by Paul Stickland

Dinosaurs bold and wondrous thunder through the pages of this book, and never fail to captivate very young children. On one level, it's a word book, but it also introduces the concept of opposites, and uses rhyme and rhythm so powerfully that it really does help children into reading. The simple text is so memorable that soon children will be joining in and pretending to read the book themselves. Only when I watched children with it did I realise that it is also a counting book, as, of course, the dinosaurs simply must be counted. A book for all children, it's absolutely packed with child appeal.

Wendy Cooling

> ## Machines and Vehicles for the Very Young
> *Trucks* by Fiona Watt (*UFBG* 55)
>
> *Can You Choo Choo Too?* by David Wojtowycz (*UFBG* 17)
>
> *Tough Machines*, **DK Snapshots** series
>
> *Trucks*, **Lift and Look** series
>
> *Diggers and Dumpers*, **Snapshot Shaped Board Books** series
>
> *Giant Earthmovers*, **Big Stuff** series

Sharing Books Right From the Start

When should I start sharing books with my baby? Start now! says **Wendy Cooling**.

It's never too early to share books; some even believe that reading aloud before birth helps the development of a calm personality and a sense of rhythm. Sharing books after birth is seldom a quiet activity, as babies will gurgle and join in with the reading well before they begin to talk, responding to the voice of the adult who loves them rather than to the content of the book.

As language develops, children will ask questions, interrupt and become serious partners in the sharing. Rhythmic language, rhyme and onomatopoeic words that you can almost taste speak to babies, and help them develop an ear for language that will lead them into reading as they get older. Most importantly, this early sharing is safe – adults often wonder about the frightening nature of some stories, but this is cancelled out by the presence of the adult sharing the adventure, journey or danger with them.

Parents and carers are the first teachers and, as they encourage feeding, walking and talking, so they encourage reading – reading as shared pleasure, of course, not pressurising children to learn to read too soon. Some adults worry about reading aloud, and even feel a bit silly trying to do the different voices in a story. But children love the voices of those who love them and are not critical; they enjoy the shared time, the warmth, the sound of the words and the details of the pictures.

The messages to the very young are that books are wonderful and reading together is fun; children receiving these messages will start school loving books and wanting to read.

The hardest thing is to find the book that will really speak to your child and become the start of his / her reading history. There are classic picture books such as *The Very Hungry Caterpillar* (*UFBG* 59); *Each Peach Pear Plum* (*UFBG* 25); *Where's Spot?* (*UFBG* 63); *Where the Wild Things Are* (*UFBG* 62) and *We're Going on a Bear Hunt* (*UFBG* 189) that every child will enjoy. There are many more, of course: books that librarians, teachers and booksellers will be happy to introduce to you.

In my family, *The Elephant and the Bad Baby* (*UFBG* 96) remains a great favourite and I simply can't count the number of times I read it to a small niece. She's now grown up and has never forgotten it, and recently asked me to read it to her when she was quite ill and in need of a little pampering. Just as we revert to boiled eggs and soldiers of toast, we go back to the comforting books that were a solid part of childhood and, of course, then we introduce them to the next generation of children. The other favourite was *Witches*, a now out-of-print book, by Colin and Jacqui Hawkins – a wonderful but quite complicated book about witches with a text far too difficult for a very young child. My niece especially loved the pages about a witch's underwear, and I would read a very edited version of the text to her. Then she began to read for herself and all was discovered – how could I have done this to her? Once stories are familiar, we simply can't skip a word, as texts will be memorised and children will begin to join in and feel that they are reading themselves. Favourite books, even if not adult choices, do have to be read again and again, and we must grin and bear it! Remembering that witch's underwear reminds me that things don't change – today's very young children love to share *Pants* (*UFBG* 153) by Giles Andreae and Nick Sharratt with anyone who will read it. It's not a naughty book, but children think it is – read it together and have fun! ●

DOING THE ANIMAL BOP
Jan Ormerod, illustrated by Lindsey Gardiner

If you want a loud and lively read, this is the book for you. There are waddling ducks, stomping elephants, ostriches that 'flim-flam flutter', monkeys that jive and jiggle, jump and wiggle, and a whole lot more. The strong, rhythmic text is perfect for making children (and, for that matter, adults) join in. You'll soon be stomping, jiving and wiggling, too. Great fun.

Daniel Hahn

* * * * * * *

DON'T PUT YOUR FINGER IN THE JELLY, NELLY! Nick Sharratt

'Don't put your finger in the jelly, Nelly... or in the pie, Guy!' This funny little story makes everyone laugh out loud. Dare you put your finger in the holes full of jelly, meringue, cheese and – urghh! – spaghetti?

Each turn of the page reveals exactly why you *shouldn't*... there are jellyphants lurking in the jelly, and choctopuses just waiting to pull you into the milkshake.

With unnervingly accurate illustrations (the spaghetti looks good enough to eat), hilarious puns and rhymes, and a happy, yummy ending, this book shows how much fun messing around with words can be.

Yzanne Mackay

Counting Books

Olivia Counts by Ian Falconer

One Duck Stuck by Phyllis Root (**UFBG** 43)

One Little Home by Dubravka Kolanovic (**UFBG** 44)

Ten Wriggly Wiggly Caterpillars by Debbie Tarbett (**UFBG** 53)

Baby Galileo Sees the Stars, **Baby Einstein** series

One Child, One Seed by Kathryn Cave

Cockatoos by Quentin Blake (**UFBG** 83)

One More Sheep by Mij Kelly (**UFBG** 150)

Everybody's Favourite...

EACH PEACH PEAR PLUM
Allan Ahlberg, illustrated by Janet Ahlberg

As satisfying to read aloud as it is to listen to, *Each Peach Pear Plum* has been delighting parents and children since 1978, and there are any number of otherwise unsentimental 20-somethings out there who, at the mere mention of the title, can recite the text perfectly, word for word. The 'I spy' game encourages close observation, and the humorous and richly detailed illustrations challenge the reader to spot the character who's the subject of the next rhyme. It's the perfect way to introduce babies to nursery rhymes, and a wonderful way to rediscover them with older children.

Kathryn Ross

As simple, as perfect, as appealing as a round, ripe plum, this classic book engages and enchants. A rhyming couplet on each page introduces a nursery character, following an 'I spy' pattern:

'Each Peach Pear Plum
I spy Tom Thumb
Tom Thumb in the cupboard
I spy Mother Hubbard'

We follow them into the cellar, up the stairs and over the woods of a sunny country landscape. Each new character picks up the thread of a humorous and beautifully paced tale, with words, story and chant fusing together to perfection.

And once you've memorised it, it's ideal for reciting on long car journeys.

Yzanne Mackay

ELMER see p.97.

★ ★ ★ ★ ★ ★ ★

FASTER, FASTER! NICE AND SLOW!
Nick Sharratt and Sue Heap

Nick Sharratt and Sue Heap have produced a number of concept books for a young audience (see also *UFBG* 49); this one is about 'opposites'.

The text is narrated in direct speech by a girl and a boy called Sue and Nick, a neat little meta-fictive joke. Their voices and cheerful appearances in every picture close the psychological space between page and viewer.

The illustrations – nothing short of exhilarating – have sensuous appeal, in a clear-line style with rich, hot colouring, and a razzle-dazzle of impetuous patterning.

Jane Doonan

★ ★ ★ ★ ★ ★ ★

FIVE IN THE BED

This is one of the books in the **Baby Fun** series, which are large and tough and will survive well in the spills of any toy box. I love the animals that feature in this delicious photographic version of the well-known counting rhyme – one that delights every new generation of babies, and one that they want to play out with their own toys. Be prepared for lots of bedtime noise and fun as you share this book! It reminds us how hard it is to beat those rhymes from our own childhoods.

Wendy Cooling

■ You will also enjoy other books in the **Baby Fun** series: *Twinkle, Twinkle Little Star*, *Old MacDonald Had a Farm* and *One Little Duck*.

FRIENDS / DRESSING / PLAYING / WORKING
Helen Oxenbury

Now over 20 years old, these small, wordless board books are still the best to be had. Helen Oxenbury's babies are warm and funny and hugely real, reflecting careful observation and love. The daily life of tiny children is at the heart of the books, and we see them surrounded by familiar objects. As they look at each page, babies will recognise themselves and the things they do.

No words, so it's up to the adult to talk to the baby as the pictures are shared and, simple as the books look, there is plenty to talk about. Talking is as beneficial as reading with the very young, and here we're given permission to chat about the most normal things.

Wendy Cooling

■ Move on to Helen Oxenbury's *Big Baby Book*, where the same babies explore the world and begin to learn about the senses and about themselves. There's lots to talk about and join in with – most popular seems to be the spread that invites babies to show off their achievements – crawling, jumping, waving and so on. Sharing this book will involve lots of noise and fun!

* * * * * * *

A GOODNIGHT KIND OF FEELING
Tony Bradman, illustrated by Georgie Birkett

A warm father / son relationship shines through the pages of this picture book. The story is a joyful one as it tells of a shared day out and describes the wonderful feelings that come with simply being together. Bradman uses rich language and introduces fine-sounding words that small children will soon be trying to get their tongues round, and he ties them together with strong rhymes and rhythm. Birkett's exuberant illustrations add to the excitement of the day, and they become softer as the story moves towards its end and a 'goodnight kind of feeling'.

Wendy Cooling

Everybody's Favourite...

GOODNIGHT MOON
Margaret Wise Brown, illustrated by Clement Hurd

A classic first picture book, which works brilliantly with very small children. Deceptively child-like illustrations are restricted to a few paint-box colours. The rhyming text is both simple and wonderfully clever. A baby rabbit is in bed in his room at night, drifting off to sleep, while an old rabbit sits knitting in a rocking chair. We see the different objects in the room in turn, and then again as the little rabbit bids goodnight to each one, ending with 'Goodnight stars, goodnight air, goodnight noises everywhere'. A perfect bedtime book, the words and their repetition form a soothing chant to send the listener to sleep.

Patricia Elliott

This is the ideal book to end a night-time 'winding-down' session. At first sight it looks rather odd, with an old-fashioned feel to the illustrations. But as you read it through, it reveals its secrets.

A little rabbit wishes goodnight to various objects, all appealing to children, who can fixate on one and follow it through each frame.

As the rabbit drifts off to sleep, objects come into the foreground and shrink back, while colours heighten and diminish, mimicking his drowsy perceptions. Relieved by grey and white pages, fluorescence intensifies the effect. The story ends with a dark room, low lights and a sleeping bunny.

Read it with a glass of hot milk.

Yzanne Mackay

HANDA'S SURPRISE
Eileen Browne

Handa is on her way to visit her friend Akeyo in the next village, in southwest Kenya. On her head she carries a basket with seven fruits (a banana, a pineapple, an avocado...) as a surprise for her friend. But in a delightful visual joke, as the text refers to each type of fruit in turn, the pictures show it being pinched from the basket by an elephant, an ostrich, a parrot... Children will love the running gag, and the surprise that awaits Handa (and them) at the end of her journey.

Daniel Hahn

* * * * * * *

HAPPY DOG SAD DOG / WHOSE TAIL?
Sam Lloyd

The dramatic shapes and colours of Sam Lloyd's illustrations in these board books really appeal to tiny children. *Happy Dog Sad Dog* is a book of opposites – it contains very few words but lots of humour. It's amazing to watch one-year-olds look at this book and giggle as they come to the 'dirty dog', and to watch them wonder at the final page, where there are no dogs at all.

Another of those simple books that isn't quite as simple as it seems, *Whose Tail?* contains an appealing guessing game, where children are shown a fraction of a tail and invited to guess which animal it belongs to, before they turn over the page.

Wendy Cooling

Nursery Rhymes

Why do nursery rhymes matter? And which collection should you choose? Author-illustrator **Ian Beck** offers some advice.

Nursery rhymes and lullabies are our primary poetry. They are part of a long oral tradition, passed on from parent to baby, and a vital ingredient of all our infancies. We first hear them from our parents or our grandparents, or from nursery teachers, and we absorb them at, or better still on, their knee or lap. Remember the gentle soothing of a lullaby as you were rocked to sleep, or those fingers striding around your baby palm followed by the delicious and endlessly repeatable surprise of 'tickle you under there'? Or indeed the sheer pleasure of the rhymes themselves? The word games, the alliterations and sprung rhythms, the sheer fun and fascination of those mysterious little stories and characters (who was Humpty Dumpty, and why was he an egg?) or of their dream-like images, 'Hey diddle diddle, the cat and the fiddle, the cow jumped over the moon'; they are impossible to better, and it would be difficult to overemphasise their importance. They remain a bedrock for the imagination, and for the development of literacy in childhood.

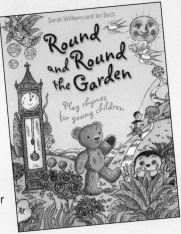

Few things can be more beneficial for infant development than the proper sharing of a good collection of nursery rhymes. I can clearly remember the singular effect and mysterious pleasure that the words of the rhyme 'Polly Put the Kettle On' had on me as an infant, and the magic still works today, nearly 60 years later. In the many school visits that I make, talking to reception or nursery children and their parents, it is interesting how few of the rhymes the children or the parents actually know. This is often as much a cultural matter, to do with background and differing oral traditions, but what a great pleasure the children take in them when they hear them, and how often I have to repeat them.

A vital part of every child's bookshelf should be a good, comprehensive collection of nursery rhymes and lullabies, and there are a bewildering variety available. If I had to offer one definitive book it would have to be *Lavender's Blue* selected by Kathleen Lines and marvellously illustrated by Harold Jones (*UFBG* 35). The book dates from the early 1950s; recently reissued, it has lost none of its sparkle, and is in any case set in a nursery-rhyme world that does not date.

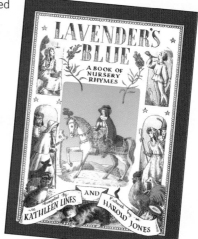

Every parent will have his or her own idea of the pictures they wish to show to their children, and many of our leading artists have illustrated rewarding collections, in a variety of styles and approaches, including historically Randolph Caldecott and Beatrix Potter, and more recently Faith Jacques, Helen Oxenbury, Lucy Cousins and Sally Gardner, among many others. Some books include CDs of the various rhymes set to music, and many are issued in baby-friendly board formats or other novelty presentations.

It is all very much a matter of personal taste, but having one good collection is essential. ●

Some Nursery-rhyme Collections in the *UFBG*

Round and Round the Garden by Sarah Williams illustrated by Ian Beck (*UFBG* 51)

Head, Shoulders, Knees and Toes by Annie Kubler (*UFBG* 32)

Lavender's Blue by Kathleen Lines, illustrated by Harold Jones (*UFBG* 35)

Mother Goose by Michael Foreman (*UFBG* 41)

My Big Nursery Rhyme Book by Julia Lacome (*UFBG* 42)

Skip Across the Ocean: Nursery Rhymes from Around the World by Floella Benjamin, illustrated by Sheila Moxley (*UFBG* 52)

HEAD, SHOULDERS, KNEES AND TOES
Annie Kubler

This is the first in a series of quite large board books that introduce well-known nursery songs – they provide the music, too! We do sometimes need to be reminded about songs like 'If You're Happy and You Know It'; songs that babies love because the texts are all interactive. It's amazing how quickly babies learn and begin to do their best to join in with the actions. Annie Kubler's babies fill the pages and are very expressive as they demonstrate the actions required. They're funny yet real, happy and active, and there's always a good ethnic mix. This one is my favourite – it's lots of fun and good exercise for both adults and babies! Kubler's pictures contain little details from a baby's world – toys, books, food and so on – so there's always plenty to talk about in between the singing.

Wendy Cooling

* * * * * * *

HELLO, LITTLE BIRD / FLUTTER BY, BUTTERFLY / THIS LITTLE CAT / RUN, MOUSE, RUN!
Petr Horáček

A series of books called **Look Inside** that uses good design to delight and fascinate children. The pages are cut into different sizes and there are holes to peep (and poke fingers) through – all cleverly adding to the story. In *Hello, Little Bird* the holes show the bird catching a worm and later feeding it to her babies. The vocabulary is good, too: we have the bird 'hop, hop, hopping / flap, flap, flapping / peck, peck, pecking' and so on through the book. There's plenty to join in with, especially the cheeping on the final page. In *Flutter By, Butterfly*, toddlers love the onomatopoeic buzzes, crunches and munches, and they enjoy the drama of the mouse's story in *Run, Mouse, Run!*.

Wendy Cooling

HOORAY FOR FISH Lucy Cousins

This book does what it says on the tin: it's full of fish and it really does make you want to say 'hooray!' Whether you're pointing out the different fish, counting, comparing opposites or looking at colours, there's plenty to keep you occupied as you follow Little Fish on his undersea journey back to Mum.

Lucy Cousins' trademark bright colours and dry humour abound, and it's a wonderfully generously sized book. Each expansive double-page spread is beautifully composed with dark blue, green and turquoise backgrounds that really make you feel as though you're floating down through the depths. Simple – but satisfying!

Helen Simmons

* * * * * * *

HUG Jez Alborough

This book contains 27 words, 25 of which are 'Hug'! It's about a chimp called 'Bobo' (that's the 26th word) who notices that all the animals in the jungle have someone to hug except him. He sets off on a hunt for a hug, helped by the animals he meets on the way. At last, with a cry of 'Mummy!' (the 27th word), his wish is fulfilled.

This book is cosy and reassuring, but not at all gooey, and the shifting expressions on Bobo's face mean that each repetition of the word 'Hug' is imbued with new meaning – a challenge for the adult who is reading aloud!

Bobo's adventures continue in *Tall* (15 words).

Susan Reuben

I LIKE IT WHEN Mary Murphy

A little penguin spends a typical toddler day with his mother: playing games, eating, having a bath and reading books. In this spare and simple story, the little penguin tells the reader what he likes about the time he and his mother spend together.

The text uses repetition to great effect, so the child will soon get to know the words and be able to join in. The illustrations use bright blocks of colour and thick black line, creating characters that are immediately identifiable. With a warm and cosy ending that's just right for bedtime, this is an exceptionally charming picture book.

Susan Reuben

* * * * * * *

I'M NOT CUTE! Jonathan Allen

I love this book! Expressive drawings and a good, short text make it an excellent first storybook.

It features the most engaging baby owl, an owl so appealing that everyone calls him 'cute'! But this is the last thing an owl needs when he's out exploring the woods and sees himself as 'a huge and scary hunting machine'. Don't read this book if you think reading time is quiet time, but if you can cope with your toddler joining in and shouting 'I am NOT cute!', you'll enjoy sharing it again and again.

Wendy Cooling

* * * * * * *

KIPPER series Mick Inkpen

Kipper has quickly become one of the iconic characters of early childhood, and with good reason. In the big, colourful illustrations, everyday objects – a box, a hairdryer, a towel – are rendered in charming detail, creating familiar scenes for children to identify with. Kipper's happy acceptance and exploration of the world around him, together with Inkpen's subtle reinforcement of social skills, make these books more than just an entertaining read. The language is simple but surprisingly resonant: freshly fallen snow is 'like an empty page waiting to be scribbled on', and a gentle humour pervades each story. Classic stuff indeed!

Laura Hutchings

■ If there's a format for young storybooks, then it's almost certain that **Kipper** will appear in it – he features in picture books; CDs read by Dawn French (*Kipper's Monster*); DVDs (of the TV series); lift-the-flap books (*Kipper's Treehouse*); concept books (*One Year with Kipper* – the months of the year); pop-up books (*Oh Where, Oh Where, is Kipper's Bear?*); touch and feel books (*Kipper's Sticky Paws*); flashcards; activity books and more!

LAVENDER'S BLUE: A BOOK OF NURSERY RHYMES

Kathleen Lines, illustrated by Harold Jones

Half-remembered lines, dimly recalled images of hushed babies, motherly geese, Jack's house, London Bridge, roses, nut trees and rabbit pie all emerge here in their full glory. Containing all the best-known nursery rhymes, and some that sadly seem to have almost disappeared from common usage, *Lavender's Blue* is as close to a definitive collection as you could wish for. Add in the gloriously old-fashioned illustrations, and you have a book that is beautiful in its own right, yet acts as the perfect nursery companion, one that hopefully will mean that this wonderful – and useful! – part of our heritage stays alive.

Leonie Flynn

* * * * * * *

LITTLE FISH

Guido van Genechten

In this simple story, Little Fish must find his mummy. He finds a red crab, an orange starfish, a green turtle, and lots of other coloured creatures, before finally being reunited with his rainbow-coloured mother.

The colours are what matter here. Deep and rich as jewels, they are wonderfully set off by the strong black background. The effect is much like those 'scratch art' pictures, where you scrape at the black to reveal the bright colours beneath.

Each colour is carefully isolated, then brought together in the rainbow at the end. It's a great introduction to colours – and perfect for a child having difficulty distinguishing between them.

Yzanne Mackay

LITTLE PRINCESS series
Tony Ross

In her white gown and golden crown, the endlessly demanding and endearingly mischievous Little Princess has shared her rites of passage with legions of toddlers and parents. Whether it's toilet training (*I Want My Potty*), bedtime (*I Don't Want to Go to Bed*), making friends (*I Want a Friend*) or being independent (*I Want My Mum*), the **Little Princess** stories employ a winning combination of slapstick humour and down-to-earth good sense to teach life's lessons. Tony Ross' hilarious illustrations and simple yet memorable texts – 'the potty's the place!' – remain brilliantly entertaining even after repeated readings. And repeated readings are guaranteed.

Kathryn Ross

■ You may also want to look out for *Say Please!*; *Wash Your Hands!*; *I Don't Want to Go to Hospital*; *I Want My Tooth*; *I Want My Dummy* and *I Want to Be*.

* * * * * * *

MAISY series
Lucy Cousins

Maisy is a mouse, one drawn with stylised simplicity and instantly recognisable. Of course, Maisy is also a pre-school classic, with a TV series of her own and with her stories available around the world, and in formats from picture books to lift-the-flaps, sticker books, board books, jigsaw-puzzle books and interactive playsets.

Maisy and her friends gently encounter all the things in a child's world, from time, colour and the weather to playschool, the dentist and holidays. It would be perfectly possible to see the **Maisy** books as just another marketing success, but they're much more than that – all of which can be put down to the sweetness of Maisy herself and to Lucy Cousins' genius at bringing Maisy, and her world, to life so brilliantly.

Leonie Flynn

■ Titles include: *Maisy's Amazing Word Book*; *Maisy's Easter Egg Hunt*; *Sweet Dreams, Maisy*; *Maisy Goes to Playschool*; *Where is Maisy's Panda?* and *Maisy's Wonderful Weather Book*.

Where is Maisy?
a lift-the-flap book
Lucy Cousins

MELROSE AND CROC series
Emma Chichester Clark

In *Melrose and Croc*, a well-to-do yellow dog and a little green crocodile are alone, and lonely, at Christmas, until a collision at the ice rink marks the start of a beautiful friendship. In *Melrose and Croc Find a Smile*, the friends, now flatmates, set off on a search to recover Melrose's lost happiness. In the last book, *Friends for Life*, the endearing duo find that their differences enrich their friendship.

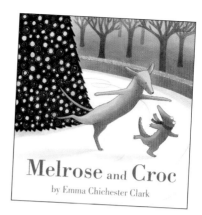

Melrose and Croc
by Emma Chichester Clark

Emma Chichester Clark explores emotions with great sensitivity in these books. Her watercolour illustrations of the pair's tender friendship reinforce the optimistic message that life is much brighter when you have a friend by your side.

Madelyn Travis

* * * * * * *

MIFFY series
Dick Bruna

She started her career as a casual drawing to entertain a toddler on a rainy day. She's reached the grand age of 50 and is still in print. She's been the subject of several international exhibitions. She has her own statue and museum in Utrecht. She holds the Guinness World Record for receiving the greatest number of birthday cards. She adorns articles from backpacks to bubble bath. She is, of course, Miffy the rabbit. Her thick black outlines and blocked colours still hold great appeal for young children. Her toddler-relevant adventures range from going to the dentist and visiting the hospital to the advent of a new baby, right through to starting school. **Miffy** stories are bright, appealing and a good starting point for discussion.

Antonia Honeywell

■ Once you've read your first **Miffy** book you'll want them all; try *Miffy at the Zoo*; *Miffy and the New Baby*; *Miffy's Numbers*; *See, Touch, Smell, Taste and Hear with Miffy*; *Miffy's Magnifying Glass*; *Tell the Time with Miffy* and various tie-ins to the TV series.

Concept Books

Books about numbers, shapes, animals and colours help us begin to understand the world around us. **Nikki Gamble** explains the benefits of 'concept books'.

Concept books are books designed to help young children learn classes of objects such as 'animals', or ideas such as 'opposites' and to recognise their defining characteristics. Concepts vary in sophistication, the simplest being 'shape' and 'colour', the more complex including 'time' and 'the alphabet'. Of course, books on their own cannot teach concepts, but they can complement other rich experiences. Multi-sensory learning – tactile, visual, kinaesthetic – should be combined with conversations, games and exploration with your child. Many concept books invite playful, multi-sensory engagement by including, for example, textured pages, sound chips or magnetic letters.

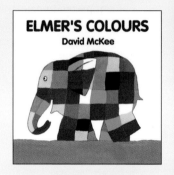

Children from as young as 15 months might begin to identify colours, starting with simple naming and later learning about colour mixing. In *Elmer's Colours* by David McKee, very young children learn about the patchwork elephant's colours. This board book is all the more appealing for its focus on a well-loved character, and is available in dual-language editions. Look out for photographic books about colour, as these often provide interesting points for discussion. For example, Jane Yorke's *My First Look at Colours* presents an array of familiar objects in varying shades and tones: the 'green' page includes a bright green apple and a sludgy green frog, prompting discussion about the 'greenness' of green. Eric Carle's *Brown Bear, Brown Bear, What Do You See?* (*UFBG* 16), with its call and response structure, encourages children to join in with the refrain. As each page is turned, a different animal is revealed, including an unexpected blue horse and purple cat. Laura Vaccaro Seeger's playful approach in *Lemons Are Not Red* uses die-cut pages to reveal the coloured objects, inviting adult and child to play a guessing game

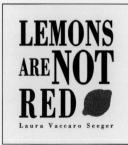

before turning the page to confirm their predictions. *Chidi Only Likes Blue* is a stunning photographic story with images of African children by photographer Ifeoma Onyefulu.

The concept of shape lends itself to a tactile approach. For the very young, Miriam Stoppard's *I Love Shapes* combines the elements of a matching game with a board book. It is packed with colourful photographs and foam pieces to help children connect mathematical shapes to everyday objects. On a similar theme, *Magnetic Play and Learn Shapes* encourages visual perception of simple forms such as stars and triangles, and includes magnetic shapes to handle so that children can feel the pointed edges and the smooth or curved lines. Stella Blackstone's colourful *Ship Shapes* teaches three-to-five-year-olds about shape through an adventure story, helping to recognise them in different contexts.

Number books include very simple stories for children from about 18 months upwards. **Baby Einstein**'s *Baby Galileo Sees the Stars*, with its raised glittery star shapes and illuminating moon, is very appealing. Mick Inkpen's *One Bear at Bedtime* and Penny Dale's *Ten in the Bed* are entertaining counting stories for three-to-five-year-olds. With lots of details in the illustrations, these are books that can sustain repeated readings. ▶

Some Concept Books Listed in the *UFBG*

Kipper's A to Z by Mick Inkpen (alphabet) (*UFBG* 121)

Bear in a Square by Stella Blackstone (shapes) (*UFBG* 13)

Mr Wolf's Week by Colin Hawkins (days of the week) (*UFBG* 137)

My Beak, Your Beak by Melanie Walsh (opposites) (*UFBG* 42)

Dinosaur Roar! by Henrietta Stickland, illustrated by Paul Stickland (opposites) (*UFBG* 21)

Handa's Surprise by Eileen Browne (counting) (*UFBG* 29)

One Duck Stuck by Phyllis Root, illustrated by Jane Chapman (counting) (*UFBG* 43)

One More Sheep by Mij Kelly, illustrated by Russell Ayto (counting) (*UFBG* 150)

Pink Lemon by Hervé Tullet (colour for the slightly older child) (*UFBG* 49)

At the top end of the age range, *Out for the Count* by Kathryn Cave features pictures of large numbers of animals: 12 wolves, 23 pythons, 36 goats, 100 shadows. The book is cleverly designed so that each number is represented in more than one way – good for conservation of number (the understanding that the number of objects doesn't change when you move the objects around).

Children are often given alphabet books long before they are ready to develop the concept of letters. Nevertheless, these books can still provide enjoyable opportunities for booktalk. For the youngest children it is important that the objects selected for illustration are familiar. A good example is Robert Crowther's delightful *Surprise ABC*. Crowther's skill in producing pop-up and novelty books for this age group is unsurpassed. There are genuine surprises here to entertain both adult and child and the illustrations have been chosen with phonics in mind. David Carter's *Alphabugs* may not depict familiar objects, but his wordplay and wacky characters will thrill children from two upwards. For a thought-provoking aesthetic experience, my all-time favourite is *A is for Artist*; discover secret cobwebs deep in the forest in this visual feast. And finally, for older children, Satoshi Kitamura's *From Acorn to Zoo* will extend vocabulary as well as developing familiarity with letters. ●

Other Concept Books to Look Out For

Jasper's Beanstalk by Nick Butterworth (days of the week)

One Year With Kipper by Mick Inkpen (months of the year)

What's the Time Mr Wolf? by Colin Hawkins (time)

Harry and the Dinosaurs Tell the Time by Ian Whybrow, illustrated by Adrian Reynolds (time)

The Bad Tempered Ladybird by Eric Carle (time)

Olivia's Opposites by Ian Falconer (opposites)

Dr Seuss's ABC by Dr Seuss (alphabet)

Black Meets White by Justine Fontes, illustrated by Geoff Waring (colour)

Ten Terrible Dinosaurs by Paul Strickland (number)

MR MAGNOLIA see p.135.

see p.135.

* * * * * * *

MOTHER GOOSE Michael Foreman

Nursery rhymes, Iona Opie reminds us in the foreword, are 'The first furnishings of the mind; the bottom-most layer of the comfortable hereditary clutter of mottos, proverbs and half-remembered tales that we use to ornament our conversations throughout our lives, knowing that they are common currency'. This big, beautiful book, containing over 200 rhymes, should be on every family's bookshelf.

What makes this edition particularly special is the quality and imagination of the illustrations. Foreman often carries pictures on over pages, offering a real enticement to the reader who will always want one page more. Mrs Hen counts her ten chicks in 'Chook Chook', but only nine are in the picture – number ten is over the page walking into the next rhyme. Georgie Porgie runs away, chased on to the next page.

This is a very special book, to be looked after and treated with care; a book to grow up with.

Wendy Cooling

* * * * * * *

MOTHER GOOSE'S NURSERY RHYMES (AND HOW SHE CAME TO TELL THEM)
Axel Scheffler, with additional stories by Alison Green

All your favourite nursery rhymes are brought to life by Axel Scheffler's beautiful pictures in this Mother Goose treasury. His work is warm and wittily detailed, in the inimitable style that will be reassuringly familiar to Gruffalo lovers. And the book has its own little narratives, too, linking the rhymes with the story of how Mother Goose came to tell them to her three goslings, and how the wise old heron wrote them down so we could all come to know and love them...

Daniel Hahn

MUDDLEWITCH DOES MAGIC TRICKS
Nick Sharratt

Naughty Muddlewitch loves 'magicking' everything around her so that things which used to look perfectly normal become madly multi-coloured and patterned. But when Muddlewitch magicks her friend Glitterwitch, she soon gets a taste of her own medicine.

When you pull the tab on each double-page spread, the colour of the picture changes in a way that seems truly magical. The book is suitable for babies and toddlers, but is also great fun for older children, who can try to work out how the colour changing works.

Susan Reuben

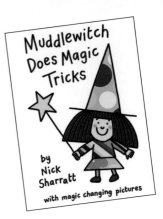

* * * * * * *

MY BEAK, YOUR BEAK Melanie Walsh

A bright book for babies and young readers, My Beak, Your Beak uses cheery pictures to show the differences and similarities between animals and birds. A smiling shark glides along the ocean bed while a little goldfish swims in a bowl. Turn the page and the shark and goldfish are nose to nose, blowing bubbles. Penguins and robins both have pointy beaks, and a friendly looking lion shares sharp claws with a pair of kittens. The book ends with a bat and a bush baby waking up when it gets dark to wish the reader goodnight.

Sarah Frost Mellor

* * * * * * *

MY BIG NURSERY RHYME BOOK
Julie Lacome

A collection of traditional nursery rhymes is an essential addition to every baby's bookshelf, as well as an essential *aide mémoire* for parents who can't quite remember how they go… This durable board book will withstand the most demanding of little readers. The 15 rhymes include such favourite nursery songs as 'Twinkle Twinkle Little Star' and 'Sing a Song of Sixpence', as well as bath and bedtime rhymes, and the big book format makes it easy to enjoy together.

Kathryn Ross

OH WHERE, OH WHERE? / NUMBER ONE, TICKLE YOUR TUM / THE BEAR WENT OVER THE MOUNTAIN / WALKING ROUND THE GARDEN
John Prater

Four delicious books, available in board as well as picture-book format, based on much-loved rhymes, and packed with fun and ideas for tickling, wiggling, climbing and other games we all love to play with babies and toddlers. Bears, too, have an endless popularity, and Prater's bears have real child appeal because they reflect the behaviour of human babies. These books just have to be shared – whether between an adult and a child, or a child and a teddy, it really doesn't matter, for either way children learn in the most enjoyable way possible. I love *Number One, Tickle Your Tum* simply because I grew up with a very similar rhyme and it was my dad's favourite – can you think of a better way to begin to learn numbers?

Wendy Cooling

* * * * * * *

OLIVIA see p.148.

* * * * * * *

ONE DUCK STUCK
Phyllis Root, illustrated by Jane Chapman

The duck gets stuck. And if you've just read a hundred books with ducks in, you might be tempted to leave it stuck. But don't! This book has a lot more imagination than most, as moose, skunks and possums all join in.

The rhymes are good and clunky (if you're not that hot on rhythm yourself, you'll be relieved to find something you don't have to practise several times), and the story both simple and funny. Fantastic original sounds, too – *zing! sploosh! spluck!*

It's all about counting, also. But like puréed vegetables in a tomato sauce, your child won't even notice…

Yzanne Mackay

ONE LITTLE HOME Dubravka Kolanovic

As a gentle introduction to counting, this book can't be bettered. Starting with one little baby, then two proud parents, each page reveals a higher number of ordinary household objects, which all add up to a lovely home.

Like the text, the pictures are warm and reassuring, with plenty of detail. I'd recommend this for parents looking for books to read to two children together – while the little one has fun naming and finding, the older one can practise counting and remembering.

Yzanne Mackay

■ In the same series are *One Little Farm*; *One Big Building Site*; *One Big Ocean*.

* * * * * * *

ORANGE PEAR APPLE BEAR
Emily Gravett

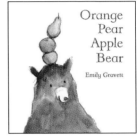

This beautiful book is a perfect example of less meaning more. On high-quality paper, the economical wash drawings show Bear, plus an orange, an apple and a pear juxtaposed through endless permutations.

Throughout, just four words (plus one last extra one!) are used to create delightful variations to intrigue both parent and small child alike. An exceptional book, which encourages sharing and the enjoyment of visual jokes at a very early age. Simple, clever and one to treasure.

Sonia Benster

* * * * * * *

OWL BABIES
Martin Waddell, illustrated by Patrick Benson

One of my all-time-favourite picture books, this is the tale of Sarah, Percy and little Bill – three baby owls – who wake up one night to find that their mother has left them alone in the nest. Sarah and Percy try to stay calm, but Bill's response to their attempts at reassurance is a repeated, until near hysterical, 'I want my mummy!'

The words and pictures work together beautifully to heighten the suspense and, eventually, to provide a deliciously comforting resolution. Benson's illustrations are suitably dark, but overlaid with the richest of colouring, creating a stained-glass luminosity. Superb!

Malachy Doyle

PEEK-A-BOO! Jan Ormerod

There are babies black and babies white in this book that introduces the joys of the 'peek-a-boo' game, something that is probably part of all our childhoods. The question 'Where's the baby?' is asked on the left of the spread and the answer is to be found beneath a tough, rectangular flap on the right. That wonderful thing of babies being sure that if they can't see you, you can't see them, is played out throughout as we see babies hiding their eyes behind teddy bears, dresses, bibs and more – until the last, quieter page suggests that bedtime has come. This really is for sharing, joining in with and generally doing a lot of laughing.

Wendy Cooling

* * * * * * *

PEEPO
Allan Ahlberg, illustrated by Janet Ahlberg

It's hard to describe quite how utterly perfect this picture book is, but I will try...

Created by arguably the greatest picture-book team ever, it's about a little baby and the world he sees around him. It's told in beautiful rhyming verse... 'Here's a little baby / One, two, three / Stands in his cot / What does he see?' with a rollicking rhythm and just the right amount of repetition to let the child join in with the familiar bits. At the joyful shout of 'Peepo!', the reader gets to peek through a hole in the page to glimpse what the baby is looking at before turning over.

The 1940s-set illustrations are so crammed with fantastic detail that you'll still be spotting things on the 100th reading – the tin bath, the kettle on the range, the daddy in the soldier's uniform... It just couldn't be bettered.

Susan Reuben

Characters to Grow Up With

Many children's books are based on a small number of familiar characters – many of which may have been around in your childhood, too. You'll find them in various formats and spin-off stories and media, and your children will form lasting friendships with them. **Wendy Cooling** explains why character books work.

I grew up in the world of Beatrix Potter; I loved the look, the size and the feel of the books and I couldn't wait for another. I still read *The Tale of Peter Rabbit* (*UFBG* 178) to any child willing to listen, and see that they all live his adventure, shudder at the threat of Mr McGregor – especially the possibility of ending up in one of Mrs McGregor's pies – and smile at the satisfactory ending. My favourite was *The Tale of Jemima Puddle-Duck*, and to this day I remember the wonder of finally being able to read it for myself.

Today, children are faced with an embarrassment of riches, but most soon find a character to love and collect, a character that may well take them into independent reading. These characters become a part of life and their very familiarity offers real comfort in a busy, sometimes impossible to understand world. Children often know the stories by heart; they 'read' them to others and to their teddy bears, and they use the books until they fall apart.

You look at **Maisy** (*UFBG* 36), **Elmer** (*UFBG* 97), the **Little Princess** (*UFBG* 36), **Chimp and Zee** (*UFBG* 17), **Kipper** (*UFBG* 34), **Wibbly Pig** (*UFBG* 63), **Poppy Cat** (*UFBG* 49), **Spot** (*UFBG* 63), **Thomas the Tank Engine** (*UFBG* 185), **Miffy** (*UFBG* 37), and still more in the library or bookshop and how on earth do you choose? Children usually make the choice themselves in ways we can't always understand; they will be given books for presents, meet characters in the library at 'bounce and rhyme' sessions, be introduced to your favourites and

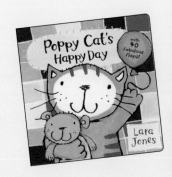

so on. And suddenly, before you know what's happening, they want a book about Maisy every bedtime. Great, as Maisy goes through many of the life experiences they do, so they enjoy becoming part of her life and, almost accidentally, learning something, too. And, as with many of these characters, Maisy appears in board books for the very young and picture books for the slightly older, so she really can take children into reading.

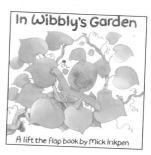

Eric Hill's ever-young Spot may well be the first character children meet. *Where's Spot?* (*UFBG* 63) really is one of the best-ever lift-the-flap books. The search for Spot is one that all want to join in with, and the finding is always so satisfactory. Children gravitate towards **Spot** books in libraries, nurseries and bookshops because they recognise a friend whose company has always been a pleasure.

More challenging, and for slightly older readers, are the stories of **Frog** (*UFBG* 103), told in expressive words and pictures by Max Velthuijs. The texts are gentle, simple and optimistic and they deal with huge issues. *Frog and Birdsong* sees Frog and his animal friends beginning to understand something of life and death, and in *Frog in Love*, Frog can't at first understand why his heart beats too fast. Big moments are looked at with gentle humour and invite the kind of discussion it is often hard to undertake with children. Every child should meet Frog and follow his adventures and his increasing knowledge of life.

For children of two or three and above, there's the memorable *Hairy Maclary from Donaldson's Dairy* (*UFBG* 110), Lynley Dodd's introduction to an excellent series. It is the language here that really makes these books winners; the rhythm and rhyme get children going and they want to join in with the stories wherever possible. The names of the dogs are a delight, and the cumulative nature of the stories helps children to predict and enjoy. The journey and the chase in that first title bring in so many doggy characters who appear in later books, and brilliantly – if you're like me and love Schnitzel von Krumm with the very low tum – get their own books as well. ▶

I love the humour and naughtiness of Tony Ross' **Little Princess** series (*UFBG* 36). Who can forget her with her dummy or on her potty? Like all children, she doesn't want to go to bed and she's not keen on going to hospital; what she does want are her mum, a sister, a cat and much more. Each of these books, again in board or picture-book format, is like the return of a friend, and the humour of the situations in the stories appeals to children and adults alike.

There is often more to these characters than children at first perceive. David McKee's Elmer (*UFBG* 97) is a good example. There is something supremely child-friendly about that patchwork elephant, and beyond this his stories are great celebrations of difference. Children will meet the **Elmer** books in school and if they are lucky enough to be read his stories at home, they will greet him joyfully like an old friend and feel the confidence that familiarity can give.

Often great characters make it to television and become even more desirable – all the children I know long for more of Lauren Child's **Charlie and Lola** titles (*UFBG* 82) faster than the publisher can produce them. Much of what is in these books reflects real life, but real life is made special by Child's quirky, fascinating illustration and her great feel for humour.

There are more examples that I have no space to detail, but it is a fact that children moving into reading with characters will feel positive about books and stories, and they will have begun one of the most influential chapters in their reading histories. These books often contain a lot of learning, but the quality of the stories and the illustration and the imagination that has created the character also mean they're beneficial for the sheer pleasure they give to young children as they collect new titles and become familiar with their chosen characters. Read them aloud again and again – both your favourites and theirs – and enjoy the sharing. ●

PINK LEMON Hervé Tullet

This is a book that explores – and delights in – colour. Tullet, known in his native France as 'prince of pre-school books', here uses his trademark bold illustrative style to wonderful effect. Each double-page spread has an image painted in the wrong colour – and on the side of the spread is a selection of other colours so the reader can choose which they think is the correct one. Yellow sea? No … black? … red? … blue!

This book contains a fabulous selection of images: from the everyday, such as eggs and lemons, to the wonderfully thought-provoking, such as tears and Martians!

Leonie Flynn

* * * * * * *

POPPY CAT series Lara Jones

There's always lots going on in the **Poppy Cat** books, which are perfect to read with small children, who'll love the jolly drawings that are a bit like the pictures they draw themselves.

With her friends, her family and her favourite Bear, Poppy gets up to all the same things as her readers, like hugging, playing, going to the park, and eating cake, which makes the stories fun and familiar. The books are full of clever tabs to pull and squishy spots to touch – be prepared to read these again and again!

Sarah Frost Mellor

* * * * * * *

■ Poppy Cat appears in just about every format imaginable, including hide-and-seek books with soft felt flaps to lift (**Poppy Cat Peekaboos**: *Snuggle Up, Poppy Cat!* and *Messy Messy, Poppy Cat!*); touch-and-feel books (*Goodnight, Poppy Cat* and *Playtime, Poppy Cat!*); **Buggy Buddies** (*Poppy Cat Splashes*); bath books (*Poppy Cat Loves Splashing*); a novelty in the form of a 3-D fold-out house, with a plush Poppy Cat toy (*Poppy Cat's Play House*); jigsaw books, drawing books and, of course, board books.

RED ROCKETS AND RAINBOW JELLY
Nick Sharratt and Sue Heap

Nick and Sue discover that they like completely different things. Nick likes red apples; Sue likes green pears. Nick likes orange hair; Sue likes purple. Yet despite their differences they discover they can be themselves and still stay friends in this exuberant story, which fairly bounces along with its simple, rhyming text. The bright, bold illustrations are done on alternating pages by the 'real' Nick and Sue, and offer lots of details to spot. This is an outstanding book for very young children – perfect for teaching colours, but a hugely enjoyable story, too.

Eileen Armstrong

■ *Alphabet Ice Cream* – a fantastic, fun-filled ABC – shows Nick and Sue learning the alphabet; *One to Ten and Back Again* sees them learn to count.

Everybody's Favourite...

ROSIE'S WALK
Pat Hutchins

This classic picture book famously has only 32 words. They tell how Rosie the hen takes a stroll around the farmyard – but the story which unfolds in the unusual, stylised illustrations is much more exciting, and the youngest child becomes a storyteller as he reads

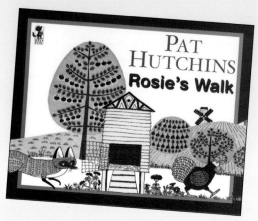

the pictures and predicts what's going to happen, both to Rosie and to the not so wily fox that's following her! For once, the child reading the pictures knows more than the adult reading the words, and that's a powerful and exhilarating position for a young reader to be in.

Kathryn Ross

Ostensibly this is one of the world's most simple picture books – yet not everyone will get the whole story! The words follow Rosie the hen as she saunters around the farmyard. The pictures also show Fox following right behind her – slobbering over the prospect of an easy catch and a tasty meal. However, as Rosie wanders obliviously through her day, Fox heads into a series of traps, from a falling bag of flour to an unseen fence, culminating in him being hounded from the farm by a swarm of vicious bees.

Jonny Zucker

Rosie the hen went for a walk

ROUND AND ROUND THE GARDEN
Sarah Williams, illustrated by Ian Beck

There are almost 40 popular rhymes assembled in this collection. Many of them ('Row, Row, Row Your Boat', 'Hickory Dickory Dock') will be rhymes you remember from your own childhood. The rhymes in this book are the ones your child will remember for ever, too.

The book now comes with a CD, and each of the rhymes has diagrams explaining the gestures that go with it; but best of all are the illustrations by Ian Beck. They are what really make this title – which was Beck's first children's book – stand head and shoulders above other, similar collections.

Daniel Hahn

* * * * * * *

SILLY SUZY GOOSE
Petr Horáček

The stunning, bright pictures, packed with humour, leap through the pages of this book and make it a real page-turner. Suzy Goose doesn't want to be like all the other geese; she wants to be different: to hang upside down like a bat, slide like a penguin, stretch like a giraffe, and more and more and more.

But Suzy soon learns that the familiar and safe feeling of fitting in with the crowd can be good – although perhaps not all the time. The giraffe stretches across a double page as does the elephant – these and other dramatic pictures have bags of appeal and really bring the text to life.

Wendy Cooling

SKIP ACROSS THE OCEAN
Floella Benjamin, illustrated by Sheila Moxley

This international collection of 32 nursery rhymes includes lullabies, action rhymes (for interactive play), poems about nature, and a 'lucky dip' section. Several are bilingual, providing the original language (such as Yoruba, Russian and Hindi) and an English translation. All are lushly illustrated in bright colours with impressionistic depictions of a multitude of countries and cultures. While some people can read rhymes aloud better than others, overall the book provides a wealth of wonderful language to enjoy. It also contains details which can show a child how people all over the world may have different experiences, but they still share some basic things (such as being sung to sleep). A brilliant bedtime read-aloud.

Laura Atkins

* * * * * * *

SOME DOGS DO
Jez Alborough

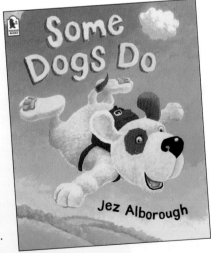

One day, Sid the dog wakes up feeling so inexplicably happy he floats all the way to school. He is brought back down to Earth by his friends, who tell him not to be so silly. They say that dogs can't fly and challenge Sid to prove that he can. But Sid finds he can't fly any more because his happy feeling has been replaced by a very, very sad one (which is shown by his face and droopy doggy posture). Luckily his dad is able to put everything right and cheer him up again.

This is an inspiring story, which shows that miracles can happen if you believe in yourself and don't let others get you down. Bouncy rhymes, just the right amount of join-in repetition and a dog painted with such fine-textured brushwork you can almost stroke him, work together for maximum feel-good effect.

Eileen Armstrong

SPOT see p.63.

* * * * * * *

TEN WRIGGLY WIGGLY CATERPILLARS
Debbie Tarbett

A bright and simple counting-down book – '*Ten* crunching caterpillars, in the bright sunshine, one fell asleep, so that left *nine. Nine* speedy caterpillars...'. The boldly coloured illustrations make each page a pleasure to the eye, but there's more to this book – ten solid caterpillar figures are embedded in the pages to touch and there's a

nice surprise on the final page. Bookshops are full of brightly coloured counting books, with not much to distinguish between them, and some work significantly better than others with their readers. For me, though, this book is the one.

Daniel Hahn

* * * * * * *

THAT'S NOT MY BEAR
Fiona Watt, illustrated by Rachel Wells

That's Not My Bear is one of a big series of touch-and-feel books, which are the very best around. There are shiny, fluffy, rough and shimmery patches to touch on every page – and the book is so tough it can be touched for ever. The search is on for a special bear, and so the text goes: 'That's not my bear. Its paws are too soft. That's not my bear. Its body is too fuzzy. That's not my bear. Its tongue is too scratchy!'

Babies love the involvement the books offer and at the same time they're developing sensory and language awareness without knowing it. Everyone has their own favourites – *Bear* and *Dinosaur* win for me.

Wendy Cooling

■ Others in the series include *That's Not My Lion; That's Not My Dinosaur; That's Not My Teddy* and *That's Not My Monster*.

TICKLE, TICKLE
Helen Oxenbury

This big board book has nice, rounded corners and is full of happy babies of all colours, drawn with Helen Oxenbury's very sure touch. The onomatopoeic words introduced – such as *squelch*, *splish* and *splash* – are great to read, and it seems that babies almost taste them as they take them in. The 'squelch' is illustrated by babies playing in the mud; on the next spread, the splashes get the babies cleaned up in the bath; then there's a quiet, gentle page of hair brushing and finally the end-of-the-day peace is under threat with a bit of tickling.

There's participation, recognition and changing tempos in this very short book. I've read it to many babies and never tire of it.

Wendy Cooling

■ There are three more appealing first books in the series: *All Fall Down*; *Say Goodnight* and *Clap Hands*.

* * * * * * *

TIGER
Nick Butterworth

Tiger isn't a real tiger. He's a small, furry kitten who likes to pretend to be a real tiger. He pretends his 'soft, little tigery paws' are 'great, big tigery claws'. He roars and growls and he definitely won't play with wool, because real tigers don't. The illustrations, which show Tiger as he really appears and then Tiger as he is in his imagination, are thoroughly engaging, and their detail provides lots of material for discussion. The little kitten's personality is one that most toddlers and their carers will recognise.

Don't miss the funny vignette on the copyright page at the end.

Antonia Honeywell

Tiger

Nick Butterworth

TRUCKS
Fiona Watt

This wonderful touchy-feely book bravely moves away from the usual fluffy bunnies and puppies, presenting a world of very different textures. The trucks on each page have pieces made from rubber, metallic materials and – my own favourite – sandpaper for 'rust', just begging a child to run their fingers over them.

Perfect for children going through their 'truck' stage, and great even for those who are not, with plenty of other touchy-feely elements (sheep, sand, and so on) to help them explore their world.

Yzanne Mackay

* * * * * * *

THE VERY BUSY BEAR
Jack Tickle

A baby polar bear bounces out from behind his mother's back as you turn the page. A moose waves his antlers on the next spread, then an arctic hare boings up in the air.

This is one of a series of books by Jack Tickle, with simple rhyming texts and friendly, cleverly designed pop-ups that make the characters seem as though they are moving as the pages turn. It's great for babies and toddlers, and my copy is still *almost* in one piece despite the pop-ups having been subjected to many weeks of my 18 month old's inquisitive fingers.

Susan Reuben

■ Other titles in the **Peek-a-Boo Pop-ups** series include *The Very Busy Bee*; *The Very Lazy Lion*; *The Very Silly Shark* and *The Very Dizzy Dinosaur*.

Just Before Bed Books

The Baby Who Wouldn't Go to Bed by Helen Cooper (*UFBG* 69)

Can't You Sleep, Little Bear? by Martin Wadell, illustrated by Barbara Firth (*UFBG* 78)

I Like it When by Mary Murphy (*UFBG* 34)

A Goodnight Kind of Feeling by Tony Bradman, illustrated by Georgie Birkett (*UFBG* 27)

Guess How Much I Love You by Sam McBratney, illustrated by Anita Geram (*UFBG* 109)

Tell Me Something Happy Before I Go to Sleep by Joyce Dunbar, illustrated by Debi Gliori (*UFBG* 180)

Novelty Books

Edgardo Zaghini takes a tour through the spinning, pop-up, 3-D world of novelty books.

A novelty book contains a distinctive device that brings the pages to life by allowing characters and objects to be explored in three dimensions. It could be anything from a simple flap that can be lifted, or a tab that can be pulled to more complicated forms of paper engineering, such as pop-ups, fold-outs or revolving discs.

Novelty books are brilliant tools for introducing children to the pleasures of reading from a very early age, and can play an important role in their literary growth and development. Novelty books also have the great advantage of stimulating interest by offering an element of surprise and awakening curiosity. Many are so complex that they can even be enjoyed as toys.

For babies, lift-the-flap books are particularly good, as they allow them to join in the book-sharing experience in an interactive way, even before they can speak. They will enjoy lifting the same flaps over and over again, showing delight at the surprise of what is underneath, however many times they may have seen it before.

Novelty books are great for reluctant readers, too: they can be explored as toys or games, encouraging dexterity but also helping to foster an interest in conventional picture books and reading in general. Partially or non-sighted children can also benefit. Shapes and textures, smells and sounds and buttons on the page make all the difference to a child unable to see the printed pictures. Particularly good is the **Head and Tails** series by Steve Cox, with titles such as *Miaow!* and *Grrrr!*, which have a combination of lift-the-flaps and touch-and-feel elements. Both titles have a clever twist at the end.

There's been a huge increase in the production of novelty books over the last few years and there's a great

wealth to choose from. So which ones should you share with your baby? It's difficult to just select a few, but here are some of the best:

Jan Pieńkowski's *Haunted House* (*UFBG* 111), published in 1979, is now regarded as a modern classic, with over a million copies sold throughout the world. Each double-page spread takes you on a spooky journey through various rooms in a haunted house. The book is packed with a wide range of mechanisms, including pop-ups, revolving discs, pull-the-tabs and lift-the-flaps.

Clackety-Clacks series: *Butterfly*

Bookstart, the national programme that brings babies to books, recommends two novelty titles in particular for 0–2s: *Hide and Seek!* by Jonathan Lambert and Emma Dodd allows babies to touch and feel the fluffy texture of the pink rabbit and lift the flap to reveal who is hidden underneath; *Animal Faces* by Caroline Davis is an innovative concept – a shake-a-rattle playbook with removable rattle, which introduces three very simple opposites: 'up and down', 'long and short' and 'open and close'.

The Blue Balloon by Mick Inkpen is a novelty without parallel: some pages can be unfolded in various shapes and formats that will amaze. And Rod Campbell has produced a number of inventive and unforgettable titles, of which the lift-the-flap *Dear Zoo* (*UFBG* 20) is a book that no baby should be without. ▶

Some Novelty Books Found in the *UFBG*

Don't Put Your Finger in the Jelly, Nelly! by Nick Sharratt (*UFBG* 24)

Muddlewitch Does Magic Tricks by Nick Sharratt (*UFBG* 42)

That's Not My Bear by Fiona Watt, illustrated by Rachel Wells (*UFBG* 53)

What on Earth Can It Be? by Roger McGough, illustrated by Lydia Monks (*UFBG* 61)

Where's Spot? by Eric Hill (*UFBG* 63)

Hello, Little Bird by Petr Horáček (*UFBG* 32)

Clackety-Clacks series by Luana Rinaldo (*UFBG* 18)

The Very Hungry Caterpillar by Eric Carle (*UFBG* 59)

And then, of course, there is Eric Carle's *The Very Hungry Caterpillar*, which uses peepholes and pages of different sizes to create an experience that combines story, counting, colours, days of the week and the concept of metamorphosis, all in a few delightfully entertaining spreads.

Lots of the classic characters have books in a huge range of formats, many of which have interactive elements. So, for a given character, you can find flap books, touch-and-feel books, pop-up books and so on. The **Spot** books (*UFBG* 63) use lift-up flaps to great effect, with surprises revealed on every spread. *Thomas Races to the Rescue* contains a grooved track and a wind-up train that runs round it, and *Maisy's House* opens out into three dimensions so you can 'walk' right around it. The range and sheer inventiveness of novelty books is increasing all the time. They're interactive, fun and often educational as well, making them a great part of the reading experience for children of all ages. ●

*Felicity Wishes
Pop-up Fairy House*

Novelty Books for Older Children

Alice's Adventures in Wonderland by Robert Sabuda (*UFBG* 207)

The Wizard of Oz by Frank L. Baum and Robert Sabuda

The Night Before Christmas by Clement C. Moore and Robert Sabuda

Perfect Punctuation by Kate Petty and Jennie Maizels

Captain Scurvy's Most Dastardly Pop-up Pirate Ship by Nick Denchfield and Steve Cox

Felicity Wishes Pop-up Fairy House by Emma Thomson

The Global Garden by Kate Petty and Jennie Maizels

Fungus the Bogeyman Plop-up Book by Raymond Briggs

Encyclopedia Prehistorica: Mega-Beasts by Robert Sabuda and Matthew Reinhart

Everybody's Favourite...

THE VERY HUNGRY CATERPILLAR
Eric Carle

This is one of *the* classic picture books – available in various versions, including a boxed set with plush caterpillar, so it's hard to believe that in 1969 its publisher was uncertain of its success. The central story is the transformation of a caterpillar into a stunning butterfly, but integrated into that are days of the week, numbers and food. The caterpillar's diet includes watermelon, salami and cupcakes, words that children love to say aloud, and then remember. And the holes the caterpillar makes as he munches his way from day to day never cease to fascinate small fingers, as does the ending with its stunning metamorphosis.

Lindsey Fraser

This modern classic continues to amaze and delight. Carle's ingenuity is boundless. Here he weaves a lesson in natural history and nutrition into a tale with instant appeal for any child with some growing up to do. Each day, a tiny, very hungry caterpillar eats his way through holes on the pages until, on Saturday, he gets a stomach ache. On Sunday he eats one nice green leaf, spins a cocoon and emerges as a beautiful butterfly.

The book is a miracle of design, from its die-cut holes and different-sized pages to its dramatic use of painted, cut tissue-paper collage.

Elizabeth Hammill

WALKING THROUGH THE JUNGLE
Julie Lacome

In this delightful adaptation of the well-known action rhyme, an authentically toddler-shaped youngster runs, swings, crawls and wades through a vivid paper-collage jungle full of wild animals. Elephant, snake, crocodile, lion – each announces its arrival with its own distinctive sound and each one is 'looking for his tea'. The page layout invites children to guess which animal is going to appear next and the lively text encourages energetic participation. A familiar rhyme, stunning illustrations in hot,  tropical colours and the opportunity to creep, leap, roar and hiss... What more could a young reader ask for?

Kathryn Ross

* * * * * * *

WE'RE GOING ON A BEAR HUNT see p.189.

* * * * * * *

WHAT DO YOU SAY? / WHAT DO YOU DO? / HOW DO YOU FEEL?
Mandy Stanley

Three excellent and entertaining first non-fiction titles all offer lots to look at and talk about. Children will learn a lot without realising it's happening because the question-and-answer format is so involving.

The first book introduces animal sounds, so involves lots of noisy joining in – often the joining in is attempted long before the book is understood. The second title teaches that hens lay eggs, cows give milk and much, much more, and the third, again through questions and answers, introduces feelings. The illustrations are bright and often very funny, making a good mix of laughter and learning.

Wendy Cooling

WHAT IS BLACK AND WHITE? / STRAWBERRIES ARE RED
Petr Horáček

Two intriguing board books, the first introducing black and white, the second looking at lots of different colours. The special thing about them is the die-cut pages that combine to offer a surprise at the end; the pages get smaller and smaller as the book proceeds and produce a wonderful stripy zebra in the first book and a delicious fruit salad in the second.

   This is a great way to begin to look at and talk about colours with small children. They see the final spreads as a kind of magic, something they want to explore again and again. Clear images and strong colours combine to make these books accessible to the very young.

Wendy Cooling

* * * * * * *

WHAT ON EARTH CAN IT BE?
Roger McGough, illustrated by Lydia Monks

It's never too soon to introduce the wonderful wordplay of Roger McGough. This interactive picture book will be enjoyed well into school as it invites children to play a timeless guessing game. Holes on the right of each spread show just a tiny part of what's to be found over the page and the repeated question, 'What on earth can it be?' invites the child to make a guess. The answer over the page is a four-line rhyme that gives a real taste of creative language – there's a crocogiant, for example, and one of my favourite collective nouns, 'a chuckle of clowns', and Lydia Monks' pictures bring them all to life.

Wendy Cooling

Everybody's Favourite...

WHERE THE WILD THINGS ARE
Maurice Sendak

Let the wild rumpus start! Ask a writer or illustrator of picture books for their own favourite in the field, and the answer you'll get most often is *Where the Wild Things Are*. And it's no wonder – it's not only the sort of wild and liberating story that children love being read to them (safely tucked up in bed), but for adults it's got originality, invention and fantastic style. One of

the great books to read aloud – even though some pages don't have words at all – it has a lovely, reassuring bedtime ending to calm you both down after all Max's wonderful mayhem.

Daniel Hahn

And when he came to the place where the wild things are they roared their terrible roars and gnashed their terrible teeth

and rolled their terrible eyes and showed their terrible claws

When Max behaves like a wild thing, he is sent to his bedroom without any supper. But such a punishment is powerless against a real wild thing. His room turns into a forest and a boat takes him to where the wild things are, and he becomes king of all wild things. But as the wild things roar their terrible roars and gnash their terrible teeth, Max has second thoughts. For the ultimate expression of childhood fantasy and the best last line of any picture book, ever, *Where the Wild Things Are* is incomparable.

Antonia Honeywell

WHERE'S SPOT?
Eric Hill

One of the best-ever lift-the-flap books, with crisp, clear pictures. Spot the puppy is an enormously endearing character and his books have huge and enduring popularity among pre-school children.

Can you help Sally to find Spot under the carpet or in the cupboard? Lift the flap and see. There is real excitement for the very youngest reader, who will soon learn to handle the flaps carefully to enjoy the surprise (even if a little sticky tape has been needed).

An ideal first book, featuring a character no child can fail to fall in love with.

Liz Attenborough

Where's Spot?
Eric Hill

■ **Spot** has been published in 60 languages as well as sign language and Braille. There are now 40 million **Spot** books in print! From the early days of *Where's Spot?* the lovable puppy has gone on to star in 16 more lift-the-flap books (*Spot Bakes a Cake* and *Spot Stays Overnight*); pop-up books (*Spot's Preschool*); board books (*Spot at the Farm*); song books (*Spot's Big Nursery Song Book*); noisy books (*Spot's Noisy Walk*) and cloth books (*Hello Spot!*).

* * * * * * *

WIBBLY PIG series
Mick Inkpen

Suitable for pre-school children, the **Wibbly Pig** books are aimed at a slightly younger audience than Mick Inkpen's Kipper. Wibbly Pig acts out the everyday lives of his readers – the minutiae of preparing for bed is explored in one volume, the excitement of playing hide-and-seek in another. Big, bold drawings in pastel colours take pride of place on every page, whilst the large, crayon-like text cleverly creates discussion topics for parents and children to share. Wibbly Pig's consistent smile is intensely reassuring; this is a safe world, where gentle jokes are acted out. It's hard to imagine a better introduction to the joys of reading.

Laura Hutchings

■ Titles include: *Everyone Hide from Wibbly Pig*; *Wibbly Pig Likes Bananas*; *Wibbly Pig's Silly Big Bear*; *Wibbly Pig Is Happy*; *Wibby Pig's Garden* and *Is It Bedtime Yet, Wibbly Pig?*

2–5 years

As varied, colourful, funny, imaginative, thought-provoking and individual as the children and families who share and enjoy them, here are over 200 personal recommendations from the thousands of books published for toddlers and pre-schoolers. This selection makes a great starting point: a springboard for your own family library, and by a happy coincidence the titles run from *A is for Africa* to Z for *Zagazoo*. Here are books about just about every creature, subject, situation and emotion on the planet – and not necessarily on *our* planet!

Is this the best time of all to be sharing books with children? Quite possibly. They're joining in with the words, empathising with characters, and delighting in details you've probably missed in the illustrations. They'll have firm ideas about which bedtime story they want, and how often they want it. They'll have favourite books and, even if they don't know their names yet, they'll be developing individual tastes for favourite writers and illustrators. And they'll be very keen to talk to you about them.

Special Features

At this age, reading and listening to stories is purely and
simply for enjoyment: a rich and colourful backdrop to a time
of great change in a child's life. Stories provide ideal emotional
and intellectual frameworks against which children can compare
their own experiences. Their horizons are widening every day –
the transition from home to nursery, 'big' school, parties,
different foods, new friends and the arrival of siblings.
Favourite, comforting, familiar books can help to make those
changes smoother and less daunting – and much more fun.
Lindsey Fraser and Kathryn Ross

A IS FOR AFRICA Ifeoma Onyefulu

Ifeoma was born into the Igbo tribe and brought up in eastern Nigeria. This is one of many books she has written about the continent in which she grew up, accompanied by her own beautiful photographs. Working through the alphabet – *beads, grandmother, yam* – we get a real sense of activity. In Ifeoma's books, she highlights aspects of life that are common to children everywhere – families, playing, food and crafts – so that the emphasis is on shared experiences, however different the setting. The photographs, together with her simple explanations, ensure that there is plenty to talk about.

Kathryn Ross

■ Other titles in the series include *B is for Brains*; *I is for India*; *J is for Jamaica* (*UFBG* 119); *K is for Korea*; *M is for Mexico*; *P is for Pakistan* and *W is for World*.

AAAARRGGHH, SPIDER! Lydia Monks

Poor Spider – all he wants is to be a family pet, but everyone is terrified of him. Whenever he tries to show what a good pet he would be, people just shout 'AAAARRGGHH, SPIDER!' and he finds himself back out in the garden. Finally Spider gives up, and it is only then that he unwittingly does something that makes the family like him after all. But watch out for the fantastic twist at the end…

Lydia Monks' style is utterly zany and joyful, and her illustrations are full of hilarious detail – check out the people's expressions in the picture on the wall in the first and second spreads.

Susan Reuben

A–Z Books

Kipper's A to Z by Mick Inkpen (*UFBG* 121)

A Is for Africa by Ifeoma Onyefulu (*UFBG* 66)

J Is for Jamaica by Benjamin Zephaniah (*UFBG* 119)

The Dinosaur Alphabet Book by Jerry Pallotta

Dr Seuss's ABC by Dr Seuss

Alphabet Ice Cream by Nick Sharratt and Sue Heap

Bob's ABC (and D to Z Too!) by Simon Bartram

My Pop-up Surprise ABC by Robert Crowther

ALFIE GETS IN FIRST Shirley Hughes

Alfie is desperate to reach his house first – head back, arms pumping, he legs it home ahead of Mum and the buggy. But being first isn't quite enough. To emphasise his triumph, while Mum is struggling up the steps, he slams the door closed, locking himself in and Mum out. What might have been a rather ordinary story escalates beautifully; the words tell of the adults' efforts to break in, while the illustrations tell Alfie's story – of his ingenuity and pride in his achievements. Hughes creates a perfect storybook with a character whose delightful mini-dramas continue to charm both children and adults.

Lindsey Fraser

■ There are lots more **Alfie** books to enjoy. Try *Alfie's World*; *Alfie Wins a Prize*; *An Evening with Alfie*; *Alfie's Feet*; *Alfie and the Birthday Surprise* and *Alfie Gives a Hand*.

AMAZING GRACE see p.207.

see p.207.

ANGELINA BALLERINA series
Katharine Holabird, illustrated by Helen Craig

Wonderfully detailed illustrations accompany the stories of Angelina, the little white mouse who doesn't want to do anything but dance. At first this ambition gets her into trouble as she's late for school, swan-dives into the neighbours' flowerbeds and makes all the boys at school cross because she spins too fast to be caught by them. Then she's enrolled in dance classes and becomes a happy and helpful little mouse. This series is unapologetically pink and pretty, but some stories nevertheless succeed in appealing to a tomboy readership, such as the adventures of Angelina's friend Henry and the tale of *Angelina's Halloween*.

Sarah Frost Mellor

■ The enchanting, dancing mouse appears in many books including *Angelina and Henry*; *Angelina's Pop-up Dancing School*; *Angelina's Lucky Penny*; *Angelina's Ballet Class*; *Angelina's Christmas* and *Angelina and Alice*.

ANOTHER NIGHT BEFORE CHRISTMAS
Carol Ann Duffy, illustrated by Marc Boutavant

Most children by the age of six have become familiar with Clement Moore's classic narrative poem. This modern rendition will capture the interest of many more. Beautifully produced for smaller hands in a square format, this is a magical book that families will bring out each Christmas so they can share the excitement and anticipation of Christmas Eve.
Sonia Benster

AUGUSTUS AND HIS SMILE
Catherine Rayner

This is one of those truly magical books that can stand reading over and over and OVER again. Augustus, the most tigery of tigers, thinks he's lost his smile and sets out to find it. The words are a delight and the pictures glorious, but it's the way the two work together that takes this book to the highest level. Adults can watch for the subtle use of typography, textures and white space; children will revel in spotting the footprints, the shadows, the tiny beetle and the way the story dances and prances or drips and plops across the page.
Vivian French

AVOCADO BABY John Burningham

Mr and Mrs Hargraves are a puny couple whose puny new baby seems doomed to grow punier by the day. But then the other Hargraves children persuade their parents to feed the baby an avocado and an amazing transformation occurs. Soon the baby is bursting with strength, seeing off a burglar and nonchalantly tossing a couple of bullies into a pond. A pared-back text and lively illustrations combine to make this into a mini masterpiece of straight-faced surreal comedy, complete with a healthy eating message. What more could an under-five want?
Tony Bradman

BABY BRAINS

Simon James

This is one of my favourite picture books ever.

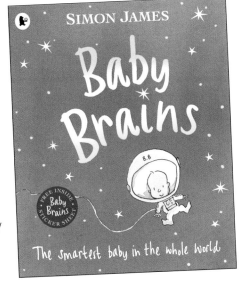

Baby Brains shows remarkable intellectual abilities, attending school at two days old and qualifying as a doctor only weeks later. He is so extraordinary that some scientists invite him to join their space mission. But on his very first space walk, Baby Brains looks at the vast emptiness around him and suddenly remembers that he is, after all, just a baby...

The amazing events of Baby Brains' first weeks are told in a hilariously deadpan way, as if his achievements are only *slightly* surprising. This book will make pre-schoolers laugh like crazy.

Susan Reuben

THE BABY WHO WOULDN'T GO TO BED

Helen Cooper

Refusing to sleep, the Baby drives his toy car down the road and away. He's determined to have fun, but everyone he meets is too tired to play. Soon even the car is sleepy, and the Baby has to push it home. Having travelled through a dream-laden landscape, peopled by toy-like characters, he eventually arrives home (with a little help from his mother). The final spread is of his mother kissing him goodnight, in a room where all his toys are revealed in their true form.

This Kate Greenaway-winning road-trip of a book is enchanting, and just perfect for bedtime.

Malachy Doyle

Choosing a Picture Book

There are so, so many picture books out there. All shapes, sizes, and styles, all those different stories and different kinds of illustration. However do you choose? What should you be looking for? **Lindsey Fraser** offers some tips...

Most of us have fond memories of a picture book to which we were very attached as children: the Ladybird edition of *The Elves and the Shoemaker* without which you couldn't go to sleep; Eric Carle's *The Very Hungry Caterpillar* (*UFBG* 59), heavily sticky-taped after a few too many vigorous attempts to poke fingers through the holes; the book you can't quite remember the name of, but it was a fourth birthday present from an aunt you liked enormously, it had a beige and red cover, it was about a bear and it smelt lovely.

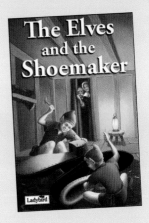

You can't possibly be sure that the book you're selecting for your child will reach that kind of mythical status, but in choosing one by which you feel enthused and intrigued, you are much more likely to bring home something that delights your child. A picture book is all about sharing. It is a joint activity, and your child – though probably not yet able to read in the technical sense – will bring as much to the experience as you.

But how do you choose?

Trust your instinct – if you like what you see, you'll respond more warmly to the story you are sharing with your child.

Try reading some of the story aloud (booksellers and librarians won't look askance – they see it all the time) to ensure that the tone of the book is one with which you feel comfortable. Success is heavily dependent on the confidence with which you read aloud.

Experiment – libraries are the perfect laboratories. Take home armfuls of books and wallow in the different worlds they reveal as you turn their pages.

Don't limit yourself to fiction – there are wonderful non-fiction picture books, and catalogue-style books like Heather Amery and Stephen Cartwright's **First Thousand Words** series (*UFBG* 234) and *You Choose* (Pippa Goodhart and Nick Sharratt, *UFBG* 200).

Don't feel compelled to start at the beginning – a particularly arresting illustration slap bang in the middle of the book can be the ideal introduction to the illustrator's style and characters. Then you can start from the beginning and work your way back to that page you already know and love.

Eavesdrop on other people's choices. Seek recommendations from your friends and relatives, and from booksellers and librarians. They won't all hit the mark, but you will soon begin to establish your own preferences and grow in confidence.

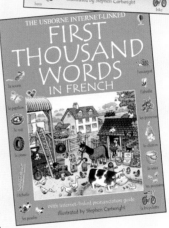

Watch children responding to the illustrations, the way in which their eyes move around the page the instant it's turned. Talk to them about what you both see – and there is every likelihood that you will be shown new ways of looking at pictures, and of telling stories.

Take books to read when you're waiting for the bus, or for a doctor's appointment – sharing books shouldn't be restricted to the half hour before bedtime.

Many parents are concerned by their child's determination to share the same book night after night... after night. In fact, that's a sign of success, but in order to maintain your own sanity, ensure that you have a varied rotation of books from which to choose.

Part of the joy of sharing picture books with children is allowing them develop their own tastes. Picture books may be slim, but most are as much works of art as anything you hang on your wall – a marriage of story and illustration that can last well beyond their golden or diamond anniversaries in the hearts, minds and imaginations of their readers. ●

BEAR Mick Inkpen

One day, a bear falls into Sophie's playpen. He's not a toy bear. He's real. He enjoys bouncing in the baby bouncer and playing with Sophie and her big brother, who tells the story. But when the grown-ups finally realise that there's a bear in the house, a serious man in a serious hat comes to decide what should be done. Which is when the reader has to step in. This beautifully illustrated story, with its unexpected yet satisfying ending, is a wonderful, interactive read.

Antonia Honeywell

BEAR AND ME Ella Burfoot

A sweetly illustrated and deceptively simple picture book that gives children permission to discover and explore the world at their own pace. A little girl takes her first steps towards independence, accompanied by her wide-eyed and not-so-confident teddy bear. One day, she tells teddy, he will be big and they'll be able to swim and fly and climb together. But for now, she reassures him, dipping their toes in the water and sitting at the foot of the stairs is 'just fine'. Perfect for those times when toddlers aren't feeling quite so gung-ho about being big boys and girls.

Kathryn Ross

BEDTIME STORIES Debi Gliori

Debi Gliori has written and illustrated her own stories for years – but then concocted this brilliant collection of familiar tales, each given a Gliori-style twist. 'The Three Little Pigs', for example, is a much more elaborate story than the original; the wolf, scuppered by Porkstone's sturdy building, tries to dynamite the house. The rhyming version of 'The Tortoise and the Hare' has an intergalactic dimension, and Hen's devious machinations in 'Nail Soup' leave you almost sorry for Fox. The often laugh-out-loud illustrations are packed with detail – this is a sharp, feisty collection that will be requested again and again.

Lindsey Fraser

■ Look out for Debi Gliori's companion volume *Nursery Rhymes*, which also gives a twist to each tale.

BEEGU
Alexis Deacon

Beegu is a yellow, rabbit-shaped alien who has crash-landed on earth. Lonely and missing her mum and dad, she tries to make friends, but nobody – or at least, no adult – seems to want her around. This despite the fact that Beegu is the sweetest of aliens, with long expressive antennae that droop with sadness or shoot straight up when she encounters a playground full of welcoming children. *Beegu*'s sombre palette might not have the instant appeal of more-colourful picture books, but this quirky story has charm and staying power, and the smudgy illustrations are full of subtle detail that children will delight in discovering. A lovely book to share.

Kathryn Ross

THE BEST PICNIC EVER
Clare Jarrett

It's the simplicity of the pictures that first catches your eye here. The crayon illustrations perfectly capture a child's attempts at drawing and colouring plants and animals. And for a good reason – this book is all about using your child's imagination.

Jack is having a picnic with his mum, but wishes there was someone to play with. Then a giraffe appears, an elephant and a few other unlikely animals. Jack has great fun galloping and leaping with them all.

This is an ideal book for any child who has to play alone at times. Ask your child at the end – do they think the animals *really* came to the picnic?

Yzanne Mackay

BIG BLUE WHALE
Nicola Davies, illustrated by Nick Maland

Nicola Davies is passionate about wildlife. Before writing children's books, she studied whales in Newfoundland and was a presenter on the BBC's *Really Wild Show*. Her knowledge and enthusiasm are evident in her outstanding narrative non-fiction books, which encourage children not only to learn about the natural world but to develop an emotional relationship with animals and the environment. *Big Blue Whale* sensuously explores what this magnificent creature feels, sounds and smells like. Its rhythmic text and repeated vocabulary makes it great for reading aloud to young children as well as for early independent reading. The text is accompanied by informative watercolour illustrations with details picked out in textured pen and ink. A big book version is also available.

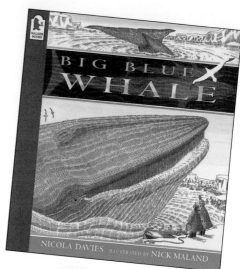

Nikki Gamble

BILLY'S BUCKET
Kes Gray, illustrated by Garry Parsons

Billy's parents are puzzled by his choice of a bucket for his birthday present, but when Billy gazes into it he can see a fantastic undersea world complete with sharks, coral reefs and submarines. Mum and Dad ask to use the bucket for mundane household tasks, but Billy warns them that they must never, ever borrow it.

The big, bold illustrations are cleverly painted in the round, creating a startling fisheye lens effect that makes us feel as if we're looking into Billy's bucket, too. Highly original, and children love the fact that the last laugh is on the grown-ups.

Kathryn Ross

BISCUIT BEAR Mini Grey

Because Horace is thwarted in his desire to eat the bear-shaped biscuit he made that day, he pops it into a tin and puts it on his pillow. But while he sleeps, the biscuit bear sets about baking a whole batch of biscuits for company. Acrobats, strong men, knife throwers – the kitchen becomes a splendid circus, with Biscuit Bear the ringmaster. But it all ends in crumbs. Mini Grey's quirky text is as sparse as it is understated. 'Bongo the dog liked biscuits. (But not in a way that was necessarily good for biscuits.)' Such gems are ripe for repetition.

Lindsey Fraser

BOB ROBBER AND DANCING JANE
Andrew Matthews, illustrated by Bee Willey

This picture book reads like an old folk tale, but is actually an original story, poetically told by Andrew Matthews. Bob Robber is a thief. He can steal 'honey from the bees and the scent from flowers'. But when he sees Dancing Jane pass nimbly by, he realises that the one thing that he can't do is dance – and this makes him sad. Bob Robber thinks the solution lies in another theft, but he finally comes to realise that asking for things can be better than stealing.

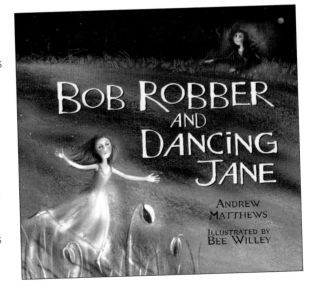

Bee Willey's illustrations are ethereal and haunting, the colours changing from dingy blues and greens to vibrant pinks and oranges as Bob Robber transforms. A quiet little gem.

Susan Reuben

BOING!
Sean Taylor, illustrated by Bruce Ingman

Readers! A fanfare if you please for The Great Elastic Marvel (five times World Trampolining Champion). An accidental bounce sees him plunging from his tower-block window, BUT... through a miraculous and amazingly coincidental series of death-defying *boings*, he escapes ravening lions, drowning and death beneath a train's wheels... only to bounce right back through his own window!

This is a veritable circus in a book. There's high drama, perfect timing, tongue-in-cheek humour and glorious flourishes; the striking illustrations experiment with colour, space, typeface and perspective, telling much more story than the deadpan text. Very theatrical – and very funny!

Helen Simmons

BORKA
John Burningham

When Borka is born without feathers, Mrs Plumpster sensibly knits a grey woollen jumper to keep her warm. But Borka's siblings tease her and when the family migrate, she's left flightless, tearfully and tragically alone on the marshes. Rescue arrives in the form of stoical Captain McAllister and Fowler, his dog, who sail upriver to London and a new home for Borka in Kew Gardens.

It's a great story – from homely beginning to darkest, deepest despair to happy ending. Underpinned by Burningham's impressionistic, atmospheric autumnal landscapes and dark, boldly black lines (revolutionary in their time), it's one I've never forgotten.

Helen Simmons

BUSIEST PEOPLE EVER
Richard Scarry

The 'people' of the title are in fact the friendly cats, dogs, mice and pigs that inhabit the world of Richard Scarry's books; here we see them doing jobs – they are ditch diggers, bricklayers, nurses, harbour police... The ubiquitous Lowly Worm (my favourite character from Scarry's world) even does a turn as a TV entertainer.

There are pieces of narrative here, but this is mainly a book of bright and busy pictures for a child who likes exploring detail. It has good words for learning ('Mummy, what's a stevedore?'), and a huge range of jobs to talk about ('What does a hay baler do, Daddy?', 'Can I be a lobster fisherman / lighthouse keeper / miner / magician / weatherman when I grow up?'). A gem.

Daniel Hahn

A BUSY DAY FOR A GOOD GRANDMOTHER
Margaret Mahy, illustrated by Margaret Chamberlain

When Mrs Oberon's son rings for help with his wailing baby, she's immediately on the case. Her backpack filled with all manner of extraneous items, she vaults effortlessly onto her trusty trail bike and sets off. The journey is challenging, to say the least, but Mrs Oberon is prepared for every eventuality from alligators, to ice vultures, to landslides. Once there, she soothes the baby and puts her feckless son straight about a thing or two. This rollicking story gleefully jettisons the stereotype of the passive, silver-haired grandparent and the illustrations are every bit as energetic as the remarkable heroine.

Lindsey Fraser

CAN'T CATCH ME!
Michael Foreman

Here's a fresh take on the nursery game of challenge, chase, catch and tickle, as Little Monkey evades his mother at bedtime. Fantasy rules, with his would-be captors ranging from large wild animals to aliens. Foreman's illustrations are as apparently effortless as Monkey's progress. Mixed media create passages of transparency and opacity with a myriad of textures, in rich greens, cerulean, tint of rose, smoky violet, and touches of light lemon. As well as experiencing a satisfying story with a surprise climax and closing twist in the tale, young readers can name the animals, find visual clues, predict, growl, roar, hrrrrumf and chant the refrains.

Jane Doonan

CAN'T YOU SLEEP, LITTLE BEAR?
Martin Waddell, illustrated by Barbara Firth

Little Bear is afraid of the dark and no matter what Big Bear does, nothing can reassure him: even big lanterns are no match for the dark outside the cave. Big Bear solves the problem by taking Little Bear out into the night to look at the bright moon and the shining stars. Little Bear falls asleep and Big Bear can finish reading his book.

The soft, expressive line and gentle colour of the illustrations capture the quiet humour of the text perfectly. *Little Bear* can be read every night for as long as is necessary, and will enthral both reader and listener every time.

Gill Vickery

CAN YOU HEAR THE SEA?
Judy Cumberbatch, illustrated by Ken Wilson-Max

Sarah's grandpa gives her a shell, telling her that if she listens to it she will hear the sea. Each day, Sarah puts the shell to her ear, but all she can ever hear are the market mammies haggling, the banana trees *swish-swishing* and the pepper stew *sput-sputtering*. Eventually she feels fed up with trying – 'That's some silly shell,' she says. It takes Grandpa's calm presence to enable her to rise above the clamour of everyday life, and finally hear the sea.

This is a simple-yet-deep story, infused with Ken Wilson-Max's paintings of African scenes in Gauguin-like colours.

Susan Reuben

CAN YOU SEE A LITTLE BEAR?
James Mayhew, illustrated by Jackie Morris

A sumptuous book that really teaches children to look at pictures. The illustrations are fabulous, from the star-studded cover and the journey on the first endpapers onwards. On one level it is a book about animals, for on the left-hand pages it tells and shows us that elephants are big, lions are yellow, parrots are green and red... But on the right-hand pages children are invited to find a little bear doing all sorts of strange things.

The rhyming text is perfect to read aloud, and the illustrations bring the information and the game together in a remarkable way, offering loads to talk about throughout. This book manages to be extremely beautiful, informative and great fun – it's one you'll want to keep for ever.

Wendy Cooling

CARS, TRUCKS AND THINGS THAT GO
Richard Scarry

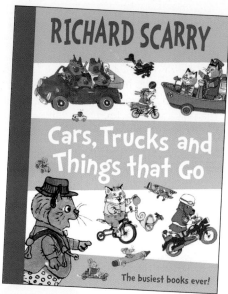

Quite simply a brilliant title for vehicle-loving toddlers. The book follows the Pig Family's journey to the beach and back again, involving all sorts of traffic incidents along the way. There is so much detail to look at and pore over. Some of the scenarios are hilarious, such as the climactic pile-up involving mustard, tomato juice, whipped cream and flour vans.

Mayhem and destruction abound, tempered with warnings to drive carefully. There is plenty to talk about, and perhaps you could even invent your own weird and wacky cars. Have you ever seen a caterpillar bus or a pickle truck? My seven-year-old still adores this book. And of course there's the cheery gold bug to spot throughout.

Jane Churchill

CATCH THAT KITTEN!
Pamela Duncan Edwards, illustrated by Rebecca Harry

Tilly is a mother cat faced with the knotty problem of getting her five energetic kittens into their basket for the night. They would much rather hide in the doll's house or drive a train. One by one, Midnight, Snowball, Ginger, Boots and Pirate escape to play with the toys in the nursery; one by one Tilly brings them back.

The pictures add personality to the story as Tilly gets more and more tired. The refrain of 'Uh-oh' each time a kitten is discovered to be missing is great fun and perfect for toddlers to join in with.

Antonia Honeywell

Everybody's Favourite...

THE CAT IN THE HAT
Dr Seuss

With Mum away for the day, the legendary Cat turns up at the house and provides his two child hosts with the zaniest and wildest display of madness and mayhem. The children are staggered by his performance, but terrified of how cross their mother will be when she returns. The Cat introduces them to amazing juggling feats, the rascally Thing One and Thing Two, and a very agitated fish. But as the tale promises to spin out of control, the Cat reluctantly tidies up his crater of mess, and escapes just before Mum appears.

This is a madcap extravaganza of poetry, humour and wackiness that has placed millions of children on the pathway to reading. Throughout the English-speaking world, children learn about the fabulousness of words through the 223 present in *The Cat in the Hat*.

Jonny Zucker

The cover says 'Dr Seuss makes reading fun', and that is true nowhere more than in this genius tale of a wet, wet, wet day when there's nothing to do... 'Till the Cat pitches up (with Thing One and Thing Two)'. The Cat makes mayhem around the house (because Mother's away) quite upsetting the fish (who does not want to play such irresponsible games). With his usual ingredients – contagious rhythms, infectiously rhymed – Dr Seuss serves up the sort of anarchic pursuits that I'm drawn to, like all children of 4, 33, or whatever, as we collude with delight in the sort of behaviour our mothers would tell us we oughtn't really to encourage. And we're given an ending that leaves even the conscientious fish happy, yet allows readers to retain a small thrill of complicity, sharing a secret, condoning illicit behaviour – because, 'Well... What would *you* do?' Irresistible.

Daniel Hahn

There's a sequel, *The Cat in the Hat Came Back*. **The Cat in the Hat Learning Library** (Tish Rabe, illustrated by Aristides Ruiz) is an American series of early-learning books for children aged 4–7 – subjects include space (*There's No Place Like Space*), the body (*Inside Your Outside*) and health (*Oh, the Things You Can Do That Are Good for You!*).

CHARLIE AND LOLA series
Lauren Child

Charlie has this little sister, Lola... She's a bright, strident personality with endearingly eccentric speech and a wild imagination. Like all children, though only small she believes she can do anything, and rails against the injustices of life – having to eat tomatoes, being told to go to sleep when you're not tired, and so on. In each story, Charlie, with preternatural wisdom and patience a parent would kill for, copes with her antics and gently talks her round. Charmingly illustrated with a mixture of artwork, photographs and textiles, the books capture the world of a headstrong little girl in a way that feels authentic and is very funny.

Steve Cole

■ Once you've read one, you'll want to read the rest of the **Charlie and Lola** books. Also available are *I Absolutely Must Do Colouring-in Now*; *I Am Not Sleepy and I Will Not Go to Bed*; *I Will Never Not Ever Eat a Tomato*; *I Am Too Absolutely Small for School* and *My Wobbly Tooth Must Not Ever Never Fall Out*.

THE CHRISTMAS STORY Ian Beck

Ian Beck blurs the boundaries between picture-book art and drama to irresistible effect in *The Christmas Story*. The layout is designed as a succession of double-page scenes set in decorative borders, showing biblical characters posed like actors, with the text as 'voice-over': the page as stage. He begins with the Annunciation in Mary's garden; a paradise teeming with flowers, plants, fruiting trees and a pair of doves. The drama gradually unfolds until, through the magic of the final page-turn, viewers are transported through time and space, and find themselves watching the close of the Reception Class Nativity play, complete with cardboard props. Perfect.

Jane Doonan

CLOWN
Quentin Blake

Quentin Blake's much-loved drawings are so full of energy and character that in *Clown* he manages to do without words altogether. It's the lively story of a toy clown, who is thrown out, along with a whole lot of other toys, and determines to get his friends rescued from the dustbin where they've been dumped.

Clown is harder to share than most picture books, as you have to find the words yourself, so it will change a bit each time, but it means you and your child can really read the pictures together (they may find it easier than you, having never lost the habit), work out what's happening, and find the details you both like. I know no better demonstration of just how eloquent pictures can be.

Daniel Hahn

COCKATOOS
Quentin Blake

Winner of the 1992 Smarties Award, *Cockatoos* is the *crème de la crème* of counting books. Every morning Professor Dupont follows the same routine, and when he's ready for the day, he greets his ten cockatoos. Until, that is, one morning when the cockatoos decide that it's time to have some fun. They escape from their conservatory and Professor Dupont searches high and low, but the cockatoos are nowhere to be seen. Or at least Professor Dupont can't spot them. Keen young eyes will have more success. Children will delight in searching the pictures to find the cheeky cockatoos and enjoy colluding in the joke with the author. A book that entertains as well as teaches. Masterful.

Nikki Gamble

Sharing Pictures, Sharing Words

Sharing picture books can mean far more than you reading the text while your child looks at the images, as picture-book editor **Susan Reuben** explains…

For children who cannot yet read, illustrations have an overwhelming importance. So while picture books can be enjoyed by all ages, they are especially valuable for the under-fives.

While you are reading the words of a picture book, babies and toddlers are seeing their own story in the pictures. Because they're not distracted by the text, they will probably notice tiny visual details that you would never spot: a picture of a dog on the jumper of a child; a cake on a table at the back of a room.

When you are sharing a picture book with a child, don't necessarily read the text straight through without pause. Expect (and encourage) frequent interruptions, as your child points out something in a picture or makes a comment on the story. By talking about and around what is on each page, sharing picture books becomes a real joy for both the parent and child, and it means that no two 'readings' are ever quite the same.

In the best picture books, the pictures and the words are like two people having a conversation. Sometimes they agree exactly, the illustrations showing precisely what is in the text. Sometimes one has something extra to say, the pictures adding a few further thoughts to the story. And sometimes they disagree completely, the illustrations saying something entirely different to the words. So, in *Mr Magnolia* (*UFBG*

He gives rides to his friends
when he goes for a scoot —

135), the story describes how poor Mr Magnolia has only one boot. And so ostensibly do the pictures. But in fact they do much more. For example, there are mice to spot on many of the spreads, although they are only ever mentioned once. And the pictures also turn the story into a counting book. Five owls are learning to hoot; turn the page and six children are going for a scoot; then seven children follow Mr Magnolia down the chute, and so on…

In *The Smartest Giant in Town* (*UFBG* 171), the town comes to life in the pictures, while the story just concentrates on the giant himself. There's a pig on the way to build a house of bricks, a squirrel reading a newspaper and a rabbit on a mobile phone. Each time you read the book together, you'll spot something new.

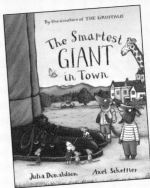

In *Rosie's Walk* (*UFBG* 50), if you read the story without looking at the illustrations, you'd think it was a very straightforward tale about a hen going for a stroll through a farm and then coming back home again. But when you look at the pictures, you see that on every spread she is followed by a predatory fox, who has frequent and entertaining accidents that prevent him from catching her. All the while Rosie marches on oblivious, with an unchangingly insouciant expression on her face.

It's possible to enjoy a book with your child long before they're old enough for the text in its full form – by simply looking at the pictures and talking about them you could tell an abridged version of the story as you go. By the time you're ready to embark together on the full text, your child will already know and love the book.

Don't resist starting in the middle, either. If your child wants to turn straight to their favourite picture of a dinosaur eating a banana, that's fine. You can always go back to the beginning once you've had a good look at it.

Eventually, most children will come to pick up a book they've never seen before, and tell the story on their own by 'reading' the pictures. It may bear no relation to the actual story, but this doesn't matter in the least.

Often the forgotten corners of a book provide more visual treats: the endpapers (the pages at the beginning and end), the title page, the back cover, even the copyright page. You may skip over them because they don't contain any story text, but for your child they are as much part of the book as the story itself, and often the illustrator has added something lovely that really enhances them.

So think of a picture book as something to meander through together, relishing the visual detail as well as the narrative. Let your child take the lead in choosing which book to look at (even if you've read the same one every night for a month), and in setting the pace as you read through it. And expect children to come back to their favourite picture books again and again, even long after they've outgrown them. ●

THE COLOUR OF HOME
Mary Hoffman, illustrated by Karin Littlewood

Hassan has just come to England from Somalia, and he feels very strange in this new place. Everything seems grey and cold, his classroom is inside instead of out, and he can't speak English so doesn't understand what his teacher or schoolmates are saying. Then the teacher asks him to paint something. Hassan produces a tranquil picture of his home and family in Somalia, but then adds guns and flames to the scene to reflect what happened to him there. The next day, a woman who speaks Somali comes to the classroom to help Hassan put his picture into words.

This is a warm, ultimately hopeful story about the world of a refugee child, and the compassion and understanding shown to him by his teachers and schoolmates.

Susan Reuben

COME AWAY FROM THE WATER, SHIRLEY
John Burningham

■ Also look out for the sequel: *Time to Get Out of the Bath, Shirley*.

John Burningham's story of a child's wildly imaginative adventures, contrasted with her staid parents' repeated warnings to be cautious, was first published in 1977 and is still fresh and funny.

On the left-hand page, simple line drawings with cross-hatched patches of pale colour show the unimaginative parents setting up deckchairs, snoozing and drinking tea. On the right, vivid washes of colour highlight Shirley, blissfully oblivious of the real world, battling pirates, digging up treasure and sailing moonlit seas. In a perfect marriage of text and illustration, Shirley's exotic and exciting fantasy takes her far away from the humdrum and mundane world of her kindly but dull parents.

Gill Vickery

THE CONQUERORS
David McKee

David McKee's *The Conquerors* is a simple story of a general and his army; the general decides to invade a small defenceless country, but finds that his soldiers are won over to the customs of the place; the soldiers don't conquer the civilians but the other way around. It's a parable that parents will appreciate, as affecting as it is clever, while children will be delighted by the story and McKee's warm and joyful illustrations. A very modern book in its way, but also an old-fashioned example of picture-book genius.

Daniel Hahn

COPS AND ROBBERS
Allan Ahlberg, illustrated by Janet Ahlberg

It's Christmas Eve and robbers are about. The dreaded Grabber Dan and his motley gang are stealing toys from children's stockings. Will the best of the cops, Upstanding Officer Pugh, catch them before the children wake up? He sets to with great panache; tying them up and bundling them into the local police cells before making sure the toys are all returned. Janet Ahlberg's warm, witty illustrations tell the story as much as Allan's rollicking verse. One of our favourite spreads is the street map marking which toys have been stolen from which property. Definitely one to return to again and again.

Jane Churchill

Cops and Robbers

Janet & Allan Ahlberg

Princess Books

The Kiss that Missed by David Melling (*UFBG* 121)

The Paper Bag Princess by Robert Munsch (*UFBG* 153)

The Princess and the Pea by Lauren Child (*UFBG* 159)

The Pea and the Princess by Mini Grey (*UFBG* 156)

Little Princesses series by Katie Chase (*UFBG* 256)

COWS IN THE KITCHEN
June Crebbin, illustrated by Katharine McEwen

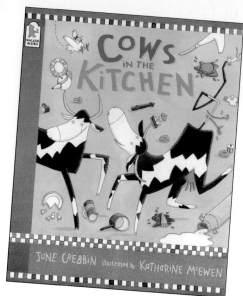

For extrovert parents, this wonderfully exuberant rhyming picture book will have total audience participation, as young children love to join in the chorus of animal voices.

At first glance, the repetitive refrain seems very simple, but the story is cleverly constructed to hold interest. First the animals and their sounds are introduced. Then we meet Tom Farmer fast asleep. It's time to wake him up, which the animals do most effectively. There is great detail in the chaotic pictures, and look out for the little white mouse, who hides throughout, finally running off into the endpapers...

Sonia Benster

CRISPIN, THE PIG WHO HAD IT ALL
Ted Dewan

Crispin really is the pig who has it all: the biggest pile of presents, the most hi-tech gadgets, all the junk food he can eat ... yet still he wants more. One year Santa leaves a very special box, which contains 'the very best thing in the whole wide world'. The problem is, there's nothing in it. Crispin thinks it's the worst present ever. But with the help of his friends, he finds that with a bit of imagination the box can be everything – space base, shop, pirate ship, castle – and is worth far more than any present he's had before.

Eye-catching illustrations hide hundreds of details to spot in this unsentimental, modern morality story, which cleverly shows that friends are worth more than any amount of possessions.

Eileen Armstrong

■ The series continues with *Crispin and the Best Birthday Surprise Ever* and *Crispin and the 3 Little Piglets*.

A CULTIVATED WOLF
Becky Bloom, illustrated by Pascal Biet

A cow, a duck and a pig are reading peacefully when a marauding wolf disturbs their afternoon. But, instead of fleeing his hungry-looking advances, they simply tell him off. 'This is a farm for cultivated animals,' they explain, pushing him away. So Wolf decides that he too wants to be cultivated. At first his efforts to read are derided, but eventually, after lots of practice, the cow, duck and pig can't get enough of Wolf's reading.

This charming, quirky story about winning friends, the challenge of reading and love of stories couldn't be a better encouragement for a new reader.

Lindsey Fraser

CURIOUS GEORGE series
Margret and H.A. Rey

George is a monkey, one with an insatiable curiosity. He sees a yellow hat and climbs into it. The owner of the hat captures him and takes him to France. On the ship he sees a gull flying, and tries that, too ... and ends up very wet. Whatever he sees he wants to try, and his adventures have him smoking a pipe, flying through the air on a handful of balloons, and even ringing the fire brigade and ending up in prison. Of course he escapes and ends up in a new home where he is very happy – the zoo.

First published in 1941, George's adventures – and those of his friend, the man in the yellow hat – have delighted generations with their unpredictability and sheer *joie de vivre*.

Leonie Flynn

■ The curious monkey appears in many more books, including *Curious George's First Day of School*; *Curious George Takes a Train*; *Curious George Goes to a Chocolate Factory*; *Curious George Goes to an Ice-Cream Shop*; *Curious George Rides a Bike* and *A Treasury of Curious George*.

DADDY'S LULLABY
Tony Bradman, illustrated by Jason Cockcroft

It's late on Friday evening and Daddy tiptoes in through the front door to find everyone asleep except the cat and a very wakeful baby. Together, Daddy and the baby walk through the house, peeping in on big brother and Mummy as they go, and finally settling down in an armchair, where Daddy sings his lullaby.

This is a peaceful, calming book, celebrating simple family life in a series of atmospheric illustrations. Its straightforward charm makes it the perfect bedtime read to share with a toddler at the end of a busy or difficult day.

Antonia Honeywell

THE DANCING TIGER
Malachy Doyle, illustrated by
Steve Johnson and Lou Fancher

From the opening line of this book, an ethereal scene is set. The 'quiet, gentle tiger' tiptoes and dances through the soothing rhythms of each page, and we see him entertaining the small girl narrator through the seasons. Every month at full moon, she comes to the woods below the hill to dance with the tiger, until the time comes at last to pass on the tradition to her great-grandchild, because her 'dancing nights are done'.

The wonderful illustrations allow us to enter unseen into the tiger's secret, mysterious world. This is an enchanting, lyrical story, infused with a beautiful feeling of calm.

Patricia Legan

A DARK, DARK TALE
Ruth Brown

Ruth Brown's gothic tale for very small children delights and scares in equal measure. Over a series of double-page spreads with minimal text, it traces a cat's night-time journey to an empty house in the dark, dark woods with a secret tucked away in a small box at the back of a dark, dark cupboard. In the first three spreads you'll need to look very carefully among the shadows to find the black cat, which is hidden in wonderfully brooding pictures full of endless detail. It's one of those books that every time you read it, you'll be amazed by things you hadn't noticed before.

Gill Vickery

DAVE AND THE TOOTH FAIRY
Verna Wilkins, illustrated by Paul Hunt

David Alexander Curtis loses his first tooth when he sneezes, and is horrified when he can't find it. He comes up with a clever plan to use his grandfather's false teeth in its place, hoping that the tooth fairy might give him money for them instead. Luckily all turns out well; Grandfather finds the missing tooth and Dave is able to buy the kite he wants.

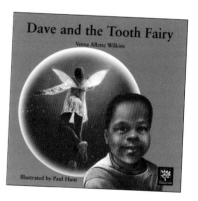

This is one of the few picture books published in the UK that features a cast of black characters. The story reads aloud well with alliterative descriptions, and the realistic pen-and-ink drawings play cleverly with perspective.

Laura Atkins

> ## Dinosaur Books
>
> *Dinosaur Chase!* by Benedict Blathwayt (*UFBG* 92)
>
> *Dinosaurs and All That Rubbish* by Michael Foreman (*UFBG* 92)
>
> *Harry and the Bucketful of Dinosaurs* by Ian Whybrow (*UFBG* 111)
>
> **How Do Dinosaurs**... series by Jane Yolen (*UFBG* 114)
>
> *Dinosaur Poems* by John Foster, illustrated by Korky Paul

DINOSAUR CHASE!
Benedict Blathwayt

The dinosaur Fin is in trouble! The bullies are picking on him and his friends, and he can't seem to outrun them – not all of the bullies run fast, but most of them can; not all of them can swim, but most can; there's one that can't jump, but the others can, and then suddenly a breathless Fin reaches the edge of a cliff and discovers that ... he can fly! He has a special gift that none of the others have! An exciting story with a charming ending, and a reassuring 'everyone is special' moral thrown in for good measure.

Daniel Hahn

DINOSAURS AND ALL THAT RUBBISH
Michael Foreman

This picture book, which brings together dinosaurs with a strong 'save the planet' message, has been a hit for over 30 years and it's not hard to see why. The story of how man destroys the Earth with his excesses of waste and pollution, and how the dinosaurs return to restore it to its natural state of beauty is simply and touchingly told.

Michael Foreman's landscapes are vividly real and his wonderful dinosaurs are both warm and engaging – more than enough to draw children into what could have been, in anyone else's hands, an overly heavy moral tale.

Philippa Milnes-Smith

DR DOG Babette Cole

Dr Dog is the Gumboyle family's pet. He is also – rather unconventionally – their doctor. So when they get sick, he's summoned back from Brazil, where he's been at a conference giving a paper on bone marrow, to take care of them. What follows is (like many books by Babette Cole) a very funny, just-rude-enough story to entertain young readers, and which has some useful knowledge about health and hygiene imparted along the way.

Daniel Hahn

Everybody's Favourite...

DOGGER Shirley Hughes

Only a heart of stone would fail to be moved by little Dave's angst when he loses his favourite toy dog, Dogger... And no one could fail to be cheered by his older sister's act of generosity when Dogger turns up at the local fête. This is my own childhood favourite – and that of many others, too. It won Shirley Hughes her first Kate Greenaway medal and is widely recognised as a modern classic. With Hughes' books we feel we are in times past – a nostalgic comfort zone. But they are more memorable than most picture books, and more moving.

Jon Appleton

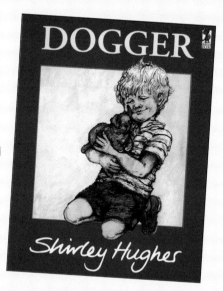

Dave loves his soft old toy, Dogger, but one day Dogger goes missing. Dave's family search the house and garden in vain. But the child audience of this book will have spotted that Dave dropped him outside the school. If only they could tell him!

Next day is the school's summer fair, wonderfully depicted in such detail that we can see all sorts of dramas going on. And on the toy stall is ... Dogger! But Dave hasn't enough money to buy him. While he desperately looks for Mum and Dad to give him the money he needs, a little girl buys Dogger, and she won't give him up! Until Dave's lovely sister Bella gives the girl the huge, smart teddy she has just won in a race, and Dogger is safely returned.

Such surging passions and drama, and the wonderful observation of family life at its best, makes this an absolute classic. Thirty years old, but as fresh as ever, *Dogger* is a visual and verbal masterpiece.

Pippa Goodhart

DON'T LET THE PIGEON DRIVE THE BUS! Mo Willems

At first glance, Mo Willems illustrations look like a child's drawings, but appearances are deceptive. In simple crayon images on a solid pastel background, the artist skilfully conveys a remarkable range of emotions as the pigeon tries every trick in the book to get his way.

In *Don't Let the Pigeon Drive the Bus!* the child reader has to play adult when the pigeon throws a tantrum. In the next book, *The Pigeon Finds a Hot Dog*, an innocent-looking duckling interrupts the pigeon at snack time and takes a subtle approach to play the pigeon at his own game. Extremely original and very funny.

Madelyn Travis

DUCK IN THE TRUCK
Jez Alborough

This is the picture book I'd recommend for all boys of around three, who can be tricky to please. It's a boisterous, cheeky, vibrantly illustrated (with lots of muddy splashes!) rhyming text that you'll want to learn off by heart and which your children will ask for again and again. The 'This is the house that Jack built'-style story is simple – duck's in his truck, driving home. He gets stuck in the muck. Bad luck! Plenty of animals try to help in ways that are both misguided and imaginative.

Jon Appleton

■ Duck went on to become a highly successful character in several sequels. Look out for *Fix-it Duck*; *Duck to the Rescue*; *Hit the Ball, Duck*; *Duck's Day Out*; *Captain Duck* and *Duck's Key: Where Can it Be?*

Animal Books

Rosie's Walk by Pat Hutchins (*UFBG* 50)

The Dancing Tiger by Malachy Doyle (*UFBG* 90)

Curious George series by Margret and H.A. Rey (*UFBG* 89)

Russell the Sheep by Rob Scotton (*UFBG* 165)

The Tiger Who Came to Tea by Judith Kerr (*UFBG* 186)

Misery Moo by Jeanne Willis (*UFBG* 133)

Slow Loris by Alexis Deacon (*UFBG* 171)

How to Speak Moo by Deborah Fajerman (*UFBG* 115)

Augustus and his Smile by Catherine Rayner (*UFBG* 68)

EAT YOUR PEAS
Kes Gray, illustrated by Nick Sharratt

Mum really wants Daisy to eat her peas. But there's one small problem: Daisy doesn't like peas. In desperation, Mum resorts to a series of bigger and increasingly surreal bribes in an attempt to get Daisy to digest the little green balls 'ganging up on her plate'. It's a hysterical menu of offerings that will resonate with every child who has ever been promised mealtime trade-offs. The consecutive pictures focusing further and further in on Daisy's face are particularly hilarious.

With Mum finally offering her daughter every supermarket, sweet shop, toy shop and bike shop in the world, plus the Sun the Moon and the stars and more, the reader is left guessing as to whether or not Daisy will cave in, right up till the hilarious twist at the end.

Jonny Zucker

■ To read more about this wonderful character, look out for the rest of the **Daisy** books, which include *Yuk!*; *Really, Really, You Do!* and *006 and a Bit*.

EDWARDO, THE HORRIBLEST BOY IN THE WHOLE WIDE WORLD
John Burningham

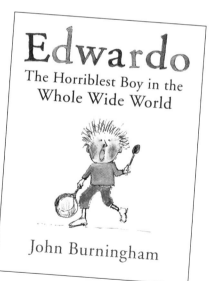

This witty account of positive parenting will keep children and their parents laughing. Edwardo behaves perfectly normally, but adult reactions to his behaviour are exaggerated until he begins to act out what he's told. He behaves worse and worse the more criticism he gets, until he does indeed become the 'horriblest boy in the whole wide world'. Then, quite by accident, he begins to do things that adults perceive as good; he responds positively to their praise and becomes the 'loveliest boy in the whole wide world'. Though you might want to explain that it's not a good idea to copy Edwardo going off with a lady who takes him back to her house.

Gill Vickery

THE ELEPHANT AND THE BAD BABY
Elfrida Vipont, illustrated by Raymond Briggs

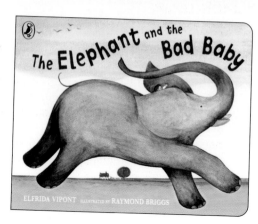

My battered hardback copy with its ragged dust jacket dates back to 1975 and reflects endless readings, for this book has been a winner with generations of small children in my family. The Elephant offers the Bad Baby a ride and they take ice creams, pies and more on their way – but the Bad Baby never says please! The chorus 'rumpeta, rumpeta, rumpeta, all down the road', is great to join in with, and the excitement builds as the baker, the butcher, the ice-cream man and other angry shopkeepers give chase. The conclusion to this romp is hugely satisfying, and you'll need to read the whole thing time and time again. This is early Raymond Briggs and his pictures, coloured on the left and balanced by black and white on the right, add life and character to a terrific cumulative story.

Wendy Cooling

ELLIE AND ELVIS
Vivian French, illustrated by Michael Terry

Elephants Ellie and Elvis are the best of friends – both love bananas and oranges and dancing together under the light of the moon. It's the perfect friendship until a misunderstanding injects a tiny element of doubt which, fanned by the duplicity of an opportunistic monkey, escalates into a full-on fall-out. Sweetness and light are replaced with suspicion and resentment. But not for long. The two friends discover that they've been duped, resolve their differences and dance their way back to happiness. Meanwhile, amidst the rich, vivid and hilarious illustrations, the unrepentant monkeys party on…

Lindsey Fraser

ELMER series
David McKee

Elmer is a patchwork elephant – a colourful creature amongst his grey friends. His sense of fun and kind nature bring a new dimension to the jungle and we are also introduced to his ventriloquist cousin, the black-and-white-checked Wilbur, Grandpa Eldo and a selection of other quirky beasts.

The genius of David McKee makes each **Elmer** story a delightful, thoughtful and immensely satisfying read. Elmer's extravagantly multi-coloured appearance makes him impossible to miss, and his warm and humorous personality makes him extremely lovable.

Jonny Zucker

■ You can meet Elmer in a range of formats including lift-the-flap books (*Elmer's Hide-and-Seek*); bath books (*Elmer's Bath*); board books (*Elmer's Colours*) and sound books (*Elmer's Concert*). And don't miss the wonderful **Elmer** picture books, such as *Elmer*; *Elmer and Wilbur*; *Elmer and the Hippos* and *Elmer and Snake*.

ELOISE series
Kay Thompson, illustrated by Hilary Knight

You can't help but love the outrageous six-year-old Eloise. Through pink and black drawings, and a chatty first person narrative, Eloise tells us about her life on the top floor of the Plaza Hotel, New York, where she orders room service and lives with her nanny. It's sad she's so alone, but she lives in her imagination, entertaining herself with the life of the hotel, gate-crashing weddings ('and I usually stay for the reception'), helping the switchboard ladies, and having larks in the shower. Although written in 1955, the story has a modern 'it' girl, Lauren Child-like style and feel.

Liz Attenborough

■ In this series: *Eloise in Paris*; *Eloise in Hollywood*; *Eloise Takes a Bath* and *Eloise Dresses Up*.

Performance Pieces

Reading books aloud is the perfect chance to release the actor in you. Your child will love it – and you'll have a great time, too, promises **Kathryn Ross**.

There can be few more pleasurable ways to spend time than in sharing a book with a child who loves the experience as much as you do. The laughter, the anticipation of favourite 'corners' of the story, the discovery of a new detail in an illustration – the best story sessions leave both readers delighted by what they have shared, and by the reaction elicited in each other.

Look for books in which the pictures tell parts of the story that the words apparently ignore. *Alfie Gets in First* (*UFBG* 67) is a perfect example of this. The child on your knee watches as Alfie calms himself and then solves the situation, while the reader concentrates on the growing chaos amongst the adults shouting instructions through the letterbox. *Handa's Surprise* (*UFBG* 29) is a sustained visual joke, as the delicious contents of the basket on Handa's head are gradually plundered by the cheeky animals. In *Rosie's Walk* (*UFBG* 50) the text remains blissfully unaware of the danger through which Rosie the hen struts, while the zebra's impatience in *Kipper's A to Z* (*UFBG* 121) provides one of those anticipatory comic moments that will go down as a family classic.

Don't be shy. The more you offer, the more you will get out of the process of sharing books. Children have excellent memories and will soon be sufficiently familiar with stories to join in or fill the gaps you leave. Rosemary Wells' brilliant

Some Wonderful Read-aloud Stories in the *UFBG*

The Kiss That Missed by David Melling (*UFBG* 121)

Tanka Tanka Skunk! by Steve Webb (*UFBG* 179)

Where the Wild Things Are by Maurice Sendak (*UFBG* 62)

Not Now, Bernard by David McKee (*UFBG* 146)

We're Going on a Bear Hunt by Michael Rosen, illustrated by Helen Oxenbury (*UFBG* 189)

Owl Babies by Martin Waddell, illustrated by Patrick Benson (*UFBG* 44)

Pumpkin Soup by Helen Cooper (*UFBG* 160)

story about sibling jealousy *Noisy Nora* has an ending so triumphant that you can't help but share in her joy. In Jack Kent's subtly understated *There's No Such Thing as a Dragon*, children will chant the refrain, giggling at the pictures, which prove against all possible doubt that there are indeed such things as dragons. And amongst the many bestsellers that have arisen from the partnership between Julia Donaldson and Axel Scheffler, *The Gruffalo*'s outstanding rhyming story is perfect for reading aloud with gusto, and then reading again.

Leave time to wonder at some of the revelations in books. In Martin Waddell and Barbara Firth's *Can't You Sleep, Little Bear?* (*UFBG* 78), take a moment to share the Little Bear's comfort at the sight of the moon in the night sky.

Michael Morpurgo and Christian Birmingham's *The Silver Swan* (*UFBG* 167) combines beauty with the raw realities of the natural world. Face the truths in such books and take the opportunity to explore what they mean. Listen to what your child has to say, and the questions being asked.

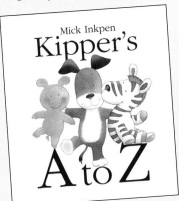

Revel in the Oscar-winning moments that books provide. Funny voices, dramatic pauses, hushed tones, raucous singing – this is an audience that won't walk out. They'll stay for as many encores as you are prepared to offer, and they'll be back tomorrow night for the next outstanding performance. ●

Some Wonderful Read-aloud Stories not in the *UFBG*

The Hutchinson Treasure of Stories to Read Aloud by Janet Schulman

Bear Snores On by Karma Wilson, illustrated by Jane Chapman

Angry Arthur by Hiawyn Oram, illustrated by Satoshi Kitamura

All Join In by Quentin Blake

Oi! Get Off Our Train by John Burningham

The Butter Battle Book by Dr Seuss

I Know an Old Lady Who Swallowed a Fly by Colin and Jacqui Hawkins

Here Come the Aliens! by Colin McNaughton

Q Pootle 5 by Nick Butterworth

Thud! by Nick Butterworth

The Snail and the Whale by Julia Donaldson, illustrated by Axel Scheffler

THE EMPEROR OF ABSURDIA
Chris Riddell

This is a delightfully silly story of the little Emperor of Absurdia, who sets off to track down the snugly scarf he has lost. His hunt takes him across a country of umbrella trees and wardrobe monsters and pointy birds and *dragons...* It's a witty and whimsical tale, but there's warmth in the story, too. Riddell's typically brilliant illustrations are full of utterly impossible detail and daft characters, and his imagining of Absurdia is every bit as wonderful and preposterous as anything he's done before.

Daniel Hahn

FAIRY TALES
Sarah Hayes, illustrated by P.J. Lynch

'Sleeping Beauty', 'The Frog Prince', 'Rapunzel', 'Beauty and the Beast' – classic fairy tales that resonate through the ages, and for any age. Retold here in a clear, straightforward way, they are wonderfully illustrated by P.J. Lynch, with his trademark realism and jewel-like colour palette. Of all the collections available, this is my favourite, as I fell in love with Lynch's work after reading his fabulous version of the Norwegian fairy tale 'East o' the Moon, West o' the Sun'.

Fairy tales have inspired some of the best illustrators, from Arthur Rackham, Kay Neilsen, Edmund Dulac, Jane Ray, Maxfield Parrish and William Heath Robinson to Margaret Tarrant. Each illustrator brings something individual and special to the well-loved stories. When you are looking for a collection of your own, hunt around through the versions available and buy one that speaks to you personally – through both the words and pictures – because whichever one you love, your child will love, too.

Leonie Flynn

FAIRY TALES
Translated by David Walser, illustrated by Jan Pieńkowski

I was first introduced to most of the classic stories in this collection – 'Cinderella', 'Sleeping Beauty', 'Hansel and Gretel' and 'Snow White' – in those old Ladybird editions, for which I will always retain great affection. But this collection, illustrated by Jan Pieńkowski, has all the virtues those old Ladybirds really didn't; Pieńkowski's silhouette illustrations brilliantly capture both the darkness and the life of these strange stories, with every spread a beauty to look at and, running alongside, a clear and elegant translation by David Walser from the Grimm / Perrault originals.

Your children are bound to meet these stories sometime – and you truly won't find a better, more dramatic, more enchanting way to introduce them than this very special volume.

Daniel Hahn

THE FANTASTIC MR WANI Kanako Usui

Mr Wani, suave in his white shirt and purple pants, is a crocodile in a hurry. He's late for the Froggies' baby's christening party. (How kind of them to ask him but a trifle risky, surely?) Four mice, Mrs Crow,

He ran and ran, faster and faster . . .

but his little legs couldn't keep up!

Bang!

He tripped, tumbled and bounced . . .

three penguins, a line of hedgehogs and an elephant are going there by the same route. The result is a series of catastrophic collisions. The visual hi-jinks are cartooned in bold shapes and elegant muted colour; nothing muted about the text though – more like an invitation for a verbal rumpus. *Bang!... Smash!... Pop!... Crash!...* Don't try sharing it at bedtime!

Jane Doonan

FARMER DUCK Martin Waddell, illustrated by Helen Oxenbury

This is the story of a long-suffering, downtrodden duck, and the chocolate-guzzling lazy farmer who exploits it (and wears his cap in bed). But love and friendship will always triumph. With a *Moo!* and a *Baa!* and a *Cluck!*, Duck's farmyard friends make their plans and bounce that fat farmer right out of his bed. (And he never comes back!)

The rain-sodden, muddy tones of Helen Oxenbury's expressive and humorous illustrations brighten into sunlight with the satisfying ending. This is a typical Martin Waddell text – not one word too many.

Caroline Pitcher

FIRST FLIGHT
Sara Fanelli, typography by Chris Bigg

Butterfly bursts out of her chrysalis and yearns to fly. Her efforts to get airborne involve meeting aeronautical experts through the centuries and across the world. Humour veers towards the surreal; images are idiosyncratic. Every picture carries significant details in Fanelli's intense and compulsive style, which includes drawing, collage elements, foreign-language print, snippets of snapshots and drawings from Leonardo's notebooks. In an intriguing tribute to perseverance and the power of love, *First Flight* will lend wings to children's minds and imaginations.

Jane Doonan

FIVE LITTLE FIENDS Sarah Dyer

Five little fiends love to admire the world around them, so one day they decide each to take away the bit they like best. One takes the Sun, one takes the sky, another the land, another the sea, and the last one takes the Moon. However, it doesn't take them long to realise that none of these treasures is any good without the others.

This is a warm and simple story for a small child, but also provides many discussion points for older children, about sharing, taking responsibility and the environment.

Susan Reuben

FROG IS FROG
Max Velthuijs

Frog is content with his lot in life, until he starts to notice the unique skills his friends possess. This unsettles him and he asks himself why can't he fly like Duck or bake cakes like Pig? Suddenly he feels the shoots of inferiority growing inside him – surely everyone is 'better' than him? It takes the wisdom of Hare to make Frog see that he has fantastic qualities as well, and he learns to celebrate the diversity of others while enjoying his own unique powers.

Jonny Zucker

■ Ever since the first **Frog** picture book, *Frog in Love*, readers have been charmed by this gentle and endearing character. Among other titles in this series are: *Frog is a Hero*; *Frog and the Stranger*; *Frog in Winter*; *Frog is Sad*; *Frog and the Treasure* and *Frog Finds a Friend*.

FUNNYBONES
Allan Ahlberg, illustrated by Janet Ahlberg

This begins as a conventional ghost story: 'On a dark dark hill there was a dark dark town...' but the heroes – a big skeleton, a little skeleton and a dog skeleton – don't manage to frighten anybody (not even the reader). Instead, there is a dog skeleton disaster. He bumps into a tree and is 'all come to pieces'. The other skeletons try to put him together again but he ends up saying *FOOW!* In the end, the dog does get fixed, so it's off to the zoo for adventures with the other skeleton animals.

The book has clear pictures in primary colours on a dark background, with big speech bubbles, and it's all lots of fun.

Caroline Pitcher

■ Allan Ahlberg went on to write further **Funnybones** tales, these ones illustrated by André Amstutz: *Dinosaur Dreams*; *The Pet Shop*; *The Black Cat*, *Skeleton Crew* and *Give the Dog a Bone*.

GEORGE AND THE DRAGON
Chris Wormell

The red dragon is a truly fearsome creature, who can smash castle walls with a flick of his mighty tail, defeat armies and sneakily carry off the beautiful princess. Alas, he has an Achilles heel...

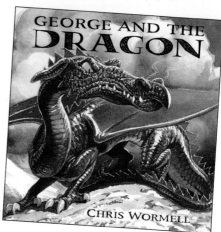

Enter George, a mouse much concerned with his creature comforts, who decides to call on the adjoining cave to borrow some sugar for his tea. George's neighbourly visit reveals the dragon's secret fear of mice. He drops the princess and flees.

Naturally, George takes up residence with the princess and guards the castle, while the mighty dragon cowers abjectly behind a snowy peak. Children are led through fear to fun and a happy ending.

Sonia Benster

THE GETAWAY
Ed Vere

Mouse-on-the-run Fingers McGraw dashes (or scoots!) across textural photographic backgrounds, while enlisting you, the reader, to help him escape with his cheesy loot. All you have to do is whistle, he tells you, if you see Ace Lawman Detective Jumbo Wayne Jr. He's a huge elephant so he'll be hard to miss – or so you'd think!

This energetic and ingenious picture book, created by fine artist Ed Vere, mixes photography, illustration and innovative design. The text has all that old time New York cops 'n' robbers flavour (including skedaddle, scram and holy macaroni). Fabulous stuff! I love this book and you will, too!

Kelly McKain

THE GIANT JAM SANDWICH
John Vernon Lord, verses by Janet Burroway

'One hot summer in Itching Down, *Four million wasps* flew into town.' How do the townsfolk deal with this problem? By getting together as a team to make the most enormous jam sandwich with which to lure the pests ... that's how! This utterly delicious book has all the right things in it: an original, ingenious plot, a lovely rhyming text and sensational, dazzlingly coloured illustrations, crammed with madcap characters, beautifully drawn buildings and delightful incidental details, all of which convey the hilarious narrative to perfection.

Nick Sharratt

GIDDY GOAT
Jamie Rix, illustrated by Lynne Chapman

If you're a mountain goat, it's best to have a head for heights. But Giddy is giddy by name and by nature. He yearns for the fields in the valley where the muttons graze, and eventually he heads downhill where, ultimately, his brave and caring nature outweighs his fear of heights. The illustrations are packed with comedy and warmth, and enhanced with inspired design in which words, too, walk up and down mountains.

Lindsey Fraser

THE GIGANTIC TURNIP
Aleksei Tolstoy, illustrated by Niamh Sharkey

You may already know the story of the old man and the old woman who kept 'six yellow canaries, five white geese, four speckled hens, three black cats, two pot-bellied pigs and one big brown cow'. They plant a turnip that grows... and grows... and grows, until it is so big that the old man can't pull it up. So the old woman and all the animals form a chain to help in the pulling... but still the turnip won't budge. This 19th-century folk tale has lost nothing of its appeal, and the expressive, fresh and creative pictures make this version the best I know.

Wendy Cooling

GILBERT THE GREAT
Jane Clarke, illustrated by Charles Fuge

A baby great white shark with big, pointy teeth seems an unlikely hero for a picture book about losing a loved one, moving through grief into acceptance and finally finding happiness with a new friend. But the unsentimental illustration style is precisely what prevents it from being too cloying or sickly sweet. The matt-blue seascape that Gilbert swims through is full of sparky sea creatures playing marine versions of childhood games, and I really loved the picture of Gilbert munching through a shipwreck (which his mum calls junk food!). *Gilbert the Great* is perfect for children who like their books with a bit of bite!

Kelly McKain

GINGER
Charlotte Voake

Lunch is not the best time to be asked about a favourite and most influential illustrator, because of snap decisions. But I was. Quentin Blake came to mind, but enough has been said about him, and about the master storyteller David McKee. I look at many artists, and to me, Charlotte Voake stands above the rest. Way way above.

Ginger is a book I would have loved to have done myself, except Charlotte Voake has done it perfectly. It is complete, with minimum lines. I have never seen a bad Voake drawing, and here absolute catness just falls off her pen. Like all masters of their skills, she understands her subject. It is a simple story, beautifully written, perceptive, funny, and a lesson in drawing. Talent makes it look easy.

Tony Ross

GIRAFFES CAN'T DANCE
Giles Andreae, illustrated by Guy Parker-Rees

I challenge you to read a child this book without dancing! I've read it to hundreds of children over the years and simply have to jig around at the front of the room – much to the amusement of my audience who are soon (of course) wanting to join in. The story:

> 'Gerald was a tall giraffe
> Whose neck was long and slim,
> But his knees were awfully bandy
> And his legs were rather thin...'

could be a sad one but it certainly isn't: it's celebratory and affirming. Gerald is unhappy to find he can't dance, but he soon discovers his own very original style that amazes all the other animals.

This is not a didactic story, but it does touch on being different in a very positive way. It also makes children smile and shows that books are something to get excited about.

Wendy Cooling

GORGEOUS!
Caroline Castle, illustrated by Sam Childs

There are books that almost unwittingly provide the secret catchphrases that bind parents and children together, and this is one of them. Once Little Zeb had arrived, 'Tip top gorgeous' was heard frequently in our house. I defy any parent to resist the charm of this little zebra as he learns new words and tries them out (not always appropriately!) on the things that he meets during the course of a long day in the African bush. Sam Childs' illustrations are perfect, adding a comic subtext all of their own.

Laura Hutchings

■ Little Zeb returns in *Happy!*; *Little Zeb's Question*; *Funny!* and *Naughty!*

Everybody's Favourite...

THE GRUFFALO
Julia Donaldson, illustrated by Axel Scheffler

A fox, an owl and a snake fancy a mouse for dinner, but the clever rodent scares off its predators by inventing a ferocious friend called a Gruffalo and describing it to them in lurid detail. Then the Gruffalo really does turn up in the deep dark wood, and the mouse's troubles begin in earnest...

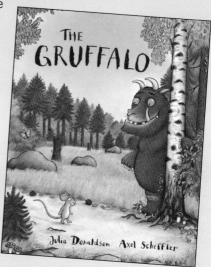

This rhyming tale of the triumph of small over mighty features illustrations that are more comical than scary, despite the beast's 'terrible teeth in his terrible jaws'. The Gruffalo is a close relation of Maurice Sendak's Wild Things, and this wild thing is sure to become a modern classic, too.

Madelyn Travis

A quick-witted mouse invents a monstrous 'Gruffalo' to frighten off his hungry predators in the wood. But when the real Gruffalo turns up, with his 'terrible claws and terrible teeth in his terrible jaws', can he outwit him as well?

The Gruffalo is a distant cousin of Sendak's *Where the Wild Things Are* (*UFBG* 62). He is a creature of vast size and comic-fierce physical characteristics, who wears an increasingly bemused expression as he becomes convinced of the tiny mouse's superior fright-power over the other animals.

A modern classic, this is a miraculously perfect picture book, where text and illustrations marry seamlessly in mood. Its gleeful rhyming text, which is a joy to read aloud, will soon have the entire family chanting by heart.

Patricia Elliott

Everybody's Favourite...

GUESS HOW MUCH I LOVE YOU
Sam McBratney, illustrated by Anita Jeram

Big Nutbrown Hare is the ultimate competitive dad. Little Nutbrown Hare is longing to explain just how much he loves Big Nutbrown Hare, but finds that his little arms, short legs and baby ideas are no match for Big Nutbrown Hare's grown-up ones. This results in an easily imitated pre-bedtime romp, which resolves into the security of Little Nutbrown Hare's soft bed of brown leaves and his absolute trust in the loving parent who settles nearby. The gentle illustrations are a lovely match for the story; the whole book is perfect for a calm, nurturing bedtime.

Antonia Honeywell

This book is the most heartfelt expression of love between an adult and child that could be imagined. Little Nutbrown Hare – and what a relief to have a hare, instead of another bunny – tries to tell Big Nutbrown Hare how much he loves him. 'This much!', stretching out his arms, or 'As high as I can hop!'. But Big Nutbrown Hare counters all with a greater love – he can hop higher, stretch further... When Little Hare is so tired that he starts pulling at his ears, Big Hare wisely lets him have the last word – he loves Big Hare right up to the moon. Gently, with perfect pace, Big Hare lays him down to sleep. And then whispers:

'I love you right up to the moon... and back'.

Guaranteed to have new parents sobbing.

Yzanne Mackay

HAIRY MACLARY FROM DONALDSON'S DAIRY
Lynley Dodd

The first of a growing number of titles about Hairy Maclary and his doggy friends. Hairy Maclary takes a walk, and one after another the neighbourhood dogs join him. Their names are brilliant; my favourite is 'Schnitzel von Krumm with a very low tum', who I'm pleased to say now has his own books. The dogs pretend to be tough and up for anything – until they meet 'Scarface Claw, the toughest tom in town', and beat a hasty retreat. Dogs with character, words to almost taste and a satisfying conclusion give the **Hairy Maclary** books the well-deserved status of classics.

Wendy Cooling

■ Other titles include *Hairy Maclary and Zachary Quack*; *Hairy Maclary's Rumpus at the Vet*; *Where is Hairy Maclary?*; *Hairy Maclary's Bone*; *Hairy Maclary Scattercat*; *Hairy Maclary, Sit* and *Hairy Maclary's Caterwaul Caper*.

HALIBUT JACKSON   David Lucas

This is a delightful tale about how even the most crippling shyness can be overcome. Halibut Jackson is so shy that, wherever he goes, he makes himself a suit that will allow him to blend, chameleon-like into the background. This works very well until an invitation to a party at the palace arrives, and his plan to attend without being noticed goes severely awry.

Halibut Jackson is set in an enticing fairy-tale world where invitations to the palace are delivered by a messenger on horseback, and the local library is full of leather chairs and winding staircases. The illustrations have a quirky, rather old-fashioned charm and are reminiscent of Ludwig Bemelmans' *Madeline* (*UFBG* 130).

Susan Reuben

HARRY AND THE BUCKETFUL OF DINOSAURS
Ian Whybrow, illustrated by Adrian Reynolds

When Harry finds a box of plastic dinosaurs in the attic, he takes them to the library to identify them and as he whispers their strange and wonderful names, he makes them his own. Harry and his dinosaurs are inseparable, until the terrible day he leaves them on a train. Will there be a happy endosaurus? The clear, richly coloured illustrations are full of atmosphere and comic touches – big sister Sam covered in milk and cereal after she's rude about Harry's lost toys – always raises a cheer!

Kathryn Ross

HARRY THE DIRTY DOG
Gene Zion, illustrated by Margaret Bloy Graham

Harry is a dog who hates having baths, so he buries his bath brush in the garden. But then he gets so dirty his family no longer recognise him. In desperation, Harry digs up the brush and persuades his family to scrub him clean.

The stylised, chunky drawings perfectly illustrate Harry's child-like emotions: his joy in being messy, his increasing desperation as his family ignore him and his relief at being recognised again.

Gill Vickery

HAUNTED HOUSE Jan Pieńkowski

'Let yourself in' says a note on the front door of this pop-up marvel. The invitation is irresistible, but beware… This is no ordinary house. It's a mock-scary mansion with unexpected inhabitants and hidden surprises. An octopus washes dishes in the sink, an alligator lounges in the bath, eyes in a painting follow you, and what's that sawing in the attic? Pulling tabs or lifting flaps allow you to let spectres and sinister creatures arrive and depart at will. The spirited, cartoon-like quality of the artwork ensures a tour that is deliciously spine-tingling and funny at the same time.

Elizabeth Hammill

Families Come in All Shapes and Sizes

Families come in all shapes and sizes, so why not mix familiar settings with some more unfamiliar in your reading, suggests **Kathryn Ross**.

C.S. Lewis, the creator of the **Narnia** series, wrote 'we read to know we are not alone'. And nowhere is this more apt than in the world of picture books.

Children undoubtedly look for a reflection of themselves in their books. They will inevitably find some disappointing, but because every child has a different reflection, every book will have a fresh chance of speaking clearly to its reader. The child reading *Five Minutes' Peace* by Jill Murphy will identify with the elephant offspring trying to gain the attention of their mother – how could she possibly want to evict them from the bathroom when they have such fascinating news to share with her? Most adults will feel in that same story a sympathy for the never-off-duty aspect of parenthood. The best picture books work on many levels, a sage nod to the adult reading alongside the child, providing a warming lift at the end of a hectic day.

But that doesn't mean that the books you share with your child should invariably mirror their domestic or social experiences. Picture books have occasionally generated copious right-wing column inches because their creators have had the audacity to set them within non-traditional domestic parameters. For a child, the story is the thing; the number of dads or mums makes no difference whatsoever. And why would it, for a child whose imagination can transform a cardboard box into a steam train, a slice of toast into a rabbit, or the shadow on a curtain into a monster? They respond first and foremost to the emotional environment of the story – how is that rabbit feeling, and why? Where is that bus going, and when will it be back?

Has the hen seen the hungry-looking fox lurking by the shed? And above all – what happens next?

Of course there has to be some anchorage in the world with which children are familiar. Lose yourselves in Mini Grey's *Traction Man* (*UFBG* 187) for an experience so surreal and hilarious that it demands endless revisiting – but is always rooted in the toy box, with which most children are familiar. The bouncing rhythm and rhyme of Kaye Umansky's *Pass the Jam, Jim* (*UFBG* 153), coupled with Margaret Chamberlain's boisterous illustrations, offers all kinds of anarchic scenarios, but at its heart is the simple excitement of party preparation which, whether real or imagined, is part and parcel of any childhood.

By all means choose books that reflect your child's cultural and social experiences, but also seek books that reflect those of other children. All human – and animal – life lies amongst the pages of children's books. Differences are to be celebrated, similarities to be embraced. Curiosity is all. ●

Some Different-sized Families to Try

All Kinds of Bodies by Emma Brownjohn

All Kinds of People by Emma Damon

Babar by Jean de Brunhoff

The Biggest Bed in the World by Lindsay Camp, illustrated by Jonathan Langley

Can't You Sleep, Little Bear? by Martin Waddell (*UFBG* 78)

The Colour of Home by Mary Hoffman, illustrated by Karin Littlewood (*UFBG* 86)

Full, Full, Full of Love by Trish Cooke, illustrated by Paul Howard

My Two Grannies by Floella Benjamin, illustrated by Margaret Chamberlain

My Granny Went to Market: a Round the World Counting Book by Stella Blackstone, illustrated by Christopher Corr

Orlando the Marmalade Cat by Kathleen Hale (*UFBG* 151)

Yum, Yum, Yummy! by Martin Waddell, illustrated by John Bendall-Brunello

HAVE YOU SEEN WHO'S JUST MOVED IN NEXT DOOR? Colin McNaughton

In this rumbustious tale about prejudice, told in verse and speech bubbles, a new family moves to a street inhabited by vampires, pigs, Hell's Angels and a cast from film, comics, folk tales and McNaughton's own books. 'Have you seen who's just moved in?' a neighbour asks. 'Pass it on', says another, setting off a running Chinese whisper. Debate moves down the street – cut-away houses offering tantalising glimpses of life inside. Jokes, and verbal and visual play abound, but McNaughton plays his biggest joke on us!

Elizabeth Hammill

HOW DO DINOSAURS... series
Jane Yolen, illustrated by Mark Teague

This series of rhyming stories asks: does a dinosaur burp, belch and stick beans up his nose when he eats? Does he stomp, roar and sulk at bedtime? Does he throw temper tantrums at the doctor's and show Mama and Papa up? Goodness me, no! These are amusing and oddly moral books, and children will enjoy the dinosaurs' bad behaviour, even if they don't emulate the good.

Caroline Pitcher

> ■ Titles in the series include: *How Do Dinosaurs Play With Their Friends; Say Goodnight; Clean Their Rooms; Eat Their Food* and *Go to School*.

HOW TO CATCH A STAR
Oliver Jeffers

This is a story about a boy who dreams about being friends with a star. He tries all kinds of ways to catch one, from getting up very early in the morning when the stars might be tired, to enlisting the help of an uncooperative seagull. The magic is in the way that both the mission and the solution are entirely in the hands of the boy. The illustrations are as charming and celebratory as the story.

Antonia Honeywell

HOW TO SPEAK MOO
Deborah Fajerman

Cows speak a language called Moo (obviously). It has only one word in it. Moo. You'd think, wouldn't you, that that would make it rather monotonous? Well, think again… With this useful guide, you and your child will be introduced to the versatility of this unique language – high moos, low moos, smooth and bumpy moos, in a tunnel, through a funnel… Have you ever tried bouncing on a jelly and mooing at the same time? What would that sound like?

A totally daft book, and hilarious; only read it, though, if you're prepared to embarrass yourself making some really silly noises. Your child will want to try too – and, indeed, how could anyone resist?

Daniel Hahn

THE HUGE BAG OF WORRIES
Virginia Ironside, illustrated by Frank Rodgers

Jenny has always been happy, with a nice family, a best friend and a lovely dog. But suddenly, some worries start to arrive. Is she getting fat? Will her friend move away? What about rows, wars and bombs? One day she wakes up to find a huge bag of worries at the end of her bed.

It follows her everywhere. She can't ignore it or throw it away. Eventually, a nice old lady comes to the rescue, sorting her worries into groups. (When she firmly sends some packing, with labels round their neck saying 'Mum' and 'Dad', because they 'belong to other people', you realise that this is a work of genius.)

This book is funny, without making fun of the situation. It shows how thoughts can become very solid and problematic. We probably all know a child (or adult) who could do with it.

Yzanne Mackay

HUNGRY! HUNGRY! HUNGRY!
Malachy Doyle, illustrated by Paul Hess

A 'grisly, ghastly' goblin invades a little boy's house. It's 'hungry, hungry, hungry' – that's why it's got such 'spidery legs' and 'skinny wee thighs'. At last, the little boy asks that well-known question from folklore, 'What have you come for?', the answer, of course, is 'you!'. But the goblin's hunger is easily assuaged by a jelly bean instead – 'That will do nicely, thank you' – for appearances can be deceptive.

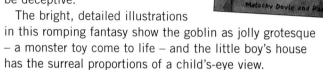

The bright, detailed illustrations in this romping fantasy show the goblin as jolly grotesque – a monster toy come to life – and the little boy's house has the surreal proportions of a child's-eye view.

Patricia Elliott

I HATE SCHOOL
Jeanne Willis, illustrated by Tony Ross

This author / illustrator partnership has given us so much, and this book is one of my favourites because it's a story for everybody. I've used it in secondary schools as well as with very small children, and seen teachers laughing their socks off and wanting their own copy. Willis' rhyming text begins:

'There was a fine young lady
And her name was Honor Brown,
She didn't want to go to school
She hoped it would burn down...'

Honor hates everything, including the teachers, the dinner ladies and her fellow children – until the end, when she realises how much she'll miss it all. The wildly creative pictures add to the anarchy and fun, but at the story's heart there's a truth that will speak to anyone.

Wendy Cooling

I LOVE YOU, BLUE KANGAROO!
Emma Chichester Clark

Lily loves her Blue Kangaroo very dearly, and every night he falls asleep in her arms. But things start to go wrong when Aunt Jemima gives her a Wild Brown Bear, who joins Blue Kangaroo in Lily's bed. Soon, more and more toys are squashing in until there is no room left for Blue Kangaroo at all...

The illustrations in Emma Chichester Clark's trademark luminous colours add so much to the story, with Blue Kangaroo's expression each time another toy arrives becoming more and more heartbreaking! The pictures tell their own story, too, as we watch Lily's baby brother becoming more and more attached to Blue Kangaroo as Lily neglects him. And take a close look at the people who bring each toy – there's more than a passing resemblance between the giver and the gift.

A wonderful story of love and loyalty.

Susan Reuben

■ Catch up with Blue Kangaroo in further titles, including *Where Are You, Blue Kangaroo?*; *Happy Birthday to You, Blue Kangaroo*; *It Was You, Blue Kangaroo*; *What Shall We Do, Blue Kangaroo?* and *I'll Show You, Blue Kangaroo*.

I Love You, Blue Kangaroo!

Emma Chichester Clark

IN THE ATTIC
Hiawyn Oram, illustrated by Satoshi Kitamura

A little boy sits surrounded by 'a million toys', but still he's bored. So he climbs the extending ladder on his toy fire engine into an empty attic that he fills with fantastic daydreams, from busy mice and flying machines to a friendly tiger who shares his games. Kitamura's surreal, detail-rich illustrations capture the attention and spark the imagination, and the spare, first-person text speaks directly to young readers. Children relish the conspiratorial, adults-keep-out ending when Mum declares that they have no attic and the boy looks straight out of the page and says, 'She hasn't found the ladder'.

Kathryn Ross

I SPY: SHAPES IN ART
Lucy Micklethwait

A fun and accessible book that proves it's never too early for children (nor too late for adults!) to be introduced to art. The artists represented include Matisse, O'Keeffe and Hockney, and the works encompass a wide and colourful range of styles and subjects. The minimal text uses the familiar game of 'I spy' to encourage readers to look closely at each painting to find a particular shape within it – square, circle, triangle, star – and the author suggests some more activities in the foreword. Looking, pointing and chatting about what you see is a great way to start enjoying art together. Stand aside, Brian Sewell!

Kathryn Ross

⁍ ⁍ ⁍ ⁍ ⁍ ⁍ ⁍

JAMELA'S DRESS Niki Daly

Set in a South African township, the **Jamela** stories of everyday life depict experiences that will resonate with young children, irrespective of cultural background. Jamela's mother has been saving for some special material to make a dress for Thelma's wedding. Jamela is charged with looking after the material when it is hung out to dry on the washing line. But dreamy Jamela imagines herself wrapped in the material parading around the town... and soon she is doing just that. What a commotion! The material is ruined! Jamela is photographed in her fine apparel and when it looks as though things can't get any worse, the photograph saves the day.

Nikki Gamble

■ Jamela is a shining heroine: imaginative, caring, playful and exuberant. She also stars in *What's Cooking Jamela?*; *Where's Jamela?* and *Happy Birthday Jamela*.

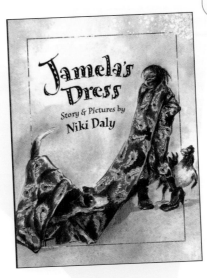

JINNIE GHOST
Berlie Doherty, illustrated by Jane Ray

Jinnie Ghost shimmers past in a shower of falling stars, as thin as the wind, with eyes like water. She is delicate and gauzy, *almost* shivery, but not quite. Jinnie casts dreams through the night. She whispers to children so that their wishes, however magical, are fulfilled as they sleep. Charlotte's toys come to life and dance, Owen boogies with the bogeyman and Tommy rides a unicorn. Then Jinnie disappears – 'Jinnie Ghost, Jinnie Ghost, where do you go?' – and in the morning, the children wake safe and sound.

   This lyrical poem is matched by Jane Ray's ethereal illustrations, full of exotic fabrics and textures and hypnotic colours. A beautiful book to own and a delight to read aloud.

Caroline Pitcher

J IS FOR JAMAICA
Benjamin Zephaniah, with photographs by Prodeepta Das

As I read Benjamin Zephaniah's lively rhyming verse with its pulling rhythm, I could hear his distinctive voice in my head. There are four lines of verse for each letter. My favourite was L for Lizards ('...they're silent, with no scent. Some live in trees, some live indoors and lizards pay no rent'). There's a rich variety of subjects in this alphabet, from Ackee, Blue Mountain, Cricket, Education, Goats, Hummingbird, Rainforest through to Ugli fruit and Yams, and the photographs are simply stunning. Plenty to talk about! Not quite as good as a real holiday in Jamaica, but a feast for ears and eyes nevertheless.

Caroline Pitcher

Everybody's Favourite...

THE JOLLY POSTMAN
Allan Ahlberg, illustrated by Janet Ahlberg

Our copy of this book has fallen apart from so much reading. *The Jolly Postman* is packed neatly with envelopes enticing the reader to sneak a look at the highly personal post inside. Discover Goldilocks' apologetic letter to the Three Bears, with a party invitation for Baby Bear, or the Witch's supply catalogue, featuring Little Boy Pie Mix and Halloween Boot in five shades of black, Jack's postcard to Giant Bigg from his Magic Carpet Tour and a writ delivered to the Wolf by Meeny, Miny, Mo & Co. on behalf of Messrs. Three Little Pigs Ltd. A magical story told in short, humorous verses, ending with the Jolly Postman cycling happily home for tea.

Caroline Pitcher

You cannot throw too many superlatives at this book. Hilarious, superbly imaginative, wonderfully rhymed and beautifully written, there is nothing else quite like it. In a world peopled by characters from nursery rhymes and fairy tales, a Jolly Postman comes:

'Once upon a bicycle,

So they say...'

And pedals round, drinking tea and champagne, through a wealth of humorous illustrations and gentle rhymes.

It would be good enough if it stopped there – but it doesn't! Six pages are envelopes, containing real letters, postcards and other novelties. The pastiches of children's letters, lawyers' demands ('all this huffing and puffing will get you nowhere, Mr Wolf' and so on) are good enough to keep even adults entertained for hours. For a child, this is a hundred books rolled into one.

Yzanne Mackay

■ There are other books about the Jolly Postman. Try *The Jolly Christmas Postman*; *The Jolly Pocket Postman* and *The Jolly Postman's Party*.

KATIE MORAG'S ISLAND STORIES
Mairi Hedderwick

If your family hasn't met the feisty, red-haired lass yet, this collection makes a fine introduction! In her trademark tartan skirt and welly boots, Katie Morag has been coping with preoccupied parents, naughty big boy cousins and a whole lot more on her Scottish island home for some years now, but her appeal is as fresh and her predicaments as relevant as ever. These are substantial, satisfying stories told with warmth and humour, and the soft, watercolour illustrations – from the crammed Post Office to the bustling quayside – are busy with captivating detail.

Kathryn Ross

■ The feisty Scottish heroine stars in more picture books, including *Katie Morag and the Dancing Class*; *Katie Morag and the Birthdays*; *Katie Morag and the Two Grannies*; *Katie Morag and the Wedding* and *Katie Morag Delivers the Mail*. There is also a short-story collection for emerging readers, *Katie Morag, Of Course!*

KIPPER'S A TO Z   Mick Inkpen

There are lots of A–Z books around, but few of them are as exciting as Kipper's. Helped by his piglet friend Arnold, Kipper sets off on an adventure that starts with a tiny ant and ends with an eager zebra. As with all his adventures, this one is noisy, messy and terrific fun. Swept along on his voyage of discovery, readers will hardly notice they are learning the alphabet as they go. Mick Inkpen has an infectious sense of mischief, and little Kipper will make parents smile and children laugh out loud.

Sarah Frost Mellor

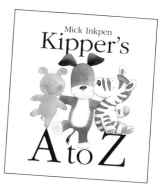

THE KISS THAT MISSED
David Melling

The King is in so much of a hurry that he simply throws his son a goodnight kiss from the doorway. The kiss misses and floats out the window! Of course, the King's Loyal Knight is sent to retrieve it. The Loyal Knight faces the dark, the snow and a frightening forest in his quest, but as the kiss floats by, it has an unexpected effect on all the wild animals, particularly on a certain hungry dragon with 'this-lot-would-be-nice-for-breakfast' eyes. The detail in the illustrations, the humour and the very satisfactory ending make this an engaging and fulfilling bedtime read.

Antonia Honeywell

THE LIGHTHOUSE KEEPER'S LUNCH
Ronda Armitage, illustrated by David Armitage

Mr Grinling takes good care of his lighthouse light, making sure that it's clean and well polished so it will shine brightly at night. Mrs Grinling always prepares a delicious lunch for her husband and sends it on a wire running from their cottage to the lighthouse.

When one day the lighthouse keeper's lunch is stolen by marauding seagulls, the young reader will understand immediately what a crisis this is. The redoubtable Mrs G must devise a plan to repulse those seagulls for good.

Cheerful, sea-watery-bright illustrations convey the optimistic spirit of this classic story.

Patricia Elliott

■ Look out for others in the series, including *The Lighthouse Keeper's Breakfast*; *The Lighthouse Keeper's Tea*; *The Lighthouse Keeper's Rescue*; *The Lighthouse Keeper's Catastrophe*; *The Lighthouse Keeper's Cat*; *The Lighthouse Keeper's Picnic* and *The Lighthouse Keeper's Christmas*.

LITTLE BEAVER AND THE ECHO
Amy MacDonald, illustrated by Sarah Fox-Davies

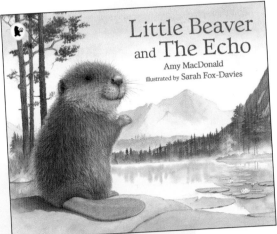

Little Beaver and the Echo was one of the jewels of my children's bedtime reading. Beautifully illustrated by Sarah Fox-Davies, it's a heart-wrenching tale of a lonely beaver who hears someone crying on the other side of the lake, and sets off to see if the distant animal will become his friend. On the way he meets some real companions – and, of course, it turns out that the unhappy beaver across the water was the echo of his own tears.

The book reads aloud beautifully. It pulls off the ultimate trick: giving children the melodious repetition they love without driving the adult reader mad.

Eleanor Updale

LITTLE GREY RABBIT series
Alison Uttley, illustrated by Margaret Tempest

These are books that hark back to a bygone age – sadly lost to us for ever, but captured in Margaret Tempest's exquisitely detailed paintings that accompany the text. Little Grey Rabbit has a host of animal friends (Hare, Squirrel, Fuzzypeg), and together they indulge in such archaic country delights as making balls from cowslip flowers and skating on frozen ponds.

These anthropomorphic tales teach gentle lessons about the value of friendship. Less witty and acerbic than *Winnie-the-Pooh* (*UFBG* 300), they conjure up Alison Uttley's country childhood and are ideal for bedtime reading.

Laura Hutchings

■ Alison Uttley wrote many **Little Grey Rabbit** stories, but note that most are out of print and hard to find. Titles include *Little Grey Rabbit's Birthday*; *Little Grey Rabbit's Party*; *The Squirrel, the Hare and the Little Grey Rabbit*; *The Story of Fuzzypeg the Hedgehog* and *Moldy Warp the Mole*.

LITTLE LOST COWBOY
Simon Puttock, illustrated by Caroline Jayne Church

Cowboy Coyote is lost in the desert. Despite much seemingly helpful advice on how to find his way home, he somehow ends up very wet, with cactus prickles in his nose and a bumped bottom, each misadventure prompting him to give a howl – 'AROOO!' Finally a toad tells him to stay where he is, but to howl his very loudest. At that, of course, Mummy Coyote finds him, and he takes hold of her tail and they go home together.

With clear, blocky illustrations, this is a good howl-along story with a great piece of advice – if you're lost, sit still and howl until your mum finds you!

Leonie Flynn

LITTLE RABBIT GOES TO SCHOOL
Harry Horse

Little Rabbit decides to take his favourite toy, Charlie Horse, with him on his first day at school. But Charlie – a wooden horse on a string – leads Little Rabbit into all kinds of naughtiness, galloping around during story time and even leaping into a bowl of cake mix. The traditional-looking watercolour illustrations, full of humorous detail, cleverly allow the young reader to work out for himself who is initiating the bad behaviour really, and to feel just a tad superior to Little Rabbit. An affectionately observed story that could provide a useful confidence boost before the momentous day.

Kathryn Ross

■ There are other **Little Rabbit** books to look out for, including *Little Rabbit's New Baby* and *Little Rabbit Lost*.

LITTLE RED
Lynn Roberts, illustrated by David Roberts

The story of 'Little Red Riding Hood' has never been so interesting. This stunning version is told as a late-18th-century American tale, all taverns, pioneers and highwaymen – with some great wigs and frocks, too. (Worn by the wolf, of course.)

It's a story of the best-ever, sweet ginger beer, and of a little boy – known as Little Red – who sets off one day into the woods to visit his grandmother... With brilliant pictures full of fun and quirky details to spot, this is one that will repay frequent rereading.

Daniel Hahn

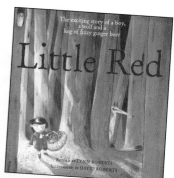

Monster Books

When a Zeeder Met a Xyder by Malachy Doyle (*UFBG* 191)

Two Monsters by David McKee (*UFBG* 187)

Monster and Frog by Rose Impey (*UFBG* 266)

Not Now, Bernard by David McKee (*UFBG* 146)

Supposing... by Frances Thomas (*UFBG* 177)

Two Left Feet by Adam Stower (*UFBG* 187)

THE LITTLE RED HEN
Jonathan Allen

The old folk tale is wittily updated in this ingenious lift-the-flap book. Sprightly Little Red Hen grows corn to make bread, and is sure her farmyard friends will help her. But, as we discover, hidden behind the flaps, Mucky Ducky, Fat Cat, Shaggy Dog, Turkey Lurkey and Funny Bunny (all with hilariously lugubrious expressions) are too busy doing nothing to be able to help – until it comes to eating the bread itself. Two mice comment sardonically on each animal's response to Henny's hopeful 'Yahoo? Who will help?' and end up gorged on breadcrumbs on the last page.

Patricia Elliott

LITTLE TIM AND THE BRAVE SEA CAPTAIN
Edward Ardizzone

This is the first of a series of adventures stories featuring the intrepid Tim and friends. Tim is one of those boys who's ordinary enough for readers to believe in utterly, while being bold enough to be a genuine hero. In this particular book, Tim stows away to encounter stormy seas, a sinking ship, a dramatic rescue and a brave sea captain and this, indeed, is entirely typical of the types of adventure Tim always seems to be able to find.

Period pieces in some ways, the combination of exciting action, vivid characters and fabulously detailed illustrations still make the **Little Tim** series enthralling.

Philippa Milnes-Smith

■ Look out too for *Tim to the Lighthouse*; *Tim in Danger*; *Tim and Lucy Go to Sea*; *Tim to the Rescue*; *Ship's Cook Ginger*; *Tim's Last Voyage*; *Tim All Alone*; *Tim and Charlotte*; *Tim and Ginger* and *Tim's Friend Towser*.

Books Reflecting Other Cultures

Publisher **Janetta Otter-Barry** celebrates the diversity to be found in contemporary picture books.

It's something I believe passionately – that books for children, from babies up, should reflect the multicultural world we live in and should celebrate the wonderful diversity of cultures around us. This isn't just something for the nurseries and schools to take care of – it's a vital part of home life, too; an important way of introducing our children to the world and passing on values.

For babies and toddlers, look for books showing all kinds of families and cultural backgrounds within a familiar domestic setting. For older children, seek out books about families living in other countries, books that show how other people live their lives, celebrating similarities as well as differences. And read stories about families from the many different cultures in our own country. There are lots of fantastic and enriching titles to choose from. If you can't find them in your local bookshop, Letterbox Library is a great mail-order resource, a book club that specialises in books celebrating equality and diversity.

For the very young, there are the delightful Helen Oxenbury board books *Tickle, Tickle* (*UFBG* 54), *Clap Hands*, *All Fall Down* and *Say Goodnight*, recently reissued and featuring an exuberant multicultural

You Can Find These in the *UFBG*

Akimbo and the Elephants by Alexander McCall Smith (*UFBG* 206)

Dave and the Tooth Fairy by Verna Wilkins (*UFBG* 91)

J is for Jamacia by Benjamin Zephaniah (*UFBG* 119)

The Jessame Stories by Julia Jarman (*UFBG* 250)

Sing me a Story by Grace Hallworth (*UFBG* 170)

band of babies. Verna Wilkins and Derek Brazell's series of books *Baby Goes*, *Baby Finds*, *Baby Noises* and *Baby Plays* (*UFBG* 12) are some of the few board books around featuring black families; and black characters also feature in another *Tickle Tickle*, this time by Dakari Hru and Ken Wilson-Max. Then try Kathy Henderson and Paul Howard's *Look at You! A Baby Body Book*, which has characterful pictures of babies from lots of different families and a lyrical read-aloud text – a great introduction to the body and the senses.

I have two other special favourites for the very young, both featuring black families. *So Much* by Trish Cooke (*UFBG* 175) is a classic, in which many different members of a big extended family come to visit, because they all want to see the baby SO MUCH. This story just begs to be read out loud, as well as being a tender homage to the new baby in the family. *Wriggle Piggy Toes* by John Agard is a magical collection of original nursery verse with a Caribbean lilt, and a wonderfully irreverent look at babyhood.

For the child of two-plus, it's exciting and stimulating to explore stories set in other countries and see the ways in which children's worlds are different as well as the universal themes of family life. Photographic picture books are a great way of doing this in an authentic and colourful way. Enter the author / photographer Ifeoma Onyefulu, whose first concept stories, set in a Nigerian village, have an irresistible blend of the exotic and the familiar. Go first for *A Is for Africa* (*UFBG* 66), a unique and exciting alphabet book. But also try *Chidi Only Likes Blue*, for learning about colours. In this warm and humorous story, Chidi discovers all the different colours – and can't decide which is his favourite. For counting there is also the lovely *One Child One Seed* by Kathryn Cave, published in association with Oxfam, which follows the growth of a pumpkin from seed to fruit in a South African rural setting, with a recipe for pumpkin pie, too!

Then there are some unmissable illustrated picture books for two-to-fives, with great characters and lots of humour. Eileen Browne's *Handa's Hen* is an enchanting story for bedtime reading, in which Handa and her friend Akeyo go looking for Grandma's hen and find all kinds of other animals instead. Niki Daly gives us the vibrant world of a South African township community in the **Jamela** books. There are four in the series, but start with *Jamela's Dress* (*UFBG* 118), in which mischievous Jamela just can't resist borrowing Mama's new material, and parades all down the street in it – until Mama finds out. *Fruits* by Valerie Bloom is a funny and atmospheric picture book in verse, about a little girl's desire to eat more and more exotic Caribbean fruit. And look out for Judy Cumberbatch's *Can You Hear the Sea?* (*UFBG* 79), a tender family story in which Sarah's grandpa gives her a special shell. Sarah can hear all the sounds of her African village in her shell, but will she still be able to hear the sea with everything else that's going on?

For five-to-seven-year-olds, the modern classic *Amazing Grace* by Mary Hoffman (*UFBG* 207) is a must. Grace wants to be Peter Pan in the school play, but there's a problem; Peter Pan is a boy, and he isn't black. But Grace's nana tells her, if you try you can do anything you want. A fantastic, empowering story. Then there's *Gregory* ▶

Cool, the story of the city boy who isn't at all keen on going to the Caribbean to stay with his grandparents. But the visit is a real eye-opener for Gregory and he has to rethink his sophisticated urban values. This is a heart-warming and special cross-cultural picture book. As is *The Most Magnificent Mosque* by Ann Jungman, the story of three boys, Jewish, Muslim and Christian, whose friendship helps to save the great Mosque of Cordoba.

Another important role for the picture book is to reflect the experience of those children coming as asylum seekers to settle in a new country, trying to understand new cultural values. Picture books can be an effective way to explore this sensitive area, and *The Colour of Home* by Mary Hoffman (*UFBG* 86) is the best one I know. In this heartrending story a Somali boy starts school in Britain, and through a painting project is gradually able to confront his past and begin a new life with his family.

Finding out about the festivals of other cultures can be approached in a really enticing way through story. Try the **Festival Time** series by Jonny Zucker and Jan Barger, which is fun and informative without being didactic. Or *Long-Long's New Year*, with beautiful artwork by the Chinese artist He Zhihong, which tells of Long-Long and his grandpa's city adventure in preparation for the Spring Festival.

Last of all, and bringing together all the values I've been talking about, I recommend *We Are Britain* by Benjamin Zephaniah. Twelve poems about twelve very different children, ready to embrace a multicultural, multicoloured land where every child is equal. It's a great book for 21st-century Britain. ●

And You Might Like to Look Out For These, Too

All My Friends by Gill Lobel

Busy Toes by C.W. Bowie, illustrated by Fred Willingham

I is for India by Prodeepta Das

Family by Isabell Monk

Hats Off to Hair by Virginia Kroll

In the Small Small Night by Jane Kurtz

LOOKING AFTER LOUIS
Lesley Ely, illustrated by Polly Dunbar

Everyone in the class knows Louis is different. When people talk to him, instead of answering he just repeats what they say. And at playtime he runs amok through the boys' football game, getting in the way without even realising.

This is a book about autism, but it's such an excellent picture book in its own right that it would be a great shame to pigeon-hole it as an 'issues' story. It's about how kind small children sometimes are to each other and how intuitive their emotional understanding can be. It has funny moments, too – particularly in Polly Dunbar's excellent illustrations, which are full of entertaining incidental detail.

Susan Reuben

LOST AND FOUND
Oliver Jeffers

A boy opens the door one day to find a penguin there, looking sad. The boy sets off to row the penguin home to the South Pole. It's only after they arrive there and the two part company that the boy realises that the penguin isn't really lost at all – just lonely.

This is a fable with a spare, simple beauty that conceals its iceberg-like depth. Oliver Jeffers manages to imbue his characters with emotion, despite them having minimal features and only dots for eyes. *Lost and Found* is a book that children will get more and more out of as they grow older.

Susan Reuben

MADELINE series Ludwig Bemelmans

It's easy to see why *Madeline* and its sequels have been read and loved for nearly 70 years. Madeline is a feisty Parisian schoolgirl who knows better than anyone how to frighten her long-suffering teacher, Miss Clavel. She lives in a boarding school with 11 other little girls, all dressed in immaculate yellow.

> ■ Books in this series: *Madeline; Madeline's Rescue; Madeline and the Bad Hat; Madeline and the Gypsies; Madeline in London* and *Madeline's Christmas*.

The elegant text in rhyming couplets is highly memorable, with lots of understated jokes. But the book shines most of all through its illustrations, with enchanting scenes of Paris lit up by the 'twelve little girls in two straight lines' who march through its boulevards and gardens.

Susan Reuben

THE MAGIC PAINTBRUSH
Julia Donaldson, illustrated by Joel Stewart

The Magic Paintbrush is a gift to a young Chinese girl. Everything she paints with it comes to life. She is able to paint feasts for hungry people, to help poor fishermen catch fish and shrimps and to give her villagers clothes and shoes. The gift comes with a warning, though – it is only to be used to help poor people, not wealthy ones. So what will she do when the Emperor puts her in prison for refusing to paint a gold-bearing tree for him? The tale unfolds in rhyme, wonderful for reading aloud together, accompanied by evocative illustrations.

Antonia Honeywell

MAN ON THE MOON
Simon Bartram

Man on the Moon describes a day in the life of Bob, the man whose job it is to keep the moon nice and tidy. (Those astronauts really don't know how to clean up after themselves.) He deals with any enquiries from tourists, too, and patiently explains to them that, no, there are no such things as aliens – *of course* there aren't.

But if you look at Simon Bartram's wonderful pictures carefully enough, you never know what you may find... With its delightfully odd and witty mixture of the old fashioned, domestic, V-neck-wearing Bob in his living room, and colourful, futuristic alien wildness, this was illustrator Bartram's first solo venture, and it's a triumph.

Daniel Hahn

THE MAN WHOSE MOTHER WAS A PIRATE
Margaret Mahy, illustrated by Margaret Chamberlain

This established favourite is a winner with children from three to well into primary school. It tells the story of a very respectable little man who works in insurance, and his wildly eccentric mother, a retired pirate. The outrageous mother and conforming son love each other, so when Mum begins to miss the sea and long for her old life, her son just has to help her. And so the journey begins, and for the son who has never seen the sea, it is a magical eye-opener; he just can't believe the wonder of it all. Mahy's writing at this point is incredible – ask children to close their eyes as you read and they will see and hear the sea. Terrific, very expressive pictures really work with the text.

Wendy Cooling

MARIANA AND THE MERCHILD
Caroline Pitcher, illustrated by Jackie Morris

This is a lyrically told, exquisitely illustrated folk tale from Chile. Mariana is a lonely old lady, laughed at and avoided by the local children, until everything changes when she finds a merbaby inside a crab shell. The merbaby's mother begs Mariana to look after her child until the sea grows calm again, and this she does with ever-increasing affection – though she knows the day will finally come for them to part.

Jackie Morris's beautiful watercolours convey great emotion. She and Caroline Pitcher have done several lovely books together, and this is one of the best.

Susan Reuben

MEET WILD BOARS
Meg Rosoff, illustrated by Sophie Blackall

According to Rosoff, Boris, Morris, Horace and Doris are the worst pets you could ever own. They'll destroy your home, fart, make fun of you, eat all your chocolate and far, far worse. But, hey, we all have friends like that. I found myself secretly applauding them for doing all the dreadful things I've always wanted to do in moments of wild boredom – for, while they have no excuse for such bad behaviour, I find it impossible not to forgive the Wild Boars.

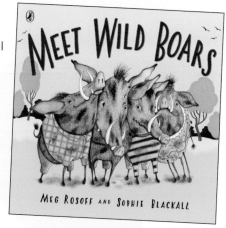

A brilliantly anarchic book with very funny, filthy illustrations. Mum, can I have a wild boar?

Jeanne Willis

MEG AND MOG series
Helen Nicoll, illustrated by Jan Pieńkowski

Incompetent witches have long provided madcap comedy and antic invention in children's books. Nicoll and Pieńkowski first created Meg, the lovable, highly stylised inky-black witch, her cat Mog and their friend Owl in 1972. The original story *Meg and Mog* and its 16 successors have everything children love: three sharply drawn, intriguing characters; distinctive use of cartoon-strip techniques, silhouettes and colour; hand-lettered texts, whose placement often corresponds visually with the activity to hand; delight in language; and plots built around spells that go wrong, or jokes that the readers – but not the characters – understand. Get a child hooked early and these books will be favourites long past the nursery years.

Elizabeth Hammill

■ Other **Meg and Mog** titles to look out for include *Meg and Mog; Mog at the Zoo; Mog in the Fog; Meg's Eggs; Meg at Sea; Meg's Mumps; Meg's Friends* and *Meg, Mog and Og.*

MISERY MOO
Jeanne Willis, illustrated by Tony Ross

Misery Moo really is a miserable old cow! She moans about everything – the weather, her birthday, even Christmas – and despite the lamb's sunniest efforts to cheer her up with parties and rainbow-coloured knitted udder-warmers she remains determinedly gloomy. Eventually her pessimistic outlook affects even Lamby Poo, and when he is overwhelmed by sadness, Misery Moo finally realises that it is up to her to make him smile again. The irreverent text and hilarious illustrations will have adults and children in stitches, but there's tenderness, too, in this useful reminder for all ages about the responsibilities of true friendship.

Kathryn Ross

MR GUMPY'S OUTING
John Burningham

This is the simple, joyous story of Mr Gumpy, who goes out for a trip in his boat, and of the children and animals who hitch a ride. Mr Gumpy agrees to take them, as long as they behave. But do they? They do not! Eventually everyone falls in the river, in a multi-coloured splash, then they wander back through the sunlit fields to Mr Gumpy's house for tea.

Burningham makes books like nobody else, and this one, which deservedly won the Kate Greenaway medal way back in 1970, is still as fresh as ever. In free-line drawings and vibrant colour he conveys each new character with supreme spontaneity, developing the story until mayhem ensues!

Malachy Doyle

MR MCGEE
Pamela Allen

Pamela Allen is a star in Australia, and should be better known across the world. Her 30-plus picture books totally focus on the world of small children, and capture first experiences with humour and gentleness. Always well designed, texts are short, often rhythmic, and the illustrations funny and uniquely stylised. Mr McGee, who lives under a tree, is a quiet, unassuming man, who is perplexed by an apple he eats and the strange things that befall him thereafter.

Jon Appleton

■ Other great **Mr McGee** books to read and reread include *Mr McGee Goes to Sea*; *Mr McGee and the Biting Flea*; *Mr McGee and the Blackberry Jam*; *Mr McGee and the Big Bag of Bread* and *Mr McGee and the Perfect Nest*.

Cat Books
Orlando: the Marmalade Cat series by Kathleen Hale (*UFBG* 151)

The Mousehole Cat by Antonia Barber (*UFBG* 139)

Catch that Kitten! by Pamela Edwards (*UFBG* 80)

Mog the Forgetful Cat by Judith Kerr (*UFBG* 138)

Six Dinner Sid by Inga Moore (*UFBG* 171)

Fred by Posy Simmonds (*UFBG* 236)

Mr Pusskins by Sam Lloyd (*UFBG* 136)

Everybody's Favourite...

MR MAGNOLIA
Quentin Blake

The story of Mr Magnolia, who has only one boot, has made children laugh ever since it was published in 1980 and won all the big prizes. The crazy rhyme is a delight to read, and children will soon join in with the refrain, but it takes them a little longer to see that it's also a counting book. Numbers are never mentioned in the text so it's up to the reader to notice that one trumpet is followed by two sisters, three pond creatures, four parakeets... These are woven, seemingly casually, into the pictures: pictures that show Quentin Blake at his wonderful best, as they're packed with comic detail, wit and movement and that extraordinary child appeal that has made him such a success. But forget about the counting: just let the book work its magic!

Wendy Cooling

One of Quentin Blake's best-loved picture books, and with good reason – it's just bursting with *joie de vivre*. Mr Magnolia has only one boot, but he takes a child-like delight in everything else in his full and varied life, whether it's juggling fruit, listening to fat owls learning to hoot or going for a scoot with his friends. The witty, rhyming text reads aloud brilliantly; the exuberant illustrations are full of quirky detail, including a secret counting game to discover, and Mr Magnolia's lack of footwear is resolved in a satisfying and typically non-conformist way. Perfect!

Kathryn Ross

MR MEN series
Roger Hargreaves

The **Mr Men** books are a brilliantly simple idea that have captivated children around the world for over 30 years. Each book features a single human characteristic personified (Mr Tall, Mr Greedy, Mr Bump and so on), making it easy for children to recognise themselves, and others, in it.

The small, square format and the simple, humorous stories are easily digestible. What sets the **Mr Men** apart, though, is the iconic simplicity of the illustrations, which are so strong that they are still published in their original 'felt-tip' rendering.

Giles Andreae

■ Along with the original **Mr Men** and the **Little Miss** books (*Little Miss Sunshine*; *Little Miss Naughty* and so on), there are new storybooks to look out for, too; try *Little Miss Lucky and the Naughty Pixies* or *Mr Bump and the Knight*.

MR PUSSKINS
Sam Lloyd

This is the cautionary tale of a cat who has it all, but throws it away on a whim. Mr Pusskins is fed up with being adored by a little girl called Emily. His life is too easy and just too boring. So one day he leaves, falls in with the wrong kind of cat and gets an exciting taste of the low life. But the excitement doesn't last. His fair-weather friends desert him, and soon he is wet and hungry and lonely. Suddenly Mr Pusskins understands what he has thrown away, and luckily for him Emily still loves him and wants him back. It is the illustrations that make this story. Mr Pusskins looks wonderfully fat, naughty, remorseful and overjoyed by turns.

Karen Wallace

MR WOLF'S PANCAKES
Jan Fearnley

Warning: read this book to yourself before reading it to children. If you don't, you might miss out on one of the most delicious of denouements.

Mr Wolf seeks the help of his neighbours to make the pancakes he's planning. But the ungracious bunch will have nothing to do with him, perhaps recalling from other stories that wolves can be duplicitous neighbours. He perseveres, however, and their fears are overcome when they catch the delicious aroma of cooked pancakes wafting from his house. In they come, greedy, mannerless and off guard... Revenge could hardly be sweeter, or tastier.

Lindsey Fraser

MR WOLF'S WEEK
Colin Hawkins

Mr Wolf's Week introduces the concept of days of the week in a highly enjoyable manner, with minimal text and a large font to help children learn to connect spoken language with written text. On each day of the week Mister Wolf dons a new outfit to match the weather and his activities: on Monday, because it is raining, he wears wellies and carries an umbrella; on Sunday, the sun is shining, so he wears sunglasses and shorts. What makes this book especially appealing is the humour captured in Hawkins' comic-style illustrations. The situation comedy conveyed in the delightful double-page spreads will amuse both children and adults.

Nikki Gamble

■ Look out for other books in this series: *Mr Wolf's Nursery Time*; *What's The Time, Mr Wolf?* and *Mr Wolf's Birthday Surprise.*

MOG THE FORGETFUL CAT
Judith Kerr

The first in a series of justly popular, warm and funny adventures of a not-very-clever family cat, who becomes a hero by mistake. The simple setting of the Thomas family home provides a backdrop for the fairly familiar event of Mog being shut outside, so she claws at the window to be let in, and manages to scare a burglar, winning her high praise from her family. In later books, Mog goes on to have a host of other adventures, with an occasional hint of fantasy, all accompanied by timeless pictures.

Liz Attenborough

■ Mog the cat returns in other titles including *Mog in the Dark*; *Mog's Kittens*; *Mog's Amazing Birthday Caper*; *Mog and the V.E.T.*; *Mog on Fox Night* and *Goodbye, Mog*. Some are available in board-book format.

MOLE AND THE BABY BIRD
Marjorie Newman, illustrated by Patrick Benson

A baby bird falls out of its nest. Mole wants to keep it. Mum Mole tries to persuade him to let the wild bird go, but Mole loves it too much. (I don't know about you, but I have played both roles in this drama...) Patrick Benson's gentle watercolour illustrations are touching, especially the one showing the baby inside the clumsy wooden cage Mole has made. Mole's grandad explains that birds are meant to fly free. After some tears, Mole makes the right choice.

This is a beautiful story by the late Marjorie Newman. She has written about a common situation with tender understatement and love. A must!

Caroline Pitcher

THE MOUSEHOLE CAT
Antonia Barber, illustrated by Nicola Bayley

This magical, moving story, inspired by an old Cornish legend, tells of Mowzer the cat and Tom the old fisherman, who brave the fury of the Great Storm Cat to sail out to open sea in the fiercest of winter weather, and save their village from starvation.

Nicola Bayley, who has made a career out of drawing cats, is triumphant here, with rich, sumptuously coloured illustrations, friezes and borders, which perfectly accompany Antonia Barber's beautifully paced and poetic narrative, celebrating courage, community, cooking and cats.

I never tire of rereading this one, or of wallowing in its beauty.

Malachy Doyle

MUNGO AND THE PICTURE BOOK PIRATES
Timothy Knapman, illustrated by Adam Stower

■ Mungo's story continues in *Mungo and the Spiders from Space*.

The Seafaring Adventures of Captain Horatio Fleet is Mungo's very favourite book. His mother reads it to him every night – several times. But when the book's hero gets fed up of all the endless heroics and decides to take a holiday, things begin to go awry – who will step into the story and save the day? Mungo has to take matters into his own hands, and dives bravely into the plot himself...

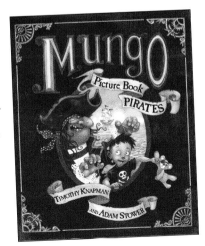

A great idea for a piratical tale, told with humour and sparky energy by Timothy Knapman, and delightfully illustrated by Adam Stower, this book will certainly face the same fate as Mungo's picture book – to be read over and over, night after night. So be warned...

Daniel Hahn

Life, the Universe and Everything

Books are there to give pleasure, but they can be useful, too. A visit to the doctor, a bereavement, the first day at school – picture books can help children come to terms with all of these and more, as **Lindsey Fraser** explains.

Booksellers and librarians have all encountered the anxious adult seeking a book to shed light on a first visit to the dentist, the first day at school, or even the first nit infestation. Usborne's **First Experiences** series by Anne Civardi and Stephen Cartwright is among those that introduce and explain some of the Big Days in a child's life.

Parents also seek stories to explain life's bigger mysteries. Such books as Alan Durant and Debi Gliori's *Always and Forever*, Judith Viorst and Eric Blegvad's *The Tenth Good Thing About Barney* and Susan Varley's *Badger's Parting Gifts* are exquisite and sensitive explorations of what it means when somebody dies. But they are also wonderful picture books in their own right, and would be well worth including routinely in a child's book collection. Children who have explored such difficult emotional areas within the safety of words and pictures in a book can draw on the resulting understanding to inform their own reactions when specific situations arise. Books aren't bandages or crutches; a five-day course won't effect a cure. But they do offer the language, imagery and perspective against which young readers – and their parents – can measure their feelings, consciously or not.

Laura Langston and Lindsey Gardiner's *Mile High Apple Pie* and Mem Fox and Julie Vivas' *Wilfred Gordon Macdonald Partridge* both tell stories in which characters are showing symptoms of Alzheimer's. But neither book should be consigned to the shelf until the prospect of encountering such a person looms. They're much too

good for that. And how better to talk the subject through with a child than in terms they recognise from a much-loved story?

Jealousy, nerves, sleeplessness, odd-one-out-ness, bullying, unhappiness, fear – look carefully enough and there will be an emotional beat of some kind to any good picture book. They don't need to be labelled like medicine bottles. Often the effect will be so subtle that it passes you by until your child refers to a particular picture, uses a particular turn of phrase, or simply requests a particular book; that choice may indicate a worry or preoccupation that a book will help clarify.

Compare Hiawyn Oram and Satoshi Kitamura's *Angry Arthur*, Debi Gliori's *No Matter What* (*UFBG* 145), Elfrida Vipont and Raymond Briggs' *The Elephant and the Bad Baby* (*UFBG* 96) and Maurice Sendak's legendary *Where the Wild Things Are* (*UFBG* 62). Each explores strong, sometimes dark emotions, but without any semblance of finger wagging or didacticism. A classroom teacher might enable her class to let off steam with a rousing rendition of *Where the Wild Things Are*, whereas a parent could explore expectations and insecurities in a gentle sharing of *No Matter What*. Or vice versa.

The best books don't teach; they simply shed light and show, leaving readers of all ages to draw their own conclusions. ●

These Are All Good Ones to Try

Are We There Yet? by Verna Wilkins, illustrated by George McLeod and Lynne Willey (disabled father)

Boots for a Bridesmaid by Verna Wilkins, illustrated by Pamela Venus (disabled mother)

Dinosaurs Divorce: a Guide for Changing Families by Laurene Krasny Brown and Marc Brown (divorce)

Don't Call Me Special: a First Look at Disability by Pat Thomas

I Love You Like Crazy Cakes by Rose A. Lewis, illustrated by Jane Dyer (adoption)

Mama Zooms by Jayne Cohen Fletcher (disabled mother)

My Brother Sammy by Becky Edwards, illustrated by David Armitage (autism)

My Name Was Hussein by Hristo Kyuchukov (persecution)

Over the Moon by Karen Katz (adoption)

We'll Paint the Octopus Red by Stephanie Stuve-Bodeen, illustrated by Pam DeVito (Down's syndrome)

Who's Poorly Too? by Kes Gray, illustrated by Mary McQuillan (illness)

MY DAD Anthony Browne

You don't have to hero-worship your dad to know that he can run faster than anyone else in the world, that his singing voice is better that Pavarotti's and that he could out-dance Fred Astaire. This book celebrates all that and more, with the brown-checked pattern of Dad's dressing gown appearing in various forms throughout the illustrations. Best of all, though, is the ending, when we find out the most important thing that makes Dad so special. It's good to be reminded that dads are for life, not just for Father's Day.

Antonia Honeywell

MY GRANDMOTHER'S CLOCK
Geraldine McCaughrean, illustrated by Stephen Lambert

A little girl quizzes her grandmother about how she tells the time if the only clock in the house, a grandfather clock, doesn't work. The answer is lyrical and affectionate – using the world shared and enjoyed by the two generations. Mondays are unmistakeably Mondays because of the baking aromas; Wednesdays are heralded by noisy dustmen. 'In one week,' Grandmother tells her, 'enough dust settles on the grandfather clock for it to need dusting.' Stephen Lambert's gently reassuring illustrations are the perfect partner for this necklace of miniature stories, all bound together through wisdom, kindness and an acceptance of the passage of time.

MY GRANDMOTHER'S CLOCK

Written by award-winning author GERALDINE McCAUGHREAN
Illustrated by STEPHEN LAMBERT

Lindsey Fraser

NEXT!
Christopher Inns

Doctor Hopper (an intellectual-looking blue rabbit) and Nurse Rex Barker (a rather butch, floppy-eared dog) work in a toy hospital. At the cry of 'Next!', each new patient comes in: One Eye Ted, whose only remaining eye has come off; Woolly Sheep, who is unravelling; Sawdust Cat, whose smile has rubbed off from too many cuddles... Each time, the medical team find an inventive solution to the problem.

This story – with zinging colours and minimal text – is very funny indeed. It manages to be both warmly touching and sharply witty at the same time, with laughs for the adult reader, too.

Susan Reuben

NICE WORK, LITTLE WOLF!
Hilda Offen

With its bubbling sense of the absurd, this is one of those rare books that makes adults snort with laughter, too. Little Wolf escapes from his pram (his mother offers only a 'small reward' for his return), and ends up with the Porkers, a lazy pig family, who are delighted to have someone to do their hard work. So Little Wolf fetches, cleans and paints, while the Porkers laze around. After digging (and tiling) a swimming pool and building a house, Little Wolf finally loses his temper, chases the Porkers off and moves his mother in.

If you've ever felt that there was another side to the story of 'The Three Little Pigs' – or had a child who thinks they have to do too many chores – buy this and have a chuckle.

Yzanne Mackay

THE NIGHT PIRATES
Peter Harris, illustrated by Deborah Allwright

The Night Pirates is a super 'all join in' book. Tucked up in bed, Tom is disturbed by strange shapes at the window, which turn out to be 'Rough, tough little girl pirates'. He joins them on their adventurous voyage to an exotic island, where they capture a treasure chest from the 'really tough grown-up pirates'. Tom returns home, to the warmth and comfort of his own bed. But there's a final surprise on the last page!

Peter Harris' rhythmic text is perfect for sharing with an individual child or a small group. It invites you to whisper the lines 'stealthy as shadows and quiet as mice', and shout the word 'PIRATES!' Take time to look at the endpapers – do the shapes of the islands remind you of anything? After reading this book, you might be tempted to draw your own maps and use them to create stories together with your child.

Nikki Gamble

NOBODY LAUGHS AT A LION
Paul Bright, illustrated by Matt Buckingham

Pa Lion is annoyed. He knows he's king of the jungle, but in fact each of the other animals is better than him at something – the monkey is better at climbing trees, the snake is better at slipping silently through the grass, the cheetah is better at running... Of course, they daren't brag about their superiority too loudly, because nobody laughs at a lion.

Pa Lion is soon so cross that he lets out a massive *ROAR!* And, well, *nobody* roars as well as a lion – Pa Lion is happy at last! Bright pictures and a repeating text make this a lovely book to share, with proud Pa as a charmingly flawed but loveable hero.

Daniel Hahn

NO MATTER WHAT
Debi Gliori

It's fairly clear that Small – a tubby little fox – is more than a little annoyed with Large. Large is on the phone, and we can tell she's been yakking for some time. So Small causes a commotion, the phone call ends and a conversation begins. 'I'm a grim and grumpy little Small and nobody loves me at all,' he explains anxiously.

There is great humour amidst the tenderness of this book – the illustrations are bursting with gleeful Debi Gliori jokes. But they never undermine the seriousness of the story. Large never wavers. She'll always love Small – no matter what.

Lindsey Fraser

NO MORE EEE-ORRH!
Lydia Monks

No one needs an alarm clock with Dicky Donkey around. When the neighbours complain, Dicky Donkey fears he will be sent away although his small owner tells him she wouldn't dream of it. The next morning she wakes up late. Dicky Donkey has lost his *eee-orrh*. He is taken to the animal hospital but nothing makes him feel any better. It is only when the neighbours oversleep and visit Dicky Donkey to tell him how much they miss him that he recovers and *eee-orrhs* triumphantly. The quirky illustrations convey much of the humour in this reassuring story, which shows that it isn't until you miss something that it's truly appreciated.

Jane Churchill

NO MORE TEASING!
Emma Chichester Clark

Mimi loves her cousin Momo, but he calls her names and tells her the Grizzly Grilla will get her. The plucky girl monkey is bewildered but undaunted. (Her retort 'I'll show you, Big Poo!' will be adopted enthusiastically by toddlers.) When Grandma finds out what's been going on, she and Mimi hatch a plan to ensure Momo gets his comeuppance.

The range and depth of colour in the jungle setting and the varied page designs maintain visual interest in a book with irresistible appeal to put-upon younger siblings.

Madelyn Travis

NOT NOW, BERNARD   David McKee

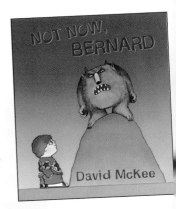

First published in 1982, *Not Now, Bernard* is a brilliant fable told simply, and clearly illustrated in David McKee's continental style, and has long since achieved classic status. Bernard is a small boy who discovers a monster in his garden. He tells his parents, but all they say is... 'Not now, Bernard.' The monster eats Bernard, only to find that Bernard's parents are too busy to take notice of him, either. Some children of a sensitive disposition find the story hard to take, but most love its relentless comic logic and deadly skewering of adult failings.

Tony Bradman

NOT SO FAST SONGOLOLO   Niki Daly

A little boy called Shepherd and his grandmother travel into the big city to go shopping. There, Shepherd presses his nose against the window of a shoe shop, comparing the beautiful bright red tackies (plimsolls) with his own battered ones.

This quiet story set in Africa has a really sensual feel: the cry of the baby and bark of the dog, the colours on Grandma's dress, and the light touch of her hands on Shepherd's shoulders. It gives an unobtrusive message about the meaning of possessions when you have very little money, and is full of understated charm.

Susan Reuben

THE OBVIOUS ELEPHANT
Bruce Robinson, illustrated by Sophie Windham

If you'd never seen an elephant before, and one turned up suddenly in the middle of your local square, what would you think it was? That's the question faced by the residents of the town, who are surprised one morning to find this huge grey whatever-it-is sitting in the square, mopping its brow with a spotted handkerchief. Is it a railway engine? A fire engine? A refuse-collecting machine? A submarine? Only Eric – a little boy much given to lying – knows the answer.

Windham's beautiful, sometimes fanciful illustrations bring warmth and wit to this charming fable.

Daniel Hahn

OLD BEAR series Jane Hissey

The everyday adventures of Old Bear, Little Bear and their friends – including Jolly the Giraffe, Sailor, Rabbit and Duck – are told with simple clarity, the stories accompanied by beautifully old-fashioned, detailed illustrations.

Each story holds a new adventure – camping out, putting on a play, rescuing a lost toy. All are ideal for copying at home, perhaps by building a toy raft of sticks or making a dragon's cave from a cloth over a chair.

While children will identify most with Little Bear, full of enthusiasm and curiosity, adult readers will appreciate the subtler points of Bramwell's pomposity and Old Bear's patience. All should gain some wonderful ideas for play!

Yzanne Mackay

■ There are many **Old Bear** stories to choose from. Titles include *Old Bear Tales*; *Little Bear Lost*; *Ruff*; *Hoot*; *Little Bear's All-Together Painting*; *Little Bear's Alphabet*; *Little Bear's Numbers* and *Jolly Tall*.

OLIVER'S FRUIT SALAD
Vivian French, illustrated by Alison Bartlett

Oliver turns up his nose when his mother gives him blackcurrant juice and tinned pears. His grandpa grows real fruit, he explains.

Mum keeps trying to entice him to eat fruit, until he admits that while he enjoys helping Grandpa grow things in his garden, he doesn't actually like eating the results. It takes a visit from his clever grandma and grandpa to persuade him, finally, that fruit can be delicious.

Alison Bartlett's mouth-watering illustrations of luscious cherries, strawberries and pears made me want to dash downstairs and dive into the fruit bowl.

Caroline Pitcher

OLIVIA
Ian Falconer

Like her heroine Maria Callas, Olivia is a wonderful mixture of elegance and charm – with a will of iron! No matter she's a small pig, Olivia is a positive whirlwind of activity: going to the beach, looking at paintings, reading and – best of all – dressing up. And in her dreams, she's a diva...

I fell in love with this book when I first saw it. Ian Falconer uses predominantly just three colours – black, white and electric red – to great effect and with immense panache. The deadpan text is perfectly paced: he knows just when to pause for an entire page of misty greys or speed up with a double-page spread of tiny, expressive vignettes of this unique pig. Entertaining and truly stylish!

Helen Simmons

■ Other titles include *Olivia Saves the Circus*; *Olivia Forms a Band*; *Olivia and the Missing Toy* and *Dream Big: Starring Olivia*, and for 0–2s, the enchanting concept book *Olivia Counts*.

ON A TALL TALL CLIFF
Andrew Murray, illustrated by Alan Snow

Busby and Puffle live on a tall, tall clifftop, but Puffle's house is closer to the edge. One day, Busby asks to borrow the contents of Puffle's shed. Then all his belongings. And finally the house itself. Puffle, struggling under teetering towers of planks, bricks and possessions, thinks 'it's a lot to ask'. But, of course, there's an excellent reason for Busby's apparently outrageous requests. The brilliantly comic illustrations make the most of the vertiginous setting, and don't miss the detailed endpapers, which tell even more stories. A fresh and thought-provoking take on the theme of trust between friends.

Kathryn Ross

ONCE UPON A TIDE
Tony Mitton, illustrated by Selina Young

Beautiful from the first endpapers onwards, this picture book is about the power of the imagination. The rhyming text tells the adventures of two children at the beach building a boat, sewing sails and setting off on an amazing adventure. They meet whales, visit islands, search for treasure, encounter pirates and arrive back at the beach ready to settle down in a house they build themselves. This dreamy journey is told as much through the pictures as the words, and is great to read at bedtime.

Wendy Cooling

Stories That Have Stood the Test of Time

The Tale of Peter Rabbit by Beatrix Potter (*UFBG* 178)

Orlando: The Marmalade Cat series by Kathleen Hale (*UFBG* 151)

The Flower Fairies series by Cecily Mary Barker (*UFBG* 236)

Little Grey Rabbit series by Alison Uttley, illustrated by Margaret Tempest (*UFBG* 123)

Curious George series by Margret and H.A. Rey (*UFBG* 89)

ONCE UPON AN ORDINARY SCHOOL DAY
Colin McNaughton, illustrated by Satoshi Kitamura

In terms of finding a harmony between words and pictures, each enhancing the effect of the other, *Once Upon an Ordinary School Day* is just about as good as it gets. McNaughton's story describes an ordinary boy, who eats his ordinary breakfast and does all the ordinary things he does on an ordinary day, but while at school something extraordinary happens – an extraordinary man brings *music* to the classroom, and everything changes... Kitamura's plain, grey pictures slowly begin to fill with colour – with blues, greens and browns... The mood-changing power of music must be just about the hardest thing to evoke with just words and pictures, but you'll feel it in this book.

Daniel Hahn

ONE MORE SHEEP
Mij Kelly, illustrated by Russell Ayto

Sam the farmer fetches his sheep home on a wild, windy night and tucks them up in bed, safe from the prowling wolf. But when Sam tries to count his flock, of course he falls asleep! Ayto's angular sheep are full of character and clearly much sharper than their kindly but woolly-headed farmer. They realise straight away that the 'little bleater' knocking at the door is no lost lamb, but a wolf in disguise.

So much more than just a counting story, this dramatic, hilarious picture book has the kind of witty, rhyming text that turns every reader into a great performer.

Kathryn Ross

THE OPPOSITE
Tom Macrae, illustrated by Elena Odrioza

This is a visually exciting book with a quirky story. It begins:

'When Nate woke up one morning, The Opposite was standing on his ceiling staring down at him.'

Nate protests and demands that The Opposite gets down from the ceiling. It responds by doing... well... the opposite, of course. It follows Nate, creating havoc in the kitchen and classroom. Whenever Nate tries to draw his parents' attention to The Opposite it disappears like Alice's Cheshire Cat, leaving behind a fading smile. You see, once the opposite has happened then it is no longer there.

This is a beguiling story with equally enigmatic illustrations. Encounters with books like *The Opposite* are vital for developing adventurous readers, who are willing to be challenged by the unfamiliar. Highly recommended.

Nikki Gamble

ORANGE PEAR APPLE BEAR see p.44.

ORLANDO: THE MARMALADE CAT
series Kathleen Hale

This series of books by author / illustrator Kathleen Hale, published between 1938 and 1972, are some of the first stories I remember reading, and spawned in me an intense and lasting love of ginger cats! The tales of Orlando, the marmalade tom 'with eyes like twin gooseberries' – along with his wife Grace and kittens Blanche, Pansy and Tinkle – range from his first camping holiday to adventures abroad, on a farm, at the seaside and zoo, and even travelling to the moon. Beautifully illustrated, they perfectly capture a bygone era, yet have completely survived the test of time.

Catherine Robinson

■ Follow Orlando and family's adventures in *Orlando Buys a Farm*; *A Seaside Holiday*; *Orlando Keeps a Dog* and *A Camping Holiday* among others.

THE OTHER ARK
Lynley Dodd

Noah's ark is full, but animals are still queuing to board, so he recruits his friend to take the flying flapdoodles, pom-pom palavers and Mongolian sneeth in his 'second best' boat. But is Sam up to the task? With a repeated refrain of 'I'm A1 efficient, I know what to do, there's nothing too tricky for Sam Jam Balu', readers know something is sure to go comically wrong – and it does!

Children will be fascinated by Dodd's visual interpretations of her weird and wacky animal creations, while the alliterations and Learesque animal names will delight readers and listeners alike.

Madelyn Travis

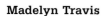

THE OWL AND THE PUSSYCAT
Edward Lear

When I was small, a man (called Ernest?) used to sing 'The Owl and the Pussycat' on *Children's Favourites* – and I still know all the words. Wistful, romantic and surreal, the poem tells of true love, a beautiful pea-green boat, of honey and money wrapped up in a five-pound note, and a wedding breakfast of mince and slices of quince. I always wanted a runcible spoon (even after I found out it was really a fork) and longed to sail to the Land where the Bong-tree grows.

My favourite illustrations for *The Owl and the Pussycat* are by Gwen Fulton, with an earnest owl deeply in love with a possibly tricky cat.

Caroline Pitcher

THE OWL WHO WAS AFRAID OF THE DARK see p.275.

PANTS
Giles Andreae, illustrated by Nick Sharratt

This is certainly one of the silliest books you will ever come across. Forget books that teach an important lesson, this one is about pants. That's all – just pants.

The rhyming text is almost tongue-twisterish, and the zingy illustrations match it in joyfulness. Little children love shouting out naughty words such as 'pants', and this book is likely to have them in stitches.

Susan Reuben

■ Look out for the sequel *More Pants*.

THE PAPER BAG PRINCESS
Robert Munsch, illustrated by Michael Martchenko

Elizabeth is a princess. She is going to marry Roland, a prince. There will be a fairy-tale wedding. Or will there? A nasty dragon gets in the way of their plans, and refreshingly it's the feisty princess who saves the prince-in-distress. Martchenko's illustrations now lend the book a slightly old-fashioned appearance, but they're lovely, and the story reads completely up-to-date, gently subverting fairy-tale tradition and creating a fine heroine to admire.

Daniel Hahn

PASS THE JAM, JIM
Kaye Umansky, illustrated by Margaret Chamberlain

This is a rollicking rhyme about a group of children preparing for a huge tea party. From the first line, 'Hurry, Mabel, lay that table!', we're off and running. The text is the voice of the adult, trying to impose some order on the increasingly chaotic proceedings, as more and more children join in slicing, spreading, pouring, spilling and eating. There are endless delicious details to look at, a colourful cast of characters to follow and it's all held together by Jim and his sticky fingers. A picture book to cheer up the dullest day and defy the deepest sulk!

Kathryn Ross

■ There's more fun with Jim in *You Can Swim, Jim* and *Need a Trim, Jim*. There is also a short-story collection for emerging readers, *Three Days With Jim*.

Truth Is Stranger Than Fiction: Non Fiction for the Very Young

Most adults read both fiction and non fiction, and there's no reason why children shouldn't, too, even from a very young age. **Lindsey Fraser** introduces some of the best non-fiction picture books.

Young children love facts – they love knowing about things and talking about what they know, and in the past two decades, some publishers have fed that enthusiasm with imaginatively devised books covering any number of subjects.

Mick Manning
Brita Granström

Is a Blue Whale the Biggest Thing There Is? (*UFBG* 248) by Robert Wells describes the concept of scale. It's a real page-turner, with a sense of anticipation that most crime writers would kill for. Mick Manning and Brita Granström's *Yuck!* invites noisy audience participation as it reveals the dietary preferences of different kinds of babies – including a lizard, an osprey, a toad and an owl. It is entertaining, informative and memorable. Karen Wallace and Mike Bostock's beautiful *Think of an Eel* (*UFBG* 184) concentrates on the life cycle of that one species – if you haven't read it, prepare to be amazed. *Growing Frogs* by Vivian French and Alison Bartlett explores more familiar territory perhaps, but with the same sense of excitement and discovery. Life – whether you're a frog, a hen or a Viking raider – is all about stories.

Mechanical things also have a life for many children. Tony Mitton and Ant Parker's **Amazing Machines** series delights in transport of all kinds with lively stories and vibrant illustrations. But if you're entertaining a stickler for technical accuracy, look no further than *The Ultimate Sticker Books* for *Tractors*, or *Cars*, *Horses* or *Puppies,* or even *Farm*... Dorling Kindersley's photographic approach satisfies even the most fact-obsessed children.

Few childhoods pass without a period in which dinosaurs preoccupy most waking hours. Straddling fiction and non fiction, there are any number of approaches to the subject, from the rhyming fun and luminous illustrations of Paul and Henrietta Stickland's *Dinosaur Roar!* (*UFBG* 21) to James Mayhew's engagingly informative *Katie and the Dinosaurs*, in which a small girl visiting the Natural History Museum has a more hands-on experience than most people.

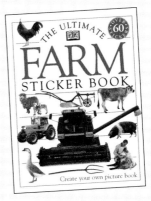

James Mayhew's Katie is an intrepid learner – during visits to art galleries she discovers all about the world of the Impressionists, the *Mona Lisa*, Van Gogh and Gauguin. How better to explore the world of art than through the pages of a beautifully painted picture book? It seems as if no subject is beyond the capabilities of the most adventurous of picture book creators. ●

Great Non Fiction for the Very Young

Best Word Book Ever by Richard Scarry

Busiest People Ever by Richard Scarry (*UFBG* 77)

Complete Book of First Experiences by Anna Civardi, illustrated by Stephen Cartwright (Going to school, doctor, moving house, new baby etc.)

I Spy: Shapes in Art by Lucy Micklethwait (*UFBG* 118)

I Wonder Why My Tummy Rumbles, **I Wonder Why** series

J is for Jamaica by Benjamin Zephaniah, photographs by Prodeepta Das (*UFBG* 119)

Kipper's Book of Weather by Mick Inkpen

Maisy's Wonderful Weather Book by Lucy Cousins

My Potty Book for Boys / Girls (potty training)

P is for Pakistan by Shazia Razzak, photographs by Prodeepta Das

THE PEA AND THE PRINCESS
Mini Grey

This is very clever! Mini Grey has the ability to take a story that everyone knows well and turn it on its head in the most delightful way imaginable. Here, the pea is the hero. Having spent long nights buried under piles of mattresses topped with one princess after another, all of whom are far too polite to say that they slept badly, the pea takes matters into its own hands and soon the prince has a bride. The story will appeal to adults and children alike, but it's the wickedly detailed illustrations that make the book. Just compare the two double-page pictures of the palace kitchen gardens…

Laura Hutchings

PEACE AT LAST
Jill Murphy

Poor Mr Bear can't get to sleep. Mrs Bear snores, taps drip and clocks tick as an ever more weary Mr Bear trails from bed to kitchen and even outside, in his quest for peace and quiet. The fuzzy-edged, moonlit illustrations are wonderfully atmospheric and expressive. Older children love spotting details such as the time passing on the various clocks, while all ages enjoy making the noises and joining in with Mr Bear's despairing cry of 'I can't stand this!' Despite its title, night-time setting and sleep-deprived hero, I can't recommend this classic book as a bedtime story – it's far too lively!

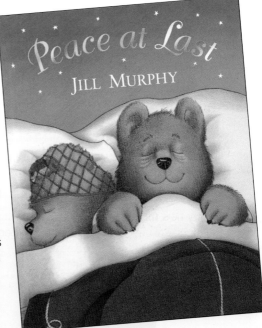

Kathryn Ross

PERCY THE PARK KEEPER series
Nick Butterworth

Life is never dull for Percy the Park Keeper and his animal friends – Owl, Mole, Fox, Badger, Squirrel, Rabbit and Hedgehog. Percy is kept busy looking after the animals when they're in trouble – and sometimes they help him, too.

There are so many different stories to choose from. Some of the books, such as *The Treasure Hunt* and *The Rescue Party*, have surprise pull-out pages. There's a special version of *One Snowy Night* complete with audio CD. And be prepared for *Percy's Bumpy Ride,* in which Percy experiences Life Beyond the Park Gates!

Caroline Pitcher

■ Other **Percy** titles include *Percy the Park Keeper: A Classic Treasury*; *One Warm Fox*; *The Owl's Lesson*; *The Badger's Bath* and *The Hedgehog's Balloon*.

PIG'S DIGGER
Simon Puttock, illustrated by Alison Bartlett

Pig receives a digger for his birthday, and as digging runs in the family he's thrilled. At first he finds plenty of excuses to use it: Cow needs a new swimming pool, Hen wants to plant the corn and Dog needs to bury all his bones. But after a few days Pig has nothing else to dig, and this is when the digger starts to bring out his wild side...

The daft text and zanily bright illustrations create an enticingly silly story. You could derive all sorts of messages from it, about self control, friendship and so on, but I wouldn't bother – just read and enjoy!

Susan Reuben

THE POLAR EXPRESS
Chris van Allsburg

I was both haunted and moved by this outstanding picture book when I first saw it over 20 years ago. On Christmas Eve, a small boy listens for the ringing bells of Santa's sleigh. What he hears is the hissing steam of the Polar Express, the night train that takes children to visit Santa's toy factories at the North Pole. So begins an extraordinary adventure, described in spare, simple text. Many years later, the narrator looks back on that night, knowing now that all things are possible for those who 'truly believe'. The illustrations have the blurred, photographic quality of dream images.

Patricia Elliott

POTTY POO-POO WEE-WEE!
Colin McNaughton

McNaughton's book highlights children's ability to blurt out the most inappropriate things at the most inconvenient times. The cheeky Littlesaurus announces the arrival of his smelly parcels with a rude refrain, making all who hear him cringe. Despairing that he may never be potty trained, his family take desperate measures. Children will love the toilet humour and adults take the moral victory over the contrary child. This book has something for everyone – warm and imaginative illustrations and the chance to sing 'Potty Poo-Poo Wee-Wee!'.

Patricia Legan

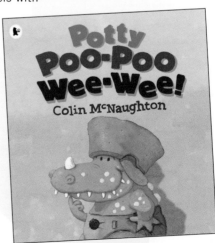

THE PRINCESS AND THE PEA
Lauren Child, photographs by Polly Borland

In this version of the classic fairy tale, Lauren Child and Polly Borland have created a magical world. They have constructed and then photographed theatrical sets in miniature, each portraying a scene from the story, with tiny objects and furniture beautifully rendered. The figures, line-drawn with fabric-print clothing, are combined with text that utilises many typefaces, to create a bold and original look.

With so many 'spins' on classic stories available, it's lovely to have a version of Hans Andersen's story that is at the same time straightforward (the plot is the original), yet visually highly unusual.

Laura Hutchings

PRINCESS POPPY series
Janey Louise Jones

With gorgeous, cup-cake coloured illustrations, these picture books are all about Poppy, and her family and friends. Each books tells a story in which Poppy usually learns a small lesson. Whether it's being too impatient to wait for her birthday, or jealous because her best friend gets the starring role in a ballet, Poppy never means any harm, and always learns from her mistakes. Each book contains an envelope, with maybe a letter from Poppy, a hint about making something (Petal Perfume in *The Birthday*) and a map of Honeypot Hill where Poppy lives. She isn't a real princess, but that's what all her family call her, and what (like many girls) she wants to be.

Leonie Flynn

> ■ More **Princess Poppy** stories? Try these: *Princess Poppy: Ballet Shoes*; *Twinkletoes*; *A True Princess*; *The Baby Twins*; *The Play*; *The Wedding*; *The Birthday*; *The Fair Day Ball* and *Friends Together*.

PUMPKIN SOUP
Helen Cooper

A warm and witty tale about sharing and co-operation. Cat, Squirrel and Duck love pumpkin soup and they always make it exactly the same way, until Duck decides that he wants to do the stirring for a change. All families will recognise the argument that follows, as harsh words fly and Duck storms (sorry, waddles...) out of the house. When tempers have cooled and Duck still hasn't returned, his friends are worried and bravely set out into the woods to find him. But Duck is scarcely home before he's stirring things again! The deliciously detailed illustrations in glowing autumnal colours are irresistible.

Kathryn Ross

THE QUANGLE WANGLE'S HAT
Edward Lear, illustrated by Louise Voce

No one can see the face of the Quangle Wangle Quee because of the enormous hat that he wears. But this does not deter many animals, mostly imaginary ones, from asking permission to camp out on its wide brim. Lear has created an unforgettable and quite delightfully silly text that not only rhymes wonderfully, but contains repetitions and musical words that makes reading it aloud a pleasure. Highly recommended for reading with young babies, who may not understand the story but will hugely enjoy the sounds, as well as Voce's colourful illustrations and simple contours that wisely retain the Quangle Wangle's mysterious identity...

Noga Applebaum

QUEENIE THE BANTAM
Bob Graham

A deliciously warm-hearted story from the pen of the wonderful Bob Graham. Caitlin's dad rescues a hen from the lake. Her mum says they must take it back to the farm over the motorway, but Queenie the hen has taken a liking to Caitlin and her family, and returns every morning to lay an egg in their dog basket. 'And that might have been the end of the story… but it wasn't.'

This beautifully presented book is all about adapting to change (including a new baby in Caitlin's family), and is illustrated in Graham's witty and deftly expressive pen-and-wash style. I just love the way he both writes and draws with the very lightest of touches, conveying with great humour and affection the centrality of relationships.

Malachy Doyle

RABBIT PIE
Penny Ives

This is a 'recipe' with a difference, describing how to get six small and cheeky rabbits to bed for the night: 'Place in warm soapy water… Gently scrub… Tuck in, sprinkling with kisses…'

Penny Ives' spare and clever text is accompanied by pastel illustrations of the rabbit family's bedtime routine – complete with naughty antics and procrastinations familiar to nurseries everywhere. The result is a book that is unashamedly cute but completely endearing, and the orange-cloth binding printed with rows of carrots really completes it. 'The perfect recipe for bedtime,' says the cover, and it's hard to disagree.

Susan Reuben

RAINBOW BIRD
Eric Maddern, illustrated by Adrienne Kennaway

This cover positively zings with vibrant citrus colours, and the illustrations inside the book are even zingier. Eric Maddern retells a folk tale set in the aboriginal Time of Dreams in northern Australia. Rough, tough, mean and scary Crocodile Man owns Fire. (And believe me, he is scary, especially when he yawns.) 'I'm boss for Fire!' he growls. But Bird Woman, an early feminist, weary of eating her food raw and shivering in the dark, wins in the end. She steals Crocodile Man's fire, and gives it to the world for light and warmth. In her triumph she dances and puts the firesticks into her tail to become the glowing Rainbow Bird. A dramatic, beautiful book with a satisfyingly right ending.

Caroline Pitcher

RAINBOW FISH
Marcus Pfister

Rainbow Fish is the most beautiful fish in the sea, but won't play with the other fish, and won't let them have any of his gorgeous shiny scales, even though he has lots and lots. So he's lonely, and it's his own fault. But will he learn his lesson?

The story has a nice 'it's good to share' moral built in, and Rainbow Fish's glittering scales are indeed lovely, with little patterned foil panels inset in every page, making this popular book a shiny visual treat.

Daniel Hahn

■ **Rainbow Fish** is available in a range of formats including board books, bath books, lift-the-flap books, games and even an interactive, computer storybook. The picture-book sequels include: *Rainbow Fish and his Friends: Hidden Treasures*; *Rainbow Fish to the Rescue* and *Rainbow Fish and the Big Blue Whale*.

ROOM ON THE BROOM
Julia Donaldson, illustrated by Axel Scheffler

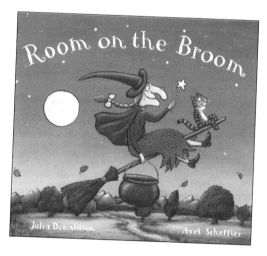

Room on the Broom is a fantastic story, written to be read out loud by frustrated thespians. The pictures are full of personality, too. The regular rhyme and rhythm mean that the story rattles along at a great pace, as the friendly witch accommodates all her friends, old and new, on her broom. The advent of an evil dragon simply extends the opportunities for funny voices and amateur histrionics, and the highly satisfying ending celebrates many things dear to parents' hearts, such as inclusion, sharing and mutual help. A real favourite that gets better and better with rereading.

Antonia Honeywell

RORY AND THE SHOOTING STAR
Andrew Wolffe, illustrated by Tom Cole

The **Rory** stories are delightful picture books about the year-round seaside adventures of red-haired Rory and his wee dog, Scruff McDuff. In this story, Rory goes in search of the shooting star he and his dad saw the night before, and which Rory is sure has fallen on the beach nearby. He meets some helpful seaside creatures and does eventually find a star lying on the sand. Whether or not it's a shooting star doesn't really matter; as far as Rory is concerned it's magic. These engaging tales, with their bright illustrations, really hit the spot.

Kathryn Ross

ROSIE'S WALK see p.50.

RUMBLE IN THE JUNGLE
Giles Andreae, illustrated by David Wojtowycz

Brightly coloured, bold and full of personality, the animals in *Rumble in the Jungle* swing, stomp and stampede their way through the rhymes that describe their antics. Each animal has its own page, so the book is good for dipping in and out of, and for choosing and comparing favourites. The follow-up collection, *Commotion in the Ocean*, has the same collage-effect illustrations and energetic verses. Both are great for acting out, too, with plenty of noises and movement to be brought to life. Not recommended for bedtimes, but great for play.

Antonia Honeywell

THE RUNAWAY TRAIN
Benedict Blathwayt

Here we have all the ingredients for a story guaranteed to capture the interest of children aged three plus – excitement, repetition and trains!

The Little Red Train sets off unwittingly without Duffy the engine driver. The chase takes the reader from the busy port station and through pastoral countryside as Duffy hitches lifts on trucks, boats, bicycles and several more unorthodox means of transport. Throughout we have the refrain '*Chuff-Chuff, Chuff-Chuff, whoo...oooo*' – until finally Duffy is airlifted from a helicopter into his engine to drive the little red train into Sandy-on-Sea, where he spends the day on the beach.

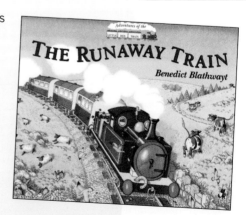

Every page is crammed with incident and interest – a veritable toddler geography lesson! However, the final double-page spread revisits all the people who have helped in the chase as the Little Red Train makes the journey home, neatly reprising the story in reverse.

Sonia Benster

■ Next in the series is *Little Red Train to the Rescue*. These wonderful stories are also available as board books – and even jigsaw books!

RUSSELL THE SHEEP
Rob Scotton

Russell is an endearing sheep with a long, striped nightcap and a frog friend. As night approaches, all the sheep indulge in the usual bedtime rituals (brushing teeth, hot drink in a mug, teddy-bear fetching, putting false teeth in a glass...) All the sheep, that is, except Russell. He tries everything to get to sleep. He counts his feet and even the stars, and thinks so hard that his hat goes ziggy-zaggy.

Then Russell counts sheep. Once he realises that he's forgotten to count one very important little sheep, he finally falls sound asleep.

Like Russell's nightcap, the illustrations are blue and white, and the layout of the words, in curves and spirals, is as delightfully quirky as the story itself.

Caroline Pitcher

SCRITCH SCRATCH
Miriam Moss, illustrated by Delphine Durand

Ever had nits? Ever panicked at the thought? Well, this is a great book for kids – and for parents and grandparents – because it makes the whole itchy infestation seem perfectly normal and wonderfully easy to deal with!

With amusing text and images, this is the everyday story of a louse, from her casual stroll into Miss Calypso's classroom to her finding a home, starting a family and then watching everyone (including the teacher) start to scratch... and scratch! Of course, all ends well, and the final pages offer factual advice on bug busting.

Leonie Flynn

THE SEAL CHILDREN Jackie Morris

Jackie Morris' first book is a tale of the tumbledown village close to where she lives in Pembrokeshire. A seal-woman comes ashore and has two children there, but eventually follows the call of the sea. Meanwhile, the impoverished villagers hope to travel to America for a better life, but are unable to raise the money. Ffion and Morlo, the children of the selkie, are enticed underwater by their mother. She gives Ffion a box of pearls to pay for the villagers' passage, but Morlo chooses to remain with his mother for ever.

A lyrical text and beautiful illustrations combine to make a haunting tale of sadness and of hope.

Malachy Doyle

SEAL SURFER Michael Foreman

One of the most heart-warming picture books I know, with an optimistic, lump-in-your-throat ending. It's the story of a boy and a seal, of the friendship they forge and the almost-accident where the seal comes to the rescue.

Looking carefully at Foreman's beautiful pictures you'll notice that the boy uses crutches – but it's never made a big deal; it's just a gentle reinforcement that this boy – like any other – can be the hero of his story.

Daniel Hahn

THE SECRET FAIRY series Penny Dann

For girls who love intricate illustrations, pink and sparkly things, tiny letters in pretty envelopes, wings and wishes, these books are delightful, from the original *The Secret Fairy Handbook* through to a vast array of novelties, including sticker books, party bags, a *Beauty Parlour Handbag* (containing, among other things, a nail file, stick-on earrings, toy make-up and a mirror), *The Secret Fairy Boutique* (with feathers, silk for making friendship bracelets and nail tattoos), *a Pop-up and Play House*, *Letters*, a *Christmas Handbook*, a *Party Book* with fairy wings and invitations, and much, much more.

Leonie Flynn

THE SHEEP FAIRY
Ruth Louise Symes, illustrated by David Sim

Being a dreamer myself, I was charmed by Wendy Woolcoat, the sheep with a secret ambition. Wendy, like all her sheep friends, eats grass – all day, every day – until she rescues a fairy entangled in a bramble bush. The fairy rewards her with a wish, which Wendy tells her 'very quietly'. The story of how Wendy's wish comes true, and more than that, how she rescues her sheep comrades from certain death, is wittily illustrated in bold, blocky colours. A perceptive and unusual theme, too: that even the most boring-seeming people may harbour secret dreams about changing their lives.

Patricia Elliott

THE SILVER SWAN
Michael Morpurgo, illustrated by
Christian Birmingham

A boy finds and befriends a swan, and watches her meet her mate and hatch a brood of cygnets – it's Nature at her most enchanting, but what will happen when the hungry mother fox gets to them? For Nature isn't sentimental about these things, and though Michael Morpurgo allows himself a little sentiment in this story he never loses sight of the real menace the beautiful swans live with... Christian Birmingham has produced soft, wintery illustrations in deep, glowing colours, which bring the beautiful words to life.

Daniel Hahn

Dragon Books

George and the Dragon by Chris Wormell (**UFBG** 104)

The Winter Dragon by Caroline Pitcher (**UFBG** 195)

There's No Such Thing as a Dragon by Jack Kent

Digory the Dragon Slayer by Angela McAllister (**UFBG** 224)

The Paper Bag Princess, by Robert Munsch, illustrated by Michael Mortchenko (**UFBG** 153)

Picture Books in Translation

Only a tiny proportion of the children's books published in the UK are translated from other languages. We need more, argues **Deborah Hallford**.

I became aware of how important books in translation were when I co-edited the *Outside In* guide with Edgardo Zaghini. Approximately 3% of books in the UK have been translated from other languages, and of these only one in a hundred is a children's title. This means that there are not many picture books available in translation from other countries. There are hardly any books translated from countries outside Europe and, even within Europe, the omissions are noticeable.

Of the books that have made it to the UK in translation, along with well-known titles such as *Tintin*, *Babar*, the unforgettable *Miffy* by Dick Bruna (*UFBG* 37) and *Frog* by Max Velthuijs (*UFBG* 103), there is a small range of contemporary picture books that deserve to have more recognition.

Max Velthuijs
Frog in Winter

Picture books from abroad often display a different style of illustration that we may not be familiar with. The books by French author / illustrator Hervé Tullet are inspirational: his bold and vibrant *Night and Day* explores opposites and *Pink Lemon* (*UFBG* 49) is a playful book about colour. The amusing *Ghost Party* and *Loch Ness Ghosts* by Jacques Duquennoy (translated from the French by Antonia Parkin), about the antics of Henry the ghost, relies on visual clues within the illustrations in order to follow the story. In complete contrast, *Tiger on a Tree* by Indian nonsense-verse author Anushka Ravishankar, is accompanied by Pulak Biswas' beautiful hand silk-screened illustrations on white, hand-made paper in a striking black and orange which complements the simple verse.

HERVÉ TULLET
PINK
LEMON

Sensitive or difficult subjects are often tackled in books from other countries. *Leo's Dream* by Antonie Schneider and Helga Bansch (translated from the German by Alison Cole) is an unusual cautionary tale of modern living. Leo's parents are too busy to have time for him, and so Leo resorts to his imagination for a solution.

Boris's Glasses by Peter Cohen and illustrated by Olof Landström is a quirky tale from Sweden about how Boris copes with his new glasses, while *The 100th Customer* by Byung-Gyu Kim and K.T. Hao, illustrated by Giuliano Ferri (translated from the Chinese by Annie Kung), is a stunning, large-format book, which shows how a simple act of generosity can bring unexpected rewards.

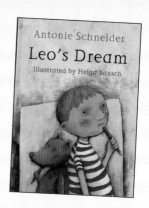

For slightly older readers, *Sweets* by Dutch author / illustrator Sylvia van Ommen is a touching and unusual book about friendship, illustrated with black and white line drawings, which beautifully portray its deep philosophical message. *Tundra Mouse Mountain* by Riitta Jalonen and Kristiina Louhi (translated by J.M. Ledgard) is an evocative and lyrical story from Finland; or take a look at *The Wizard, the Ugly and the Book of Shame* by Argentinean author / illustrator Pablo Bernasconi, with its striking collage-type illustrations.

Reading books in translation helps to break down the barriers of geography, language and race, and build bridges between nations. By enabling different audiences to access, explore and enjoy books from other countries, a diverse literature can help develop a greater understanding of – and tolerance for – other beliefs and cultures. There is a wonderful array of rich tradition and culture in children's literature from around the world that needs to be experienced by British readers. ●

Some Translated Picture Books to Try

The Bad Mood! by Moritz Petz, illustrated by Amélie Jackowski, translated from the German by J. Alison James

Blue & Square by Hervé Tullet

The Little Flower King by Kveta Pacovská, translated from the German by Anthea Bell

The Magic Pocket by Michio Mado, translated by the Empress Michiko of Japan

A Night-Time Tale by Alexandra Junge, translated from the German by Kate Connolly

Poppy's Biggest Wish by Maxim Biller, illustrated by Sybille Hein, translated from the German by Alyson Cole

The Story of the Little Mole Who Knew It Was None of his Business by Werner Holzwarth, illustrated by Wolf Erlbruch, translated from the German (*UFBG* 176)

Yellow & Round by Hervé Tullet

SIMPLY DELICIOUS!
Margaret Mahy, illustrated by Jonathan Allen

Mr Minky buys a double-dip-chocolate-chip-and-cherry ice cream with rainbow twinkles and chopped-nut sprinkles for his son, who is at home on the other side of the jungle. Then Mr Minky sets off on his bicycle, ice cream held aloft. But in the jungle are lots of animals, who really fancy a taste. 'Simply delicious!' they cry as they give chase.

The rollicking, cumulative text has lots of places to join in noisily. Will Mr Minky manage to deliver the ice cream to his son before it melts or gets gobbled? You'll have to read the book!

Susan Reuben

SING ME A STORY
Grace Hallworth, illustrated by John Clementson

Five traditional Caribbean tales, featuring turtles and tigers, mermaids and kings, are retold by excellent storyteller Grace Hallworth. John Clementson's collage illustrations are as vibrant and lively as the stories they depict.

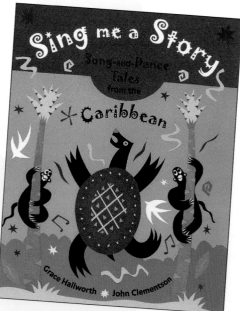

This is a story collection with many layers. Each story involves a song and / or dance, and music and dance steps are included throughout, making the book useful for anything from a cosy bedtime read, to a group activity where the stories are told, then the songs and dances learned and even performed.

Susan Reuben

SIX DINNER SID Inga Moore

Sid is a wily black cat who lives at six different addresses and scoffs six dinners every day. His secret is rumbled when he develops a cough and is taken to the vet six times. The angry neighbours restrict his dinners to one a day, so Sid moves to 1–6 Pythagoras Place. Here the neighbours are friendly and communicative, so they know about Sid's ruse from the start and don't mind.

Inga Moore's witty drawings complement her laugh-out-loud text and make the book a delight to read.

Gill Vickery

SLOW LORIS Alexis Deacon

This is the story of Slow Loris (who is a slow loris), who the other animals think is quiet and dull, but who really – secretly – spends his nights doing things FAST! When the animals discover his secret they want to join in, too. The odd humour in the weird, brown-grey illustrations won't be appreciated by very young children, but when they're old enough they'll love the character and the detail and the dots of colour, and you'll laugh at it all together. Especially the hats.

Daniel Hahn

THE SMARTEST GIANT IN TOWN
Julia Donaldson, illustrated by Axel Scheffler

George is the scruffiest giant in town, until he buys himself a brand-new outfit. As he walks home, though, he gives away his new clothes one by one: his shoe becomes a house for a little white mouse, one of his socks is a bed for a fox and his belt helps a dog who is crossing a bog...

Julia Donaldson's brilliant cumulative rhyme will have children joining in in no time, and Axel Scheffler has conjured up a society of animals, people and giants, who interact completely naturally.

Susan Reuben

THE SMELLY BOOK Babette Cole

The Smelly Book is a riot of revolting pongs, accompanied by suitably foul pictures of rotting food, rubbish tips and, of course, Dad's whiffy feet. Children will hold their noses, and are likely to get giddy with the fun of being encouraged to laugh at stink bombs in the classroom and similar outrages. Best of all, the book rhymes, making it easier to remember and read (repeatedly, of course) at the end of a long day. Babette Cole is a dab hand at the unsentimental antidote to stories with morals and uplifting endings. Her *The Sprog Owner's Manual* is another firm favourite.

Sarah Frost Mellor

THE SNEETCHES AND OTHER STORIES
Dr Seuss

There are so many fabulous Dr Seuss books, and *The Sneetches* is definitely up there near the top of my list. This collection of stories is classic Dr Seuss genius. Brilliantly madcap (and silly) rhymes, brilliantly madcap (and silly) illustrations, with crazy creatures and zany contraptions and a good moral heart. The title story is an allegory of how daft racism is, and it's wonderful, but they're all pretty glorious to tell the truth. Did I ever tell you that 'Mrs McCave / Had twenty-three sons and she named them all Dave?'

Daniel Hahn

Bear Books

Biscuit Bear by Mini Grey (**UFBG** 75)

Bear by Mick Inkpen (**UFBG** 72)

Bear and Me by Ella Burfoot (**UFBG** 72)

Can You See a Little Bear? by James Mayhew (**UFBG** 79)

Can't You Sleep, Little Bear? by Martin Waddell (**UFBG** 78)

Old Bear by Jane Hissey (**UFBG** 147)

Peace at Last by Jill Murphy (**UFBG** 156)

The Very Small by Joyce Dunbar (**UFBG** 188)

Oh Where, Oh Where? by John Prater (**UFBG** 43)

Everybody's Favourite...

THE SNOWMAN Raymond Briggs

Words like 'magical' are bandied around all too often in connection with children's books, but here's one that can make legitimate claims to the tag. A soft-hued picture book that's actually designed more like a comic book, with around 170 panels spread over 32 pages, *The Snowman* uses no words at all to tell its tale of a boy's friendship with a magical snowman.

The story is simple – boy builds snowman, snowman comes to life, boy and snowman share their worlds – but it's the haunting, poignant ending that ensures that, while magic may be found only fleetingly, this story lingers warmly in the memory for a lifetime.

Steve Cole

The Snowman is a classic story that is every child's number one Christmas fantasy. There is a quality about the book that is almost otherworldly, while at the same time it is completely down-to-earth and charming. The pictures that tell the story are breathtaking. Some of them almost float off the page. When asked how he came to make such a book, Briggs said he would 'assume that something imaginary is wholly real and proceed logically from there'. What is magic becomes real, but what's even better is that in books like *The Snowman* what is real becomes magic. *The Snowman* should be on every child's shelf for years and years to come.

Karen Wallace

SOMETHING ELSE
Kathryn Cave, illustrated by Chris Riddell

Something Else tries so hard to be like all the others, but they won't let him join in. Then, one night, a perky oddball creature marches into his house, saying it's just like him – for it's something else, too. Something Else sends it away, but has recognised a bit of himself and what has happened to him in its saddened face, runs after it and invites it back for oodles of fun.

A story which shows that friendship and acceptance shouldn't depend on being alike, and the perfect book for reassuring a child that being different can be a very positive thing.

Malachy Doyle

SOMETIMES I LIKE TO CURL UP IN A BALL
Vicki Churchill, illustrated by Charles Fuge

For a little furry wombat, life is full of amazing and enjoyable things to do. Whether it's putting his tongue out and pulling funny faces, running round in circles until he falls over, shouting at nothing or getting muddy in puddles, wombat has to try them. But there is one thing he likes to do best of all... which is reassuringly revealed right at the end of this brilliant bedtime book!

The artwork is amazing: expressive, warm, richly coloured and textured, with imaginatively used double-page spreads. It's impossible to look at little wombat and not smile back!

Eileen Armstrong

■ Wombat has more adventures in *Found You, Little Wombat* and *Swim, Little Wombat, Swim*, all about making new friends and appreciating that we're all very different.

SO MUCH
Trish Cooke, illustrated by Helen Oxenbury

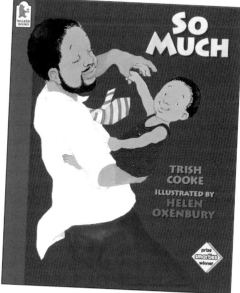

Get ready for a good time in this vivacious, heart-warming tale. Listen to the rhythmic, cumulative patois as an Afro-Caribbean family gather together for a surprise party for Dad. They weren't doing anything, Mum and the baby, nothing really... Then 'DING DONG! Oooooooh!'... Turn the page. In comes Auntie Bibba who wants to squeeze the baby so much. Other relatives follow, each wanting to kiss, eat or fight the baby because they love him so much.

Anticipation and arrival bubble through a story that sees Oxenbury daringly experimenting with colour, texture and gouache to bring a close-knit family dancing to life.

Elizabeth Hammill

STELLA STAR OF THE SEA
Marie-Louise Gay

This adorable picture book introduces Stella and her younger brother Sam, during Sam's first trip to the seaside. Afraid of the water, Sam asks a constant barrage of questions ('Does a catfish purr?') to avoid swimming with Stella. Her answers are imaginative and fun ('You can ride a seahorse bareback'), and she finally convinces Sam to join her for a swim.

Pen-and-ink drawings awash with pastel colours evoke the sounds and smells of the ocean, and provide a whimsical atmosphere for this playful book – the first in a series about Stella.

Laura Atkins

■ Other titles include *Stella Fairy of the Forest*; *Stella Queen of the Snow* and *Stella Princess of the Sky*.

THE STORY OF THE LITTLE MOLE WHO KNEW IT WAS NONE OF HIS BUSINESS

Werner Holzwarth,
illustrated by Wolf Erlbruch

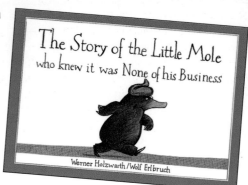

This scatological book features a mole, who finds that someone has done a poo on his head. He tries to solve the mystery of who has done it by asking various animals (such as a horse, a pig and a cow) if they were the culprits. Each shows that when they 'do their business' it looks different. Finally, with the help of some flies (experts in this area), the mole's detective work is successful.

Cartoon-like drawings with humorous touches add a quirky feel. While some parents may shy away from direct discussion of faeces, children love exploring how their bodies work and the potty humour is a sure child-pleaser.

Laura Atkins

SUDDENLY!

Colin McNaughton

The first book in the **Preston Pig** series (now a popular animated TV series) is pure pantomime. When Preston walks home from school, he has the strangest feeling that he is being followed. In fact, unbeknownst to him but evident to the reader, Preston is being stalked by Mister Wolf. Each time the hapless wolf is ready to pounce, SUDDENLY! something happens and disaster is averted for Preston, while Mister Wolf is left nursing his pride and licking his wounds. Enjoy the tension and drama of turning the page as your child anticipates what will happen next.

McNaughton is a comic genius and children lucky enough to experience this book will learn a lot about how stories work.

Nikki Gamble

> ■ Preston Pig features in other titles including *Oops!*; *Shh! (Don't Tell Mr Wolf)*; *Oomph!*; *Boo!* and *Goal!*

SUPPOSING...
Frances Thomas, illustrated by Ross Collins

Little Monster is positively aquiver with worries – black holes, outsize spiders, fire and endless falling – which he shares with Mother Monster in mildly accusatory tones. '...I called you, and you didn't answer,' he tells her. Mother Monster patiently acknowledges his anxieties, but instead of offering solutions or platitudes, she presents a different picture – one in which such lovely things as pancake eating, bun toasting, and balloon flying happen. And Mother Monster is never far away. It's an excellent lesson in positive distraction techniques, with stunning illustrations that play with perspective and colour, leaving us looking down on an idyllic bedtime scene.

Lindsey Fraser

SUSAN LAUGHS
Jeanne Willis, illustrated by Tony Ross

Susan laughs, Susan sings, Susan flies, Susan swings... Susan can do so many things, and it's only in the final illustration, and never in the words, that we discover she's in a wheelchair.

An optimistic, understated and unsentimental offering from the picture-book dream-team of Willis and Ross, with a deliciously simple rhyming text and cheeky, cheerful illustrations, this is a wonderfully refreshing approach to the subject of living with a difference. I found, and still find, it extraordinarily uplifting.

Malachy Doyle

Everybody's Favourite...

THE TALE OF PETER RABBIT
Beatrix Potter

Of Beatrix Potter's much-loved tales, this is perhaps the best known. Mother Rabbit tells Peter and his sisters to run out and play, but not to go into Mr McGregor's garden. Because – she says matter-of-factly – their father had an accident there and 'was put in a pie by Mrs McGregor'. But greedy Peter, being the naughty one in the family, doesn't heed her warnings, and finds himself in the forbidden vegetable garden being chased by an irate Mr McGregor.

In some respects it's an unusually threatening tale for such young readers; but, of course, no one really minds the danger so long as it's being read to you while you're safely tucked up in bed yourself; and those classic watercolours really are lovely.

Daniel Hahn

THE TALE OF
PETER RABBIT

BEATRIX POTTER
The original and authorized edition

For small children of a nervous disposition, be careful which Beatrix Potter book you choose, for she tells it how it is – the true nature of nature. Some have distinctly sinister undertones and all have strong moral messages. But they are deserved classics, with their beautifully detailed illustrations and acute observation of animal behaviour, while the balanced, rhythmic text makes them a pleasure to read aloud.

In this, her first published and most famous story, Peter Rabbit, like any young creature of spirit, disobeys his widowed mother (her husband was 'put in a pie' by Mrs McGregor) and runs into the forbidden territory of Mr McGregor's garden. A terrifying chase begins, as Mr McGregor tries to flush Peter from his various hiding places. Lost in an adult and dangerous world, Peter's tears are useless and only courage and resourcefulness can save him from the same fate as his father.

Patricia Elliott

■ Other Beatrix Potter tales include *Squirrel Nutkin*; *Jeremy Fisher*; *Mrs Tiggy-Winkle*; *The Tailor of Gloucester*; *Benjamin Bunny* (Peter's cousin) and *Jemima Puddle-Duck*.

TANKA TANKA SKUNK!
Steve Webb

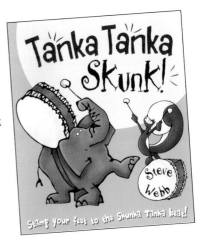

Steve Webb's innovative book, with its bold, blocky pictures of animals, teaches scansion, rhythm and rhyme almost incidentally. If only every child could come across *Tanka Tanka Skunk*! when they were young, poetry would be so much easier to appreciate later on! This book is huge fun and has to be read out loud. I defy any adult to resist its final instruction: 'Once more from the top...' The only problem will be turning the pages fast enough.

Laura Hutchings

THE TEDDY ROBBER Ian Beck

While reading in bed one night, Tom has his teddy stolen away from under his nose. He sets off in hot pursuit and soon finds himself in the robber's domain, at the top of a mighty staircase. The robber turns out to be a tenderhearted, courteous, muddled-thinking giant with broken fingernails, who has turned to a life of crime because he's mislaid his own teddy. Beck's style, which mimics dry-point engraving, creates an intriguing effect; viewpoint and scale are skilfully juggled to construct settings for a small boy's figure in an oversize world. Sharp-eyed children may interpret Tom's adventure as a dream.

Jane Doonan

Pig Books

Crispin, the Pig Who Had It All by Ted Dewan (*UFBG* 88)

Wibbly Pig by Mick Inkpen (*UFBG* 63)

Cars, Trucks and Things that Go by Richard Scarry (*UFBG* 80)

Olivia by Ian Falconer (*UFBG* 148)

Pig's Digger by Simon Puttock (*UFBG* 157)

Suddenly! by Colin McNaughton (*UFBG* 176)

The Sheep-Pig by Dick King-Smith (*UFBG* 284)

TELL ME SOMETHING HAPPY BEFORE I GO TO SLEEP
Joyce Dunbar, illustrated by Debi Gliori

It's bedtime and Willa (a small rabbit) is anxious. 'Tell me something happy before I go to sleep,' she begs her big brother Willoughby, who's in the bunk bed above hers. So Willa and Willoughby set off on a tour of the house, looking for happy things, large and small – from the slippers waiting for Willa's feet to slip into them, to the night-time waiting for the morning to travel around the world.

This is an incredibly cosy and reassuring book for bedtime, and any child who is frightened by going to sleep can talk about their own list of 'something happys'.

Susan Reuben

THAT PESKY RAT
Lauren Child

A sweet, quirky tale about everyone's need to belong – even a dustbin-dwelling brown rat deserves some creature comforts. Rat longs to be somebody's pet and to have a proper name, not just 'that pesky rat', so he decides to do something about it, by putting a notice in the pet shop window. Amazingly, Rat's poor paw writing and his new owner's bad eyesight lead to a lucky case of mistaken identity, and Rat's dream comes true!

Child's distinctive illustrative style is a busily attractive combination of collage, zingy colours, photomontage and spiky, hand-drawn line, and children love it.

Kathryn Ross

THAT RABBIT BELONGS TO EMILY BROWN
**Cressida Cowell,
illustrated by Neal Layton**

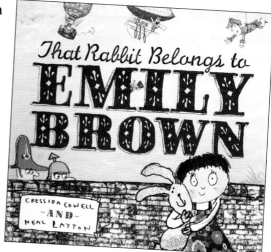

The Queen wants Emily's toy rabbit Stanley for herself, so she sends her servants to demand that Emily gives him to her. But Emily's rabbit is 'not for sale!'. So the Queen arranges for Stanley to be stolen.

Emily stomps to the palace and takes him back. But she also gives the Queen a stiff new bear and tells her to 'Play with him all day. Sleep with him at night. Hold him very tight and be sure to have lots of adventures. And then maybe one day you will wake up with a real toy of your OWN'. She's very wise, as well as being feisty, is Emily Brown.

This exceptional picture book has wonderfully energetic and funny illustrations. It is simple and funny, yet profound.

Pippa Goodhart

THERE WAS AN OLD LADY WHO SWALLOWED A FLY
Traditional, illustrated by Pam Adams

Pam Adams' version of the old rhyme is deservedly a classic. The hole at the middle of each page gets bigger and bigger to accommodate the ludicrously expanding menagerie that the old lady swallows (bird, cat, dog, cow), and the rhyme cleverly reassembles itself through the holes on facing pages, getting longer and sillier till we reach the very last (the horse, which finally kills her off). Great fun to read aloud or sing, the building repetitions make it easy for your audience to join in, too.

Daniel Hahn

Dual-language Books

A relative newcomer to the world of children's book publishing in the UK, dual-language books can bring benefits to English-speaking and non-English-speaking children and parents alike, as publisher **Mishti Chatterjee** explains.

The linguistic map of Britain has changed substantially over the past 15 years. In London, for instance, the number of languages spoken now nears 300, and it is estimated that one third of children in schools in the capital speak a language other than English at home. While this level of language diversity may only be indicative of London and other inner cities, nevertheless most areas of Britain are now host to many language groups.

There is a diverse range of dual-language books that can be read and enjoyed by all. For second-generation British children who are bilingual, the books can help develop literacy skills in their home language and keep them in touch with their culture; for refugee children and new arrivals with little or no English, the books can help with their learning of English and with inclusion both at school and in the home; for monolingual children, the books are an important tool to introduce them to the wealth of languages and cultures; and for parents and carers, they can bridge the gap between home and school and can allow parents who have little or no English to read to their children and share in the school experience with them.

The range of languages and genres of bilingual books has also increased. In 1997, bilingual books were published in 12 different language editions. This number has since increased to over 40, to reflect changing language needs. Bilingual books are available for all young readers and include picture books, board books, myths, folk tales and fables, series by well-known illustrators such as Jan Ormerod, picture dictionaries with interactive CD-roms in 40 language editions and other multimedia resources.

Some of the other things readers can now enjoy include:

- dual-language versions of popular books originally written in English, such as *The Very Hungry Caterpillar* (*UFBG* 59), *Dear Zoo* (*UFBG* 20), *Elmer* (*UFBG* 97), *Handa's Surprise* (*UFBG* 29), *Amazing Grace* (*UFBG* 207) and *The Wheels on the Bus* by Annie Kubler;
- original titles, such as the award-winning *Journey Through Islamic Art* by Na'ima Bint Robert, illustrated by Diana Mayo, and *The Little Red Hen and the Grains of Wheat* by Leigh Ann Hill;

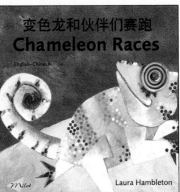

- books focusing on issues, such as Laura Hambleton's *Chameleon Races* (helping others), and Henriette Barkow and Sarah Garson's *Ellie's Secret Diary* (bullying);
- books for the teaching of French and other European languages in a fun and engaging way to young children.

A new creative tool, the *Talking Pen*, which narrates text from the printed book in a variety of different languages, was launched in 2007. This teaching tool is designed for the many children whose first language is not English, and whose reading skills may not be as good as their speaking and listening skills. They too can now enjoy stories in their home language. ●

Useful Websites

www.codework.f9.co.uk/bsm (b small publishing)

www.mantralingua.com (Mantra Lingua)

www.milet.com (Milet)

www.talkingpen.co.uk (Talking Pen Publications)

THINK OF AN EEL
Karen Wallace, illustrated by Mike Bostock

In this book, the amount you learn about eels in around 600 words is frankly astonishing – from the inauspicious hatching in the 'salty, soupy' Sargasso Sea, the exhausting and perilous three-year swim, and the pre-determined (and determined) search for a muddy home, to the sad, silent journey back to where the eel was born, before reproducing and dying. The gorgeous, dreamy illustrations of an eel's strange and fascinating life echo the sinuous, sensual prose perfectly, and the combination pushes every possible button – emotional, informative, visual and poetic. This is from Walker Books' **Read and Wonder** series and, really, you have to.

Nicola Morgan

THIS IS THE BEAR
Sarah Hayes, illustrated by Helen Craig

When a much-loved teddy is deposited in the dustbin by the family pet, its young owner is determined to find it. After much searching, the dog redeems himself and restores order in this reassuring tale. The repetitive structure and rhyming couplets ensure that this is a story that young readers will quickly learn by heart and they will supply the rhymes if you pause to encourage them to predict what comes next:

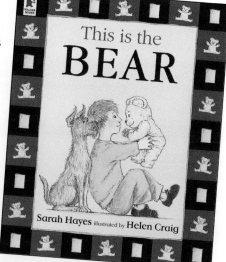

'This is the bear who fell in the bin, This is the dog who pushed him...'

Helen Craig's gently humorous illustrations cleverly reveal the dog's feelings. Was he jealous of the boy's affections? Does he feel guilty about what he's done? Also available with an audio version read by Harry Enfield.

Nikki Gamble

THOMAS THE TANK ENGINE series
The Rev. W. Awdry

Thomas products are everywhere, but before you buy the pyjamas, cups and videos, try to get hold of the original series of books by the Rev. W. Awdry. More than 50 years on, their intricate illustrations and well-paced stories outshine most of the derivative spin-offs. The formula is simple: we get to know and love (or in Diesel's case, despise) the cast of engines, and then in each book a heart-stopping crisis resolves into a happy ending. Few humans are involved, but The Fat Controller must rate as one of the great creations of children's literature: a puffball of pomposity everyone will recognise in later life. Sow the seeds with these books and you will be able to forgive your children's demands for the bric-a-brac that now shares the brand.

Eleanor Updale

THE THREE LITTLE WOLVES AND THE BIG BAD PIG
Eugene Trivizas, illustrated by Helen Oxenbury

Trivizas has written a hilarious role-reversal tale about three cute, sweet-natured wolves menaced by a pig. Helen Oxenbury's illustrations make the pig look positively evil as – with a glint in his terrible little eye – he demolishes the wolves' houses with a sledgehammer, a pneumatic drill and a ferocious quantity of dynamite. In the end, the wolves convert the pig in a completely unexpected way and, in the best traditions of folklore, they all live together happily ever after. It's impossible not to laugh out loud at both the story and illustrations, with their sly references to the traditional tale. And it's now available in a skilfully paper-engineered pop-up version, too.

Gill Vickery

Everybody's Favourite...

THE TIGER WHO CAME TO TEA
Judith Kerr

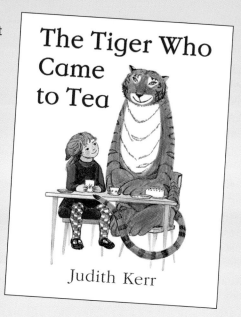

It's hard to say anything fresh about a book that has enchanted children since it was first published in 1968. The visit of Sophie's tiger represents something we would all love to experience. The tiger is more like a very large cuddly cat and is never frightening, even when he's eaten absolutely everything in the house. The illustrations reflect a different era and may make adult readers feel rather nostalgic, but children respond to their charm, which adds to the dream-like quality of the book. For days after hearing the story they will be saying, 'Do you think the tiger will come back?'

Wendy Cooling

One ordinary day, a big, furry, stripy tiger rings Sophie's doorbell and asks to stay for tea. Far from sending the man-eating carnivore about its business, Sophie's mummy invites him in, and the adventure starts. The tiger eats and drinks everything in the house, from the supper cooking in the saucepans to Daddy's beer. When Daddy comes home, they have to go to a café – after all, how can you have a bath or cook a meal when the tiger has drunk all the water in the tap?

It's the sheer plausibility of the impossible that makes this story such a joy, and has left four decades of readers hoping that the tiger might, one day, come for tea with them.

Antonia Honeywell

TRACTION MAN Mini Grey

An action hero like no other, perfectly outfitted for each death-defying mission, Traction Man's fearlessness knows no bounds! But his ego is dented when he's forced to don Grandma's Christmas present – an all-in-one, green, knitted romper suit with matching bonnet! However, heroism will out, and the suit plays a life-saving role in his next daring rescue.

I love the parodic humour, verbal and visual, in this tongue-in-cheek action-adventure: Grey's idiosyncratic illustrations unfold a witty narrative, creatively presenting the everyday anew.

Helen Simmons

TWO LEFT FEET Adam Stower

Rufus is a monster, and monsters (as everybody knows) love to dance. But Rufus has two left feet, so when his friends start getting ready for the ballroom dancing competition at the Glittering Palace, no one wants to be his partner. That is, until he meets Maddie, who has... two *right* feet! And of course they spin, skip and glide their way to the prize. The moral – it's OK to be different – is comfortably reassuring, but not heavy-handed, and the whole book fizzes with movement and energy.

Daniel Hahn

TWO MONSTERS David McKee

A must-read fable for our time. Two argumentative monsters, on either side of a mountain, refuse to see eye-to-eye. They start by hurling verbal abuse at each other, escalate to flinging rocks, and eventually collapse the entire mountain between them. Only to discover that, once they meet, the world looks much the same to them both and they don't need to argue any more. All about tolerance and reconciling difference, and full of exuberant over-the-top insults, this book is a joy.

'That was rather fun,' giggled the first monster. 'Yes, wasn't it,' chuckled the second. 'Pity about the mountain.'

Malachy Doyle

THE VERY HUNGRY CATERPILLAR

see p.59.

ᴠ ᴠ ᴠ ᴠ ᴠ ᴠ ᴠ

THE VERY NOISY NIGHT

Diana Hendry, illustrated by Jane Chapman

Little Mouse is too scared to sleep alone, as he hears in turn the huffing, puffing wind, a tapping branch, the owl hooting and a dripping tap... But Big Mouse doesn't want to share his bed. All young children will identify with Little Mouse and his night-time fears, and delight in spotting the small, familiar objects that furnish the mouse house – beads, a dice, stamps, matchboxes, cotton reels – in the detailed, poster-bright illustrations. A charming story, told with warmth and humour, and complete with loud, night noises of course.

Patricia Elliott

ᴠ ᴠ ᴠ ᴠ ᴠ ᴠ ᴠ

THE VERY SMALL

Joyce Dunbar, illustrated by Debi Gliori

A hugely warm and satisfying tale of a Giant Baby Bear who finds a lost little something in the woods. Giant Baby Bear takes him home and tries to cheer him up by creating the sort of family life a Very Small might enjoy, in miniature. The illustrations play brilliantly with scale, and children will adore such details as the tiny swing made from a pencil, a matchbox and some string and the soap-dish bath. By bedtime, all The Very Small wants is his own family. The cosy domestic routine, the ingenious resolution and the tenderness of the pictures make this the sort of bedtime story that will easily become a favourite.

Jane Churchill

Everybody's Favourite...

WE'RE GOING ON A BEAR HUNT
Michael Rosen, illustrated by Helen Oxenbury

Michael Rosen's text swishes and stumbles and tiptoes along, as an intrepid family braves all sorts of challenging terrain in their hunt for a bear.

The story alternates between optimism: 'What a beautiful day! We're not scared', and concern: 'Uh-uh! A snowstorm! A swirling whirling snowstorm!' Then, when the family finally reaches the bear cave, we get a bear's eye view of them squinting into the darkness – until they turn round and dash back home, the bear in hot pursuit!

The text has stacks of repetition and lovely noisy words, which make it perfect for joining in with. Helen Oxenbury's illustrations – in alternating black and white, and colour – are full of the excitement of adventure – with the family shown small against the wild landscape. The final close-up of everyone huddled under the duvet is wonderfully cosy in contrast. An all-time classic.

Susan Reuben

I was working with struggling readers in a secondary school and they all said they had never enjoyed a book. Then I arrived one day to see them round a large table in the library listening to one boy reading this story. They were swishy swashying and generally joining in, just as they had done when they were very young. When I reminded them that they had never enjoyed a book, the answer was, 'This is not a proper book.' Well, what could I say? It has great illustrations, a brilliant rhyming text, a big adventure that you're invited to join in with – what more do you want?

Wendy Cooling

THE WHALES' SONG
Dyan Sheldon, illustrated by Gary Blythe

The Whales' Song is an evocative, atmospheric picture book in which a little girl experiences the truth of her grandmother's memories. Averse to fairy tales, Uncle Frederick maintains that whales are nothing but a source of blubber and meat; Grandma, though, says that sometimes the whales will sing to you if you offer them a gift. The pictures are beautifully executed, with the moonlight and the seascapes offering the same dream-like charm as the expressions on the faces of Lilly and her grandmother as they share their secret. *The Whales' Song* is a soft, magical way to share quiet time.

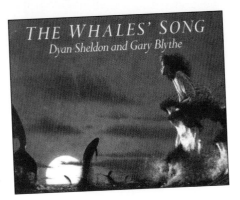

Antonia Honeywell

WHAT PET TO GET? Emma Dodd

Jack really wants a pet, and his mother agrees that he can have one. But for some reason she doesn't like any of his suggestions. 'An elephant would be nice, dear, but not very practical. How would we take it on holiday?' Eventually they agree on a type of pet, but a fold-out page at the end shows that Jack and his mum still aren't thinking along *quite* the same lines...

Huge, comical-looking animals fill the pages in this entertaining take on the 'choosing a pet' theme. The lion looks like he's about to jump out and eat you up; the giraffe is so tall that you can only see a bit of him. Great fun.

Susan Reuben

WHEN A ZEEDER MET A XYDER
Malachy Doyle, illustrated by Joel Stewart

Xyderzee is tall, green and hairy. Zeederzoo is small, bald and blue. Each is lonely and yearns for companionship – but surely they are too different ever to be friends? Happily, they recognise the twinkle in the eye, the something special inside that makes a friend – and Pazoom! There are 37 little Xyderzeeders – and they are never lonely again!

Stewart's illustrations, with their glowing turquoise and lilac washes and echoes of Mervyn Peake and John Tenniel, create a strange, beautiful, magical world for these eccentric creatures; Doyle's rhyming, strongly rhythmic text reads aloud beautifully. A wonderful picture book.

Helen Simmons

WHEN SHEEP CANNOT SLEEP
Satoshi Kitamura

The perfect bedtime book, this is almost incidentally the perfect counting book, too.

It's bedtime, but Woolly the sheep is wide awake, and his endeavours to get to sleep lead to an encounter with a butterfly, a couple of napping ladybirds, a trio of owls, four bats... The alert reader will notice the number pattern and want to count the apples, stars, doors, peas, as the story develops. By the time Woolly is contemplating his 21 relatives, going round and round in his head, he's just about ready to doze off. And your child will be too – unless, of course, he wants this lovely book read again, and again...

Daniel Hahn

WHERE THE WILD THINGS ARE see p.62.

WHERE'S MY TEDDY? Jez Alborough

This was one of my son's favourite books when he was three years old. Be warned, he carried it with him everywhere demanding repeated rereadings! Eddy loses his favourite teddy bear in the woods and must try to retrieve it, even though the forest is a dark and frightening place. His encounter with a real bear terrifies him, until he realises that the bear is just as scared, and that he too has lost his comforting teddy bear. When the teddies are restored to their rightful owners, Eddy and the bear become good friends. Very satisfying.

Jez Alborough is the master of bounce-along rhyming text that carries the story forward effortlessly. After a couple of readings, don't be surprised to find your child reciting the words when you read it.

Nikki Gamble

THE WHISPERER Nick Butterworth

There are not many authors today who could get away with telling a 'Romeo and Juliet' story in the style of Raymond Chandler and aimed at two-to-five-year-olds, but Nick Butterworth has managed just that!

The eponymous Whisperer is a rat: one who keeps the gangs of rival cats fighting each other, and not hunting him and his kind – a status quo he's quite keen to maintain. But the best-laid plans can be overturned by true love, for when Amber (a Ginger) and Monty (a Black and White) meet, they have to be with each other. There's a balcony scene to rival Shakespeare's, a banishment and an ending involving the cutest, stripiest kitten you've ever seen. All of which adds up to a funny, gloriously illustrated plea for tolerance – one endorsed by Archbishop Desmond Tutu!

Leonie Flynn

WHO'S AFRAID OF THE BIG BAD BOOK?

Lauren Child

The unfortunate Herb falls into a book. And it's not a pretty book filled with nice people and flowers: it's a book of fairy tales. So he's suddenly faced with Cinderella's ugly stepsisters, a stroppy Hansel and Gretel, a shrieking Goldilocks and worse, as he madly attempts to escape back to the safety of his bedroom.

If you've never read Lauren Child's books before, you'll be dazzled by the inventiveness of it all: the magnificently mad typography, the clever humour and the visual imagination… (If you have, you don't need me to tell you what a genius she is.)

Daniel Hahn

WHO'S IN THE LOO?

Jeanne Willis, illustrated by Adrian Reynolds

This clever picture book recommends itself on several levels. First, of course, there's the ever so slightly naughty (but not too gross) breaking of the loo taboo. Parents and children can allow themelves to giggle at the very witty toilet humour of the text and the pictures. Next, Jeanne Willis' text is an impeccable piece of lyric writing in which she shows herself a very accomplished poet. Her content is a wonderful sequence of playfully imaginative but ludicrous answers to the question

'Who's In The Loo?'. Adrian Reynolds responds to her fantastical flights with an array of animal (and some human) characters in a style with abundant child-appeal. Even the most prudish parents must surely be won over by the innocent exuberance of this book.

Tony Mitton

193

WILL AND SQUILL Emma Chichester Clark

Will the boy and Squill the squirrel have been friends since infancy, despite their mothers' disapproval. They play together, share meals and sometimes a bed. In an attempt to distract Will from his wild mate, his parents buy him a sweet kitten. Will is delighted; Squill, on the other hand, feels neglected. Will their friendship withstand the test? This large-format picture book is packed with vivid illustrations and is delightful to read aloud – the many tongue-twisters involving the words 'Will' and 'Squill' will prove a real challenge for you, and a good laugh for your child.

Noga Applebaum

WINNIE THE WITCH series
Valerie Thomas, illustrated by Korky Paul

■ Luckily for us, Winnie's outrageous adventures continue; look out for the rest including *Winnie's Magic Wand* and *Winnie at the Seaside*.

Winnie the Witch lives in a house with black carpets, black walls, black doors, black sheets, black chairs, even a black bath. Unfortunately Wilbur, her long-suffering cat, is also black, which means Winnie spends quite a lot of time tripping over him. The only solution is for Winnie to cast one of her infamously unsuccessful magic spells to make sure she can see Wilbur wherever he goes…

The lively storylines of the **Winnie** books are perfectly partnered with wonderful illustrations every bit as wacky as Winnie herself. Children will love exploring their witty details, which bring out the black humour and almost tell another story on their own.

Eileen Armstrong

Dog Books

The Hundred-Mile-an-Hour Dog by Jeremy Strong (*UFBG* 244)

Hot Dog Harris by Rose Impey (*UFBG* 242)

Dr Dog by Babette Cole (*UFBG* 92)

Harry the Dirty Dog by Gene Zion (*UFBG* 111)

Big Dog and Little Dog Go Sailing by Selina Young (*UFBG* 211)

Dogs' Night by Meredith Hooper (*UFBG* 227)

THE WINTER DRAGON
Caroline Pitcher, illustrated by
Sophy Williams

Rory is afraid of the dark until he makes the Winter Dragon, with his glitter eyes, painted crest and glowing scales 'green as an apple in deep magic' to keep the night at bay. Together they share fiery, fearless adventures in the dragon's dreamtime world – until the spring comes and the dragon longs to return home.

A vividly lyrical text, full of the wonder of unexplained things yet ultimately comforting and uplifting, is complemented by glowing, misty pictures that convey the magic and mystery of a child's interior world.

Patricia Elliott

WOLVES
Emily Gravett

Intriguing and extremely entertaining, this book is a fascinating artefact in itself and children will love discovering its hidden jokes and references. West Bucks Burrowing Library notifies Rabbit that *Wolves* by Emily Grrrrabbit is now available. Unfortunately, Rabbit's so engrossed in the facts about wolves that he fails to notice he's being followed until it's too late. The ending is a shocker! So much so that the author has provided a spoof alternative ending for readers of a sensitive nature. The illustrations are spare, but wonderfully expressive; thick bristly pencil for the wolf, delicate line and wash for Rabbit and a deep meaningful red for the library-book cover…

Kathryn Ross

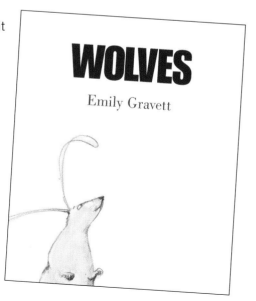

Gift Books

What makes a really good gift book? Of course, any book can be a gift, but certain ones lend themselves particularly to present giving. **Simon-Peter Trimarco** has some suggestions...

When I was little, presents under the tree at Christmas always included a few big books that, once unwrapped, delighted me with pictures of stars and planets, with graphs of orbits and blazing comet trajectories. I remember one book, now long out of print, that had glorious pictures of people riding giant wasps into battle against black, hooded creatures on saurian demons, with an accompanying text full of battle cries and clashing swords. My sister's favourites were of Roman and Greek myths, and she would read to me these muscular tales of gods and men, passion and heroics as we looked at the old-fashioned colour plates of people in strange clothes being menaced by giants or swans! These were 'gift books', a name given to books that tend to be lavishly produced – they're often in hardback, printed on thick, glossy paper and adorned with beautiful illustrations.

Treasuries collecting a whole series of stories together are common – all the **Winnie-the-Pooh** stories in one volume, for instance. Or boxed sets, containing individual books – like the tales of Beatrix Potter, which are ideal for gift giving. There's something immensely tactile and rewarding in owning a sturdy, open-ended box housing several beautifully produced books. It's also very satisfying to have the whole 'set' of something. While cheaper books may end up with bent covers, torn flaps and so forth, there's something about a beautifully produced gift book that makes you want to treasure it and keep it for years and years. And often they contain classic stories that endure just as the book itself is made to.

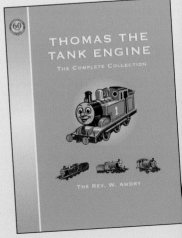

There are a whole range of gift books to choose from. Many classic characters have treasuries devoted to them. *Dr Seuss: A Classic Treasury* with its wonderfully repetitive and hilarious alliteration is great for kick-starting an interest in words and reading. Other examples include *The Roald Dahl Treasury*, *Curious George: the Complete Adventures with CD*, and *Thomas the Tank Engine: The Complete Collection*.

Another type of treasury concentrates on a theme rather than a specific character. Michael Foreman's *Nursery Rhymes* has lots of colour and detail in the illustrations, which ramble over the pages and perfectly complement the clear text. Also worth looking for are *The Hutchinson Treasury of Children's Literature* and *The Hutchinson Treasury of Children's Poetry*, both collected by Alison Sage.

Among the many boxed sets are *The Winnie-the-Pooh Collection*, *Peter Rabbit's Bookshop: 23-copy Miniature Collection Box* and *The Mr Men Library*. ▶

Some Gift Books To Start a Child's Library

Winnie-the-Pooh: the Complete Collection of Stories and Poems by A.A. Milne and E.H. Shepard

Thomas the Tank Engine: The Complete Collection by The Rev. W. Awdry

A Collection of Rudyard Kipling's Just So Stories by Rudyard Kipling, illustrated by Jane Ray et al

Alice in Wonderland by Lewis Carroll, illustrated by Helen Oxenbury

The Brambly Hedge Collection by Jill Barklem

The Night Before Christmas: Pop-up by Clement C. Moore, engineered by Robert Sabuda

Horrid Henry's Ten Terrible Tales Box Set by Francesca Simon, illustrated by Tony Ross

The Macmillan Treasury of Nursery Rhymes and Poems by Anna Currey

Dragonology by Dugald Steer

The Barefoot Book of Stories from the Opera by Shahrukh Husain, illustrated by James Mayhew

The Barefoot Book of Ballet Stories by Jane Yolen, illustrated by Heidi Stemple

Novelty books lend themselves particularly well to gift giving. Lauren Child's pop-up version of *Beware of the Storybook Wolves* is a delight, and slightly older children will love Robert Sabúda and Matthew Reinhart's pop-up series **Encyclopedia Prehistorica**; choose from *Sharks and Other Sea Monsters, Mega Beasts* or *Dinosaurs*. In my experience, you can't go wrong with dinosaurs. For more about novelty books, see the feature on p.56.

Myths and legends are perennial favourites, and a good gift book will be revisited again and again. Take a look at *Greek Myths for Young Children* by Heather Amery and Linda Edwards or *The Orchard Book of First Greek Myths* (*UFBG* 234) by Saviour Pirotta and Jan Lewis.

Everyman Children's Classics are beautifully produced, with bookplate illustrations. They look and feel wonderful, and will be treasured into adulthood. Start off with *Mother Goose's Nursery Rhymes* and work up to *The Thirty-Nine Steps...*

The choice of gift books out there is fantastic, and ultimately the best ones are those that the giver enjoys giving and the receiver enjoys owning – both as a reading book and as a lovely possession to have in their own library of much-loved books. ●

More Gift Books You Might Enjoy

The Horse and Pony Treasury by Rosie Dickins and Leonie Pratt

The Chronicles of Narnia by C.S. Lewis, illustrated by Pauline Baynes

Britannia: 100 Great Stories from British History by Geraldine McCaughrean, illustrated by Richard Brassey

Collected Poems for Children by Ted Hughes, illustrated by Raymond Briggs

The Oxford First Encyclopedia by Andrew Langley

The Orchard Book of Aesop's Fables by Michael Morpurgo, illustrated by Emma Chichester Clark

The Complete Tales of Uncle Remus by Joel Chandler Harris, illustrated by William Holbrook Beard

Our Island Story: A History of Britain for Boys and Girls, from the Romans to Queen Victoria by H.E. Marshall

WOOLLY JUMPER
Meredith Hooper, illustrated by Katharine McEwen

Remember the nursery rhyme 'The House That Jack Built'? Well, this is the story of how wool goes from sheep to woolly jumper, in similar format and rhythmic style. A mind-opening array of processes is introduced, including farming, shearing, grading, pressing, transport, milling and weaving; yet it's simultaneously a lovely story with lyrical language and warm pictures. Perfect for two entirely different types of reader: the systemising fact-grabber who wants to know how things work, and the emotionally driven reader who wants to *feel*. Importantly, you *could* read it again and again. And you will quite probably be asked to.

Nicola Morgan

THE WORLD CAME TO MY PLACE TODAY
Jo Readman, illustrated by Ley Honor Roberts

This is a great start to being aware of the wider world and how it affects us without our noticing. George can't go out because he's ill, but Grandpa shows him how so many things in the house have actually come from other countries – so the world has come to him. Stories for this age group need warmth, and this one has it in duvet-loads. Great illustrations, too, in a mixture of collage and photos, emphasising the real-world aspect. A perfect example of how a story can sometimes be the best vehicle for facts.

Nicola Morgan

YERTLE THE TURTLE AND OTHER STORIES
Dr Seuss

A fabulous collection of moral tales with a great deal more heart, depth and humour than Dr Seuss' better-known books. Each story pricks a human failing – arrogance, vanity, boastfulness – with delightfully triumphant results.

Dr Seuss' verse is so agile and playful that it can't fail to imbue the reader with a real love for words. Young readers also find this kind of rhyming text tremendously helpful in guiding them towards the end of each line with confidence.

Dr Seuss' distinctively crazy illustrative style perfectly complements the exuberance of the worlds he creates. This is a real gem.

Giles Andreae

YOU CHOOSE
Pippa Goodhart, illustrated by Nick Sharratt

This is a mind-expanding book. Each double-page spread is packed with illustrations on a different theme – food, transport, animals and so on – introduced with an invitation to choose your favourites. You might pick any number of fascinating characters to expand your existing family or any number of exciting beds in which to sleep at night. The choice of clothes is fabulous – including a Marie Antoinette dress and an Elvis outfit, and an option (just out of shot) not to wear anything at all. *You Choose* is all about chat – a great vocabulary enhancer, but above all a source of infinite fun.

Lindsey Fraser

YOU'RE A HERO, DALEY B!
Jon Blake, illustrated by Axel Scheffler

A rabbit is having an identity crisis. Who is he? Where should he live? Why are his feet so big? Daley B needs help. But he isn't the brightest rabbit in the burrow, and his answers miss the truth by a mile. Meanwhile, Jazzy D, a weasel on a mission to kill, arrives, providing a timely distraction. When her intentions become clear, rabbit instinct kicks in – literally and metaphorically – and Jazzy D is propelled by those huge rabbit feet back to where she came from. Daley B still doesn't really know who he is, but all the other rabbits know he's their hero.

Lindsey Fraser

ZAGAZOO
Quentin Blake

George and Bella are a young, happy couple, who one day take delivery of a parcel containing Zagazoo, an adorable small baby. Things start to go awry when Zagazoo changes into a huge baby vulture, who makes the most terrible screeching noise. Then, just when they think they can stand it no longer, they discover he has turned into a small elephant. And so it goes on…

It takes someone of the calibre of Quentin Blake to create a picture book that is absolutely relevant and enjoyable both to a two-year-old (who won't see the message in the story, but it doesn't matter), to the two-year-old's grandparents (who certainly will see the message), and anyone in between.

Susan Reuben

5–7 years

Your child has started going to school, and is beginning to learn to read. You might think that this is where it gets serious. NEVER let it get serious! Reading should be as much fun as it was when you recited nursery rhymes to your baby, watched his face as you pointed to pictures, listened to his excited attempts to point at them himself, or told a much-loved picture-book story to your sleepy toddler in the cosy glow and milky smell of the nursery.

The trouble is, because learning to read is so crucial for a child's development, this is a stage that can be fraught with worries for a parent. Sometimes those worries can be transferred to the child – and this is something to be avoided at all costs. As the founder of The Child Literacy Centre, I know very well the stress that parents can find themselves under as their children approach reading at different speeds and with different degrees of ease.

In this section, there is advice for parents who may have concerns, and there are tips for *all* parents about how to have the best possible experience helping their children become

Special Features

happy readers – but most of all, it is full of wonderful, enjoyable books. Because we must never forget that books are, above all, meant to be enjoyable.

So, forget *teaching* reading for a while, and just think about books, beautiful books. In the pages that follow we share the joys of the books we have loved and we hope you will share those joys with your child. Writing a wonderful children's book is a billion times harder than it looks – reading or listening to one is the easiest thing in the world, and yet one of the most valuable. The talented authors whose books we're recommending have done the hard part – the easy part, the fun, is all yours. And, far more importantly, your child's.

Enjoy!

Nicola Morgan

The symbols are a rough indication of the relative difficulty of the title, from 1 (easiest) to 3 (most challenging).

ABEL'S MOON Shirley Hughes

Abel's Moon celebrates children's imaginative powers. Abel Grable has to work abroad; when he's home he writes stories about his adventures for his three sons, sitting in the garden at a folding table. When Abel goes away again, the two older boys create games with the table, turning it into a shelter, a boat, even a moon machine to take them to Abel.

Hughes brings to visual life an almost palpable world of robust, endearing characters through her expressive line, free brushwork, dappled hues, and emphasis on modelling through tone. The Moon sheds its symbolic light on the text in several ways.

Jane Doonan

* * * * * * *

ADVENTURES OF THE LITTLE WOODEN HORSE
Ursula Moray Williams

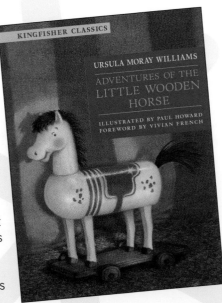

For me, the bridge between nursery rhymes and independent reading will always be linked by two small but heroic figures: Mrs Pepperpot and the Little Wooden Horse – both, strangely enough, made out of wood. *Adventures of the Little Wooden Horse*, however, contain a poignancy that *Mrs Pepperpot* does not. He doesn't want to be a hero: he wants to be at home with his beloved master; but the fates conspire against him, and out in the wide world he has one thrilling adventure after another. Perfect for reading together before bedtime, I'm delighted to see that this has recently been reissued.

Laura Hutchings

AESOP'S FUNKY FABLES
Vivian French, illustrated by Korky Paul

2,500-year-old Greek fables are brought bang up to date with rollocking rhymes, rhythms, raps and refrains, which just beg to be read aloud rather than kept on the page. Korky Paul's scratchy illustrations and vibrant colours are every bit as energetic, bringing the well-known characters from the fables boldly into life. This is storytelling as it should be, keeping to the oral tradition while making it relevant for the current generation of listeners.

Eileen Armstrong

■ **Funky Fables** fans should also look out for **Funky Tales** – eight fairy stories given a very modern makeover.

* * * * * * *

AIRY FAIRY series
Margaret Ryan, illustrated by Teresa Murfin

If you worry about all the pink, sparkly fairy books, with their perfect size-0 supermodel fairies who never get anything wrong (except perhaps for mis-matching their accessories…) then Airy Fairy is the perfect antidote. Yes, she's a fairy attending Gropplethorpe's Academy for Good Fairies; yes, she has wings and yes, she can do magic; but is she perfect? No way! Her adventures all come about through her unerring ability to get things wrong. She flies into windows, can't spell (in either sense of the word), magics goats instead of the required coats, hates sport and has a wonderfully inventive nemesis in Scary Fairy. Funny and beautifully written, these are great stories, perfectly illustrated with hilarious line drawings by Teresa Murfin.

■ The **Airy Fairy** books: *Magic Music!*; *Magic Mischief!*; *Magic Mess!*; *Magic Muddle!* and *Magic Mix-Up!*.

Leonie Flynn

205

AKIMBO AND THE ELEPHANTS
Alexander McCall Smith

Akimbo lives in the heart of Africa, on the edge of the game reserve where his father works. One day, he and his father find an elephant that's been slaughtered for its tusks by poachers – and an orphaned baby elephant. The horrifying sight starts off a fast-paced story in which Akimbo helps his father and the other rangers track down the poachers.

Fast-paced, and lush with descriptions of Africa and wildlife, each of the **Akimbo** stories is an enthralling read. Alexander McCall Smith manages the skilful trick of writing realistic tales that don't talk down to children at all, yet are easily accessible to emerging readers.

Leonie Flynn

> ■ Akimbo is a great character, and there are now several stories about him, and about African life and animals. His adventures continue in *Akimbo and the Lions*; *Akimbo and the Crocodile Man* and *Akimbo and the Snakes*.

* * * * * *

ALICE GOES TO HOLLYWOOD
Karen Wallace, illustrated by Bob Dewar

Alice is content to live like all other anteaters, snoozing in the sun and, of course, eating ants. Then she finds a *Fabulous Film Star* magazine stuck in a thorn bush and decides to change her life. But how does an anteater become a film star? Her only chance is to ask for the help of Cornelius the crocodile – as long as he remembers his manners and doesn't gobble her up.

This witty and highly original story explores the idea of a child beginning to search the world around them, embarking on an adventure filled with wondrous discoveries as well as pitfalls. As with its sequel *Alice Goes North*, the story is fast paced, funny and thought-provoking (why shouldn't anteaters get Christmas presents?) and children cannot fail to love the feisty determination of Alice, the far from average anteater.

Martin Remphry

ALICE'S ADVENTURES IN WONDERLAND
Robert Sabuda

Alice's Adventures in Wonderland is amazing, but then so are all Robert Sabuda's pop-up books. He's done retellings (*Wizard of Oz*), books about sharks and dinosaurs, and other fantasies (*Winter Wonderland*), each of them demonstrating new skills on the part of their masterful creator. They're quite robust, given the mind-boggling intricacies of the construction, and they're witty; but above all they're dazzlingly imaginative and beautiful – some of the spreads are simply breathtaking. You'll keep wanting to close the book, just to be able to re-open it and watch that magic thing happen again, as it springs suddenly to life. You've really never seen a pop-up book till you've seen one of these…

Daniel Hahn

* * * * * * *

AMAZING GRACE
Mary Hoffman, illustrated by Caroline Binch

When the part of Peter Pan comes up in a school play, Grace sees herself as the perfect candidate. Her life is filled with dressing up and imaginary games, where she takes on the role of a swashbuckling hero or a dazzling saviour. But other children in her class point out that she's not eligible: Peter Pan after all isn't a girl, and he's certainly not black. But with the help of her family and the fairy-tale story of a strong role model, Grace begins to see that *anyone* can be *anything*.

■ In this series: *Grace and Family*; *Starring Grace*; *Encore Grace!*; *Bravo Grace!* and *Princess Grace*.

This was a groundbreaking book about race and gender when it was first published, and it remains an absolute standard – brilliantly told with superb artwork.

Jonny Zucker

How Teachers Will Teach Your Child to Read

Few parents really understand the processes and techniques that the teacher will be using to teach their child to read. **Margaret Meek** sheds some light on the mysteries...

Be assured, your child *will* learn to read. With encouragement and example, most children do. Curious about everything, they have been natural learners since birth. Books come into their lives as toys. Then real reading begins when an adult turns the pages and a rhyme or a story comes out. The next time this happens, the words are still the same. This important element in children's learning to read is not directly taught. Like all other skills, reading needs practice and experience. Helping children to learn to read is a home / school partnership.

School is where reading and writing become official – obligatory learning, as set out in the first part of the National Curriculum, which is designed to ensure that all children become literate. In state schools, teachers are expected to follow systematically the Primary Framework for Literacy in a 'broad and rich language curriculum' where 'talking and listening are important parts of learning'.

Before long you will be invited to meet your child's teacher, who will tell you about the school's reading policies and practices. Take this opportunity to look around for other signs of reading and writing. Is there a library with new books as well as computers? Do you feel that here 'every child counts', as the official documents state?

Primary school teachers of this generation have had the most extended education since the beginning of compulsory schooling. They are expected to understand the complexities of learning to read throughout the first five years of school, including the continuing debates about phonics and spelling. Their explanations to parents about how they structure their lessons include the part played by the Literacy Hour. Their competences are regularly inspected.

In the beginning, the best teaching practice brings together the components of word recognition. Children learn the letters of the alphabet, their shapes and sounds. Parents are usually keen to help, selecting alphabet books and indicating the initial letters of words on signs and adverts. 'Do not enter box unless your exit is clear' was an important sign text in our family. Endless games of 'I spy' softened the tedium of journeys.

Still in the early stage, there is the other important reading skill of 'blending' letters together. This is usually demonstrated by the teacher, who is aware of recent debates about the nature and place of phonics in teaching children to read and the obligation to explain this to parents. The general agreement now seems to be that phonics teaching is necessary, 'but not in itself sufficient to develop effective and enthusiastic readers'. The nature of the English spelling system does not make this easy, as this poem by Mike Jubb makes clear:

'An <u>ho</u>nest <u>ho</u>rse
made his <u>ho</u>me in a <u>ho</u>use
on the <u>ho</u>t <u>ho</u>rizon
Every <u>ho</u>ur
He put on a <u>ho</u>od
dipped his <u>ho</u>oves in <u>ho</u>ney
and <u>ho</u>isted a flag... to celebrate
eleven different ways
of pronouncing 'ho'.'

There is no single approach to reading that guarantees initial success. Individual readers have different views of learning tasks and different motivations for learning. Experienced teachers encourage confident beginners to take risks reading aloud without worrying about 'miscues' (not 'mistakes') when they move from single words to sentences. Miscues occur when readers are trying to make sense of the text, and their 'discerned response' is different from the teacher's 'expected response', which provide the teacher with revealing information about how the learner is trying to gain meaning from the words.

There is no doubt about the teacher's central role. The content and the pace of their lessons keep the children's interest and promote their competences and confidence. Their wide appreciation and knowledge of contemporary books for children ensure their enthusiasm for reading throughout their time in primary school. Teachers know that most parents are relieved when their children seem to be making progress. They want to tell them that when fluency increases, children feel some of the power of reading, and delight in discovering what the words mean. If they stumble while reading aloud and correct themselves, they are confident readers. It is never a good idea to reproach inexperienced readers when they are out of their depth. There is no point at which adults should retire and leave children to 'go it alone'.

In fact, most children who are making progress read at three levels. The first is their confident, fluent return to the books they enjoyed when their parents read to them; the closeness of these encounters comes back with the story. At the same time, reading lessons in class engage them in a series of exercises designed to enhance their awareness of written language. When their teacher reads a gripping story, leaving the class in suspense before the end, then you know that 'what happens next' is the nature of continuous text that keeps the committed reader in thrall and promises a new stage in the pleasure of reading. Teaching children to read is one thing; helping to make enthusiastic, competent readers is something more lasting. ●

ASTROSAURS series Steve Cole

So you thought dinosaurs were wiped out thousands of years ago? Wrong! Steve Cole has found out the truth – the dinosaurs didn't die out, they became astronauts, and they're dedicated to fighting evil across the vast expanse of outer space.

These are great books for boys. Girls can read and enjoy them, too, but find a reading-shy boy, pop *Riddle of the Raptors* (**Astrosaurs** book one) in his hands and stand back. There are jokes (many truly dreadful jokes, just right for *Beano* enthusiasts), friendship, blood-tingling excitement, fast-paced action and collector cards in every book! What more could a reader want?

Leonie Flynn

■ Titles include: *Riddle of the Raptors*; *The Hatching Horror*; *Seas of Doom*; *The Mind-Swap Menace*; *The Skies of Fear* and *The Planet of Peril*.

* * * * * * *

THE BEAR Raymond Briggs

The Bear arrives quite unexpectedly one night. He is soft and furry and huge, and his presence causes some difficulties for the little girl who has to look after him. He needs to be fed. He takes up a great deal of space. He doesn't understand that life inside a house has different rules from life outside. And the grown-ups don't understand that looking after a bear is a demanding occupation that doesn't necessarily fit in with their usual routines. *The Bear* is a book for anyone who has an imagination – or who lives with someone who does.

Antonia Honeywell

Some Books a Confident Reader Will Still Enjoy Having Read to Them, or With Them

Winnie-the-Pooh by A.A. Milne, illustrated by E.H. Shepard (**UFBG** 300)

When We Were Very Young by A.A. Milne, illustrated by E.H. Shepard (**UFBG** 298)

Adventures of the Little Wooden Horse by Ursula Moray Williams (**UFBG** 204)

Milly-Molly-Mandy stories by Joyce Lankester Brisley (**UFBG** 264)

Moomin series by Tove Jansson (**UFBG** 267)

The Sheep-Pig by Dick King-Smith (**UFBG** 284)

BEETLE AND THE HAMSTER
Hilary McKay, illustrated by Lesley Harker

Hilary McKay understands what matters to children. We *hate* being kept out of a secret. But sometimes there is a reason for a secret to be kept. Beetle has promised Lulu that he won't 'tell' how he won his hamster from her. It was all to do with the promise of a kiss. But Lulu changes her mind about wanting a kiss when Beetle emerges, having chased the escaped hamster through a compost heap, under a spidery shed and a fallen oily bike! This is a funny farce of a story, revolving around the statement that 'a promise is a promise'. Served up in short chapters and with colourful illustrations, it makes a very pleasing read for young children.

Pippa Goodhart

■ The series continues with *Beetle and the Bear*; *Beetle and Lulu* and *Beetle and the Big Tree*.

* * * * * * *

BIG DOG AND LITTLE DOG GO SAILING
Selina Young

The title tells you the plot, but it can't convey the charm and warmth of this delightful first reader. Colour illustrations accompany the story of two friends as they spend a day on their boat. They fish, dive, water-ski, go for a walk on an island and, quite by accident, meet someone special. With picture-book elements – there is often something going on in the pictures that isn't in the text – to ease the transition to chapter books, this is a perfect introduction to independent reading for both boys and girls.

Leonie Flynn

■ The canine duo get up to further adventures in *Big Dog and Little Dog Go Flying* and *Big Dog and Little Dog Go to the Moon*.

* * * * * * *

BIG WIG Colin West

Hilarious – with a level of humour that works for both children and adults. Big Wig is a gentle giant with a giant-sized ginger wig – until the wind blows it away. It's found by a Little Person, who uses it on his cottage roof as the 'snazziest thatch in the land'. What follows are Big Wig's efforts to retrieve the thatch, while at the same time not letting the love of his life, Toothy Peg, see him hairless. I love the warmth of the story, and the delicious, playful use of language.

Nicola Morgan

BILL'S NEW FROCK
Anne Fine

A delightfully surreal, yet at the same time grounded, story. Bill struggles to deal with an unexpected experience – waking up one morning to find himself outwardly transformed into a girl. Things get worse when he's sent to school in a pink dress, with pearl shell buttons... He soon discovers many ways in which boys and girls are treated differently, by adults and each other. Although, like all good books, the story is more important than the message, it's also surprisingly eye opening, for children *and* for adults who think they know everything about gender stereotypes.

Nicola Morgan

> ■ Anne Fine has written many books for newly adventurous readers – try *Loudmouth Louis* (*UFBG* 258), especially with a child that has trouble being quiet!

* * * * * *

BILLY BONKERS
Giles Andreae, illustrated by Nick Sharratt

The most incredible, madcap adventures just will keep happening to William Bertwhistle Benedict Bonkers – Billy Bonkers to his family and friends. Too much porridge and suddenly he's an airborne burglar deterrent. A family jaunt to the beach finds Billy donning a pair of jet-propelled rocket boosters (a.k.a. over-inflated armbands) in a daring sea rescue. And over-eager bouncing on his birthday trampoline leaves him stranded in outer space... The forces of physics interact with over-the-top silliness, non-stop action and bouncy illustrations to create three very funny, easy-to-read stories.

Helen Simmons

'Utterly bonkers! A riot of fun! I loved it!' Harry Enfield

Billy Bonkers

Giles Andreae
illustrated by Nick Sharratt

BILLY WIZARD   Chris Priestley

Starting a new school is pretty bad for Joe. Why on earth did Dad insist on moving to Little Hartley, which is so far from all Joe's friends? The only people who talk to him in the new school are the school bully, and that weirdo, Billy. Billy's new, too, and definitely not cool, and worse still, he thinks he's a wizard. Yikes... But, as Joe learns, different people cope with being new boys in different ways.

A funny story, which entertains as it gently reassures young readers that big changes needn't be a big deal.

Daniel Hahn

* * * * * * *

BLOBHEADS series
Paul Stewart, illustrated by Chris Riddell

The Planet Blob is peopled by some peculiar, purple, highly intelligent aliens. They first arrived in Billy Barnes' life through an alpha-gamma-space-time wormhole, popping up suddenly one day in his toilet. In the first book in the series, the aliens are in search of the Most High Emperor of the Universe in Billy's bathroom, while in the second, the aliens reveal their 'mental tentacle', an intergalactic superpower which allows them to make all electrical appliances spring unbidden into life.

Easy-to-read text, amusing, minutely detailed line drawings, crazy characters and imaginative incidents guarantee the hilarious Blobheads will become a firm favourite, whether children have seen the TV series or not.

Eileen Armstrong

BOOJER Alison Prince

Boojer the rabbit is a family pet – but the family seems to have forgotten all about him. He's neglected and lonely, but far from downhearted. Boojer is resourceful and has no intention of moping alone in his hutch. Off he goes in search of appreciative friends and plentiful carrots. Written from our hero's perspective, this has all the wit, opinions and optimism that we'd expect of a rabbit.

Alison Prince has a mischievous touch, which chimes beautifully with newly fluent readers who, like Boojer, are looking for fun.

Lindsey Fraser

* * * * * * *

BRICK-A-BRECK
Julia Donaldson, illustrated by Philippe Dupasquier

This is the story of a boy called Stephen who is crazy about cereals and invents his own. 'Brick-a-Breck' makes him famous, gives his mother back her job, and eventually leads him to change his diet completely. The great thing about this book is that while the structure is simple, the language is rich and funny and the subject matter is absolutely up to the minute – when Stephen's prize-winning cereal gets him on television, we read about him 'brandishing' a milk jug, and when the chaotic interview is over, the interviewer takes us on 'to the Brazilian rainforest'. Stephen's new-found fame then leads him into the world of making commercials where, by the 14th take, he ends up being sick all over his cereal. *Brick-a-Breck* is as much a gentle satire as a story and all the better for it. Philippe Dupasquier's colour illustrations are detailed and full of life.

Karen Wallace

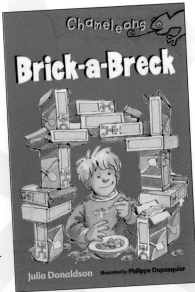

Chameleons

Brick-a-Breck

Julia Donaldson   Illustrated by Philippe Dupasquier

Your Child's School Reading Book

Your child will be taught to read at school, and you can increase the pleasure in reading by buying or borrowing books to read together. But what about when your child brings their reading book home from school? What should you be doing with it? **Julia Eccleshare** offers some suggestions...

Long before most children start school, they will have been exposed to some kind of background to reading. The three Bookstart packs will at least have given them book ownership and, hopefully, their first opportunity to enjoy books by sharing them with adults. It is just the preparation they need. They need to hear stories read aloud, to join in with rhymes and poems and to see print around them. It is from this that they can begin to engage with the real purpose of reading; what it is for and how it can be enjoyed. From there, children can approach the first steps of reading with confidence that it will be worthwhile and enjoyable.

When they bring a book home from school, it is important that you share it with them rather than simply having them read it to you.

• Look at the meanings of words and sentences, making sure that not only are the words read, but also understood and put into context – this helps an inexperienced reader to begin to predict what might be going to happen in the book.

• Talk about the pictures. What they say will tell part of the story and help reinforce the meaning of the words. They also help the child predict what will happen next.

• Pick out words – maybe a name, or something simple like 'dog' or 'cat' that they have seen many times before – and talk about them. Find other words that sound or look the same and match them.

• Choose a group of favourite words (for instance active verbs or rhymes, or animal words or colours), or ones that sound or look the same, and turn them into a game that can be played without the need of the book itself.

Never lose sight of that fact that the main point of reading is to get pleasure. All work on individual reading development should be underpinned by an embedded enjoyment of stories. Reread as often as the child wants. Too often, reading is seen as a ladder to be climbed. Enjoyment and confidence is far more important: even when you know your child can read the story comfortably, allow them to revisit it.

In whatever way learning to read progresses, and it is often more in fits and starts than along a smooth curve, never give up reading aloud. Knowing the wider scope of what books can offer is the best possible spur to becoming an enthusiastic reader. ●

CAPTAIN UNDERPANTS series
Dav Pilkey

Overcoming his own learning disabilities and hyperactivity, author / illustrator Dav Pilkey started writing because there'd been nothing fun for him to read at school. But nowadays any boy who thinks there is nothing fun to read hasn't encountered the **Captain Underpants** books! Perfectly pitched for young boys, they are full of cartoon images, disgusting happenings, aliens, superheroes and really very silly humour. They are interactive (flip'o'rama!), have the longest titles (*Captain Underpants and the Perilous Plot of Professor Poopypants* or *Captain Underpants and the Invasion of the Incredibly Naughty Cafeteria Ladies from Outer Space – and the Subsequent Assault of the Equally Evil Lunchroom Zombie Nerds*) and are pretty much guaranteed to have any boy in fits of giggles and clamouring for the next title.

Leonie Flynn

* * * * * * *

THE CAT MUMMY
Jacqueline Wilson

Frankly, I cried. Several times. This is an incredibly moving book about grief and love. It's about letting go but holding on, and moving on. Jacqueline Wilson understands what children worry about, and her books allow them to share their worries with a caring adult. Children need to know that bad things do happen and that when they do we hurt horribly, but friends and family help us through them. This book tackles the difficult questions that children have when a person or animal dies, and all in the cushioning context of a story with a powerful heart.

Nicola Morgan

C.I.A.: COWS IN ACTION Steve Cole

Pat Vine and his sister Little Bo Vine belong to a rare breed of super-intelligent cattle, the Emmsy-Squares. Clever they might be, but not as clever as someone else who lives on the farm: Angus McMoo – *Professor* Angus McMoo! He's a scientist, and so brainy that he's invented a time machine. But, before they can start exploring, a visitor arrives from the future – a ter-moo-nator, sent by the F.B.I. (the Fed-up Bull Institute) to destroy the professor! Luckily, they manage to knock the would-be assassin out, just before two more visitors arrive and invite our bovine trio to join the C.I.A. – Cows In Action – a crack team of time-travelling cow commandos, dedicated to saving the world!

With daft names, glorious puns, appalling jokes (cowpats feature, as you can imagine), fast dialogue and even faster adventure, this is a wonderfully groan-aloud / laugh-aloud treat, suitable for strong readers.

Leonie Flynn

* * * * * * *

CLARICE BEAN series Lauren Child

With her usual mix of collage, colourful drawing and some wild typography, Lauren Child brings to life her greatest creation, the sublime Clarice Bean.

Her family is wonderfully peculiar (and yet somehow rather familiar); it includes Mandarin-learning Mum, Dad who hides in the office, brothers Minal Cricket (younger – whiny and annoying) and Kurt (older – dark and moody) and boy-mad sister Marcie, as well as Grandad (asleep) and cousins, uncle and more... And at the heart of all the chaos is Clarice, with one of the most distinctive and alive voices in picture books, and heaps of charm.

Daniel Hahn

■ Start with *Clarice Bean, That's Me*, which introduces the characters; further books include *What Planet Are You From, Clarice Bean?* and *My Uncle is a Hunkle, Says Clarice Bean*.

CLEVER POLLY AND THE STUPID WOLF
Catherine Storr

In these twelve linked stories, readers will recognise and delight in Storr's modern twists on favourite fairy tales in which brave, clever Polly outwits scheming Wolf again and again. Here, Wolf haunts a suburban street, intent upon eating Polly. But his slow wits are no match for hers. In vain, he turns to fairy tales for help, but Polly knows her fairy tales, too. Her knowledge and poor Wolf's inability to get anything right in the modern world invariably thwart him. Polly remains in control throughout – like the reader, her imagination, fairy-tale knowledge, and common sense means she remains one step ahead of Wolf all the way.

Elizabeth Hammill

Catherine Storr
CLEVER POLLY
AND THE
STUPID WOLF
INTRODUCTION BY BABETTE COLE

* * * * * * *

CLIFFHANGER
Jacqueline Wilson, illustrated by Nick Sharratt

There's nothing that appeals less to Tim than the idea of going on an adventure holiday. His dad has booked one for him, but Tim is convinced he's going to hate it. And, sure enough, it isn't long before Tim and his team (the Tigers) are facing the most horrifying challenge of all: *abseiling!* Then canoeing, then an obstacle race... And Tim really, really *does not* like sports. He can't even catch. Then one day the Tigers have to do a Crazy Bucket race, and Tim has a brilliant idea...

An exciting, funny and reassuring book (and a Jacqueline Wilson title a boy would read!). Tim's adventures continue in *Buried Alive!*

Daniel Hahn

CLOUD BUSTING Malorie Blackman

This is a wonderful and original story about being true to your real friends and daring to be different. It is, I warn you, very moving. Amazingly, it's also entirely in verse, in a variety of forms, yet reads as naturally as simple prose. It's a tall order to write a story about guilt for this age group (though we're talking the upper end of the age range) and yet keep it safe and warm, but that's just one of the things that makes this book very, very special.

Nicola Morgan

* * * * * * *

COSMO AND THE MAGIC SNEEZE
Gwyneth Rees

Cosmo is no ordinary kitten: he's a magic witch-cat, just like his father Mephisto. Witch-cats help their witches to do spells, by sneezing (magically) into the potion. But Cosmo's witch is up to something suspicious and only Cosmo and his friend Mia can find out what.

This is a long book with a number of important plot details to remember, so it's not an easy read; but for an advanced reader it's a fun, satisfying challenge.

Daniel Hahn

Picture Books For All Ages

Ug by Raymond Briggs (*UFBG* 294)

Father Christmas by Raymond Briggs

Wolves by Emily Gravett (*UFBG* 195)

Zagazoo by Quentin Blake (*UFBG* 201)

Where's Wally? by Martin Handford (*UFBG* 298)

Window by Jeannie Baker (*UFBG* 299)

Eloise by Kay Thompson, illustrated by Hilary Knight (*UFBG* 97)

CRAZY CAMELOT CAPERS series
Tony Mitton, illustrated by Arthur Robins

OK, to give a taste of this I have to quote from the first lines of *Excalibur and the Magic Sword*:

'Back in the Middle Ages,
Brave knights wore suits of tin,
Whenever they changed their underwear
It made a monstrous din.'

Written in verse, these books tell the 'King Arthur' story in a totally hilarious way, while the illustrations add to the general feeling of mayhem. Good for newly confident readers, they give a good grounding in the legends whilst keeping the reader in fits of giggles. The first title is *King Arthur and the Mighty Contest* and tells the story of the sword in the stone.

Leonie Flynn

* * * * * * *

THE DANCING BEAR
Michael Morpurgo, illustrated by Christian Birmingham

Set in a little mountain village, this is the story of Roxanne and the bear cub she meets. She brings him home and calls him Bruno, and for years the two are inseparable. But when a film crew comes to the village and wants to make Bruno dance for their cameras, it all turns sour.

Morpurgo is brilliant at giving real depth and warmth to even his simplest stories, and this one is no exception: it's perfectly pitched, gentle and touching. But it's not overly sentimental, and you'd be wise not to set your heart on a happy ending.

Daniel Hahn

THE DAY I SWAPPED MY DAD FOR TWO GOLDFISH
Neil Gaiman, illustrated by Dave McKean

With a title this long and an author better known as an adult writer you would expect something different from the norm. This book is precisely that – unusual, quirky and quite profound.

Dad, left in charge, is preoccupied with his newspaper to the exclusion of everything, including his children, and is therefore unaware that he has been swapped by his older son, after some negotiation, for two goldfish. Little sister provides a running commentary on events, and when Mum returns, they are both ordered to take back the goldfish and retrieve their father who, in the meantime, has been exchanged many times, and is eventually located in a rabbit run – still reading his newspaper.

Despite its picture-book format, this is a complex read and brilliant for expanding the reader's imagination. Look out for the same partnership's *The Wolves in the Walls*, which is seriously scary.

Sonia Benster

* * * * * * *

DETECTIVE DAN
Vivian French, illustrated by Alison Bartlett

This is the story of how Dan and his best friend Ben solve a mystery at their school. There is pace, humour, a reassuring whiff of a happy family life, a cat called Minnie and, central to the story, the distinctive aroma of a sardine sandwich. Vivian French is a master at writing for this age group. Her background in storytelling ensures that the text has an engaging rhythmical quality that is perfect for reading aloud. The sentences are short, simple and funny, and she knows exactly where repetition will most engage the reader.

Karen Wallace

How Should I Read With My School-age Child?

The time has come when your child is starting to be able to read more or less without your help – but don't let that mean you stop sharing books, says **Margaret Meek**. There's still a lot you can do to build confidence and encourage the pleasure in stories.

No one can really tell you exactly; there are no rules. If you have already enjoyed picture books together you are both probably experienced in book holding, looking at detailed illustrations, repeating familiar words and phrases and making friends with the heroes and heroines. The pleasure of these activities – genuine reading lessons – carries over into the next phase, where young readers can follow a longer storyline and come to see groups of letters as words.

You can count on a certain degree of confidence when your child takes the initiative and reads the title of a new book. Children don't leave their early reading behind. It's part of their growth in both language and in what reading *feels* like. Don't abandon the picture book. Ask the child to tell you the story from the book as if they could read it. You'll hear them using some of the author's words.

Reading aloud with children should be less formal, and more varied than school reading lessons. If you are about to read a new story together, explain something about it so that your listener is curious. Their anticipation sketches the action ahead of the telling, as when an adult reads a review on the back of a new novel. At this stage, most stories are adventures, with the possibility of surprise hinted at in the opening pages. These point the way forward, but don't hurry. Invite your child to do more than listen. Let them see the words you say, and from time to time they might like to read the words of a dialogue with you. When you do this, don't correct them. Encourage them to go on a little further and they may correct themselves.

What should you read together? It's amazing how long nursery rhymes linger in the memory. They are fundamental literature. When children know them by heart, they are surprised that they can see what they say. It feels like real reading. I like to vary the kinds of texts in early reading, but the main thing is the reader's grasp of what is happening – what the words mean. Short poems, stories in verse, are the most memorable. Try the collection of poems *Under the Moon and Over the Sea*, selected by John

Agard and Grace Nichols. In the wordplay
you'll discover another important reading
lesson children have to learn: that words
often mean more than they say.

Do you think that traditional tales are
old hat? Have 'Little Red Riding Hood'
and the 'Three Little Pigs' had their day? I
can't imagine childhood without 'The
Emperor's New Clothes', 'Beauty and the
Beast' and 'Hansel and Gretel', stories
featuring children who wrought their own
salvation with diligence. As long as you
are both enjoying the experience, your
child will not only learn to read, but also
learn about reading. It's worth taking
time to read to each other so that the
actuality of the voice on the page, first
heard aloud, goes inward as another part
of understanding reading.

'Growing into reading' is best with good roots. So
children who have made a good start by being read to
can safely take refuge, from time to time, in rereading
their early books – whether it's
Each Peach Pear Plum (*UFBG*
25), Maurice Sendak's *Where the
Wild Things Are* (*UFBG* 62) or
John Burningham's *Mr Gumpy's
Outing* (*UFBG* 134), the Opies'
Oxford Nursery Rhyme Book or
Quentin Blake's *Green Ship* or
Clown (*UFBG* 83). These familiar
books confirm children's progress in
learning how a story works, and
what is implied rather than stated.
The new reader has a pact with both
the author and the adult reader who
has been showing them how to do it.
Soon they will read, on their own,
a longer, continuous text, and
meet new authors; in the meantime,
returning to these old favourites
will have established those
necessary roots. ●

THE DIARY OF A KILLER CAT Anne Fine

The urban legend of the dead pet rabbit is given a fresh (and hilarious) twist by Anne Fine. This tale is told by Tuffy, the killer cat – a quick-thinking wise guy – who one morning drags a rabbit in through the cat flap. A dead rabbit. Their neighbours' pet rabbit! Tuffy has already killed two small, fluffy creatures so his owners have no reason to suspect he didn't kill Thumper, too. Tuffy's cool justification for his behaviour – it's in his nature – will sound familiar to parents, but the story has more twists to come.

Gill Vickery

■ The saga goes on in *Return of the Killer Cat* and *The Killer Cat Strikes Back*.

* * * * * * *

DIGORY THE DRAGON SLAYER
Angela McAllister

A charming, *funny* story from Angela McAllister, this is the tale of Digory, an ordinary young boy who – quite by accident and altogether against his wishes – finds himself knighted by the local squire, and sent off into the world to (eek!) slay dragons, and (oh, the horror!) marry a princess! All those knightly things he's so afraid of happen, and then some – he does meet a jaw-dripping, bone-crunching dragon (who comes to a most unusual end) and also a very special princess, called Enid.

Challenging for younger readers, but you needn't wait till they're older, as this is a lovely read-aloud book, too.

Daniel Hahn

■ Read more about Digory in *Digory and the Lost King*.

* * * * * * *

DILLY THE DINOSAUR series
Tony Bradman, illustrated by Susan Hellard

Dilly is a young dinosaur, who thinks of life as one long adventure. He's always up to mischief, annoying his parents and especially his sister in the process. Life is never dull as he bounces through a series of hilarious exploits. Children love to imagine themselves in Dilly's shoes and, when things are not going their way, let out one of his infamous 150-miles-per-hour super-screams!

The short, fast-paced stories are exciting to listen to, but children will also enjoy reading them for themselves.

Patricia Legan

■ Dilly's adventures continue in *Dilly Goes to School*; *Dilly Goes on Holiday* and there are many more to choose from, too.

DINOSAUR'S DIARY
Julia Donaldson

Most dinosaurs have some way of protecting themselves: big teeth, or clubs at the end of their tails, or armour-plating. But alas, not Hypsilophodon (H for short). All she can do is run... Then, one day, she finds herself toppling into a puddle and surfacing in a modern-day farm! Fortunately, a friendly family of swallows is on hand to help her find her way around this strange world. And by the time she returns to her swamp she's got a unique new weapon, and 13 new dinosaur babies, too! An exciting story with appealing characters and some longer chapters to challenge the more confident reader.

Daniel Hahn

* * * * * * *

DIRTY BERTIE series
Alan MacDonald, illustrated by David Roberts

The three stories in *Fleas!* feature a child called Bertie, who has all the unsavoury habits of any seven-year-old boy with a few extra ones thrown in for good measure. The writing is spare, funny and colloquial and just the sort of thing a reluctant boy reader would enjoy. Bertie's dog is called Whiffer. His enemy at school is Know-All Nick. The cast of fleas, hapless parents, pathetic teachers, tough inspectors and a school caretaker who is 'a vampire with a broom', is tremendous.

> ■ Three more revolting stories about Bertie are told in *Worms!* and *Pants!*.

David Roberts' illustrations are superb. A modern take on the genius of Ronald Searle, they are a perfect mixture of wacky and naughty with a whiff of the gothic to make the whole concoction irresistible.

Karen Wallace

DOGBIRD AND OTHER MIXED-UP TALES

Paul Stewart, illustrated by Tony Ross

Three short yet perfectly formed stories about crazy, mixed-up creatures. There's a budgie who refuses to talk, but barks like a dog, sending the whole family barking mad; a cautionary tale about a greedy boy who risks turning into a were-pig from eating one Mars bar too many, and a frightened watch frog who ends up saving the day. Imaginative, entertaining and superbly illustrated in Tony Ross' characteristic, scribbly style, these stories are presented in a large typeface with just the right number of words on the page for newly independent readers.

Eileen Armstrong

* * * * * * *

THE DOG IN THE DIAMOND COLLAR

Rebecca Lisle

Theo, Laurie and Joe are brothers. One day, when they're playing outside, a black-and-white dog wanders into their garden. A stray dog, wearing what looks suspiciously like a diamond collar. (Nearly) four-year-old Theo is the only one who thinks they're real diamonds. But then Theo also thinks the dog is his and instantly names it – much to his brothers' disgust – Clinky Monkey. But who does Clinky really belong to? And what about the boy on the news, the one who's been kidnapped?

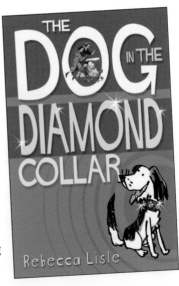

This is a story that involves wicked villains, a dog who really doesn't like being dressed as a baby, three squabbling – yet fiercely supportive of each other – brothers, one rich kid, a butler, a safari park and a wonderful gorilla. Boys and girls will enjoy solving the mystery of Clinky's ownership and trying to work out exactly who the crooks are.

Leonie Flynn

DOGS' NIGHT
Meredith Hooper, illustrated by Allan Curless

Get to know Meredith Hooper as both a great storyteller and a master of non-fiction picture books for young readers – a rare combination. Each year, the dogs from paintings in London's National Gallery leave their poses and run wild through the gallery for one night. Usually they return to their correct places – but this time they end up back in the wrong paintings! Confusion abounds amongst the humans! It takes another year for the dogs to return to their proper homes. Reproductions of actual paintings, with notes, combine with playful illustrations.
A perfect introduction to museum visits (and an ideal souvenir to return home to) – and great fun.

Jon Appleton

* * * * * * *

THE ENORMOUS CROCODILE
Roald Dahl, illustrated by Quentin Blake

In this, the first collaboration between Roald Dahl and Quentin Blake, the eponymous crocodile fancies some nice, juicy children for lunch and has thought up secret plans and clever tricks to achieve his ends. Dahl's trademark diabolical ingenuity is very much at the fore as the crocodile tries to disguise himself so as to lure his prey – only to be foiled by other animals, one of whom ensures he will never be hungry again... The simple, repetitive structure of the book, the promise of potential bloodshed and the rough justice meted out in the shout-along ending make this a compelling, memorable read.

Steve Cole

ESIO TROT and THE TWITS
Roald Dahl, illustrated by Quentin Blake

Roald Dahl's wicked and non-conformist humour is legendary. In *Esio Trot*, typically, he is uninterested in obvious moral messages – old Mr Hoppy successfully woos the love of his life by pure deceit. Dahl's consummate storytelling speaks to readers of all ages and this is a perfect introduction for newly fluent readers, or a bedtime tale for not-quite-yet readers. In *The Twits*, Dahl is at his gleeful best in the portrayal of revolting, horrible Mr and Mrs Twit and their irredeemably nasty behaviour.

Children love these perfectly structured, subversive books, and they will return to them again and again, eagerly looking forward to his more difficult titles as their reading prowess develops.

Nicola Morgan

FANTASTIC MR FOX
Roald Dahl, illustrated by Quentin Blake

Mr Fox is on the run. Three nasty farmers are hot on his tail after his repeated thefts of their choicest poultry. However, Mr Fox has many mouths to feed at home and is determined to beat the farmers at their own game. Clever animal that he is, he comes up with a truly fantastic and utterly hilarious plan to outsmart his enemies. Simple words and short chapters make this book a great introduction for first readers to Dahl's quirky humour. Blake's illustrations capture the grotesque farmers as well as the flair of Mr Fox.

Ariel Kahn

THE FARAWAY TREE STORIES
Enid Blyton

Some children have more adventures than most. It helps if you have an Enchanted Wood at the bottom of your garden, and friends like Silky the elf, Moon-Face and Saucepan Man, the inhabitants of the Faraway Tree. Every week, at the top of this magic tree, there is a different land to visit – from the irresistible Land of Treats to the Land of Bad Temper. The children sometimes find themselves in trouble, but never any real danger – they always manage to get back in time for tea. The stories may be slightly old-fashioned, but they have a vividness and sense of magic that more sophisticated books can lack. And there are things that will always appeal to children's imaginations – sweets that turn from hot to cold in your mouth, a cat that can tell fortunes, a Land of Birthdays...

Katie Jennings

* * * * * * *

FELICITY WISHES series
Emma Thomson

These books are unapologetically girly. Felicity is a fairy. She lives in Little Blossoming and, with her three friends, Holly, Polly and Daisy, attends The School of Nine Wishes, where she is learning to be a Friendship Fairy. Her favourite colour is pink, and wherever she goes, Little Blue Bird isn't far away. Every storybook contains – along with three short stories – a wish, little aphorisms ('gather friends like flowers, they make a beautiful bouquet') and delicate drawings of Felicity and her friends.

Felicity's popularity in the non-fairy world means that as well as the paperback storybooks, there are pop-up books, books with letters, colouring books, activity books and picture books.

Leonie Flynn

Transitional Readers

The transition between being read to and becoming an independent reader can be tricky – but there are ways to make it easier! Here **Leonie Flynn** offers some help.

Fluency in reading isn't something that happens overnight; instead it happens in incremental stages – stages that children go through at differing times and speeds. The process starts with the earliest familiarising of a child with books, and progresses through books being a shared experience, with you reading aloud and the child following along, to the words of much-loved and often-repeated texts being spoken out loud by the child as he or she chants along with you. All this eases the child into the act of reading.

Early years schooling with its structured lessons in the mechanics of reading follows, and your child will work his or her way through one of the graded reading schemes that are available, the aim of which is to bring the child to the point where reading is no longer a hesitant process of decoding, but a fluent translation of letters into words and then, finally, words into both literal and emotional meaning. As your school's method of teaching reading will vary, so will the graded reading scheme, and most schools use more than one, tailoring the books to the individual needs of the child. The point when your child moves away from graded readers to 'free' reading will also vary; there are no hard and fast rules here.

Apart from the graded readers there are many other books available that are written specifically for the beginning reader and will help lead your child, step by step, towards reading independence. Most children's publishers have a series of books aimed at this market. If you look at the early years shelves (often labelled 5–7) in your bookshop, you can spot them – slim, bright, attractive volumes that progress from simple stories with lots of illustrations through to complex stories with fewer illustrations.

There are some wonderful authors writing in this field and far from being dry books that are simply a means to an end – as used to be the case – they are now a vibrant and exciting part of children's literature. So, how do you choose one? You can liaise with the form teacher to find out how your child is progressing and when he or she launches into chapter books and independent (sometimes called 'free') reading, or you can take your child to the nearest library or bookshop and choose together, making sure you keep the level of difficulty appropriate – this is not a stage when you want to push the reader past his or her limits; this is about enjoyment, fun and a gradual build-up of reading skills.

Whatever interests your child, there will be books there that will suit, be it funny stories, or stories about animals, fairies, naughty boys and girls, everyday experiences or aliens. Your child will have preferences – indulge them. This intermediate stage in reading needs to be fun and exciting – and if it is, then it won't be long before it's left behind, and the whole world of children's books will be a treasure trove for your child to enjoy.

Ladybird Books offer a selection of graded reading schemes: **Read with Ladybird**, **Read it Yourself** and **Read it Yourself Non Fiction**. They also offer a selection of classics and fairy tales.

The Egmont **Bananas** series is graded by colour.

Green Bananas (reading age 4+). Try:

I Win! by Lynne Richards, illustrated by Melanie Williams

Shout, Show and Tell! by Kate Agnew, illustrated by Lydia Monks

Blue Bananas (reading age 5+). Try:

Monster Eyeballs by Jacqueline Wilson, illustrated by Stephen Lewis

"Here I Am!" Said Smedley by Simon Puttock

Red Bananas (reading age 6+). Try:

Dilly and the School Play by Tony Bradman, illustrated by Susan Hellard (*UFBG* 224)

A Dog Called Whatnot by Linda Newbery, illustrated by Georgie Ripper

Yellow Bananas (reading age 7+). Try:

My Brother Bernadette by Jacqueline Wilson, illustrated by David Roberts

Long Grey Norris by Malachy Doyle, illustrated by Sholto Walker

Puffin offer **Happy Families** by Allan Ahlberg as first transitional readers.

Follow them with a **First Young Puffin:**

The Monster Muggs by Jeremy Strong, illustrated by Nick Sharratt

Bella at the Ballet by Brian Ball, illustrated by Hilda Offen

Blessu by Dick King-Smith, illustrated by Adrienne Kennaway

And then for more confident readers try the **Colour Young Puffins:**

Robodog by Frank Rodgers

Goblinz! by Kaye Umansky, illustrated by Andi Good

Dumpling by Dick King-Smith, illustrated by Jo Davies

Orchard Colour Crunchies are perfect for building reading confidence:

Monster Mountain series by Karen Wallace, illustrated by Guy Parker-Rees

Scout and Ace series by Rose Impey, illustrated by Ant Parker

Orchard Crunchies for beginner readers, but without colour illustrations:

Little Horrors series by Shoo Rayner

Raps series by Tony Mitton, illustrated by Martin Chatterton

Happy Ever After series by Tony Bradman, illustrated by Sarah Warburton

Scholastic's **Colour Young Hippos** are in the same vein:

Creepy Crawlies series by Tony Bradman, illustrated by Damon Burnard

Mermaid Rock series by Kelly McKain, illustrated by Cecilia Johansson

As are A & C Black's **Chameleons** series:

Milo in a Mess by Emma Damon

Dino Doggy by Tony De Saulles

Spookball Champions by Scoular Anderson

Mouldylocks and the Three Clares by Sally Grindley, illustrated by Nathan Reed

Walker Starters include:

Brian the Giant by Vivian French, illustrated by Sue Heap

Buck and his Truck by Vivian French, illustrated by Julie Lacome

Miss Trim and Miss Jumble by Ed Boxall

Scary Dog by Scoular Anderson

Or try one of Random House's **Flying Foxes**:

Jed's Really Useful Poem by Ragnhild Scamell, illustrated by Jane Gray

Magic Mr Edison by Andrew Melrose, illustrated by Katja Bandlow

Moonchap by Mary Murphy

Corgi Pups are black-and-white chapter books for beginner readers:

The Invisible Vinnie by Jenny Nimmo, illustrated by Sue Heap

Chalk and Cheese by Adèle Geras, illustrated by Adriano Gon

Snow Dog by Malorie Blackman, illustrated by Sami Sweeten

Or for more confident readers, try **Young Corgis**:

Zeus on the Loose by Paul Dougherty (*UFBG* 305)

Billy and the Seagulls by Paul May

The Big Day by Rob Childs

Usborne Young Readers are an excellent series that focus on writing for the beginning reader; look out for classics retold such as *Alice in Wonderland*, *The Amazing Adventures of Hercules* and *Robinson Crusoe*; as well as the **Stories of**... series in which each book has a few very short stories, each focusing on a specific subject such as *Mermaids*; *Giants*; *Princesses* and *Knights*. There is also a series of famous lives, such as *Julius Caesar* and *Anne Frank*.

When your child is ready for less-structured reading, move on to other titles in the 5–7 section. All the entries are graded according to difficulty; choose the easiest ones and progress upwards – though be guided by your child's enthusiasm for titles / authors / series.

These are some of the excellent easy, independent reading recommended in this guide, all of which are perfect for keeping the reading momentum going:

The Woman Who Won Things by Allan Ahlberg, illustrated by Katharine McEwan (*UFBG* 301)

The Worst Witch by Jill Murphy (*UFBG* 304)

Flat Stanley by Jeff Brown, illustrated by Scott Nash (*UFBG* 235)

The Legend of Spud Murphy by Eoin Colfer (*UFBG* 252)

Mr Majeika by Humphrey Carpenter (*UFBG* 265)

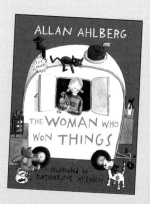

FIRST GREEK MYTHS series
Retold by Saviour Pirotta, illustrated by Jan Lewis

These six retellings of Greek myths are short and well-balanced and the language is fresh and immediate. The full-colour illustrations throughout the book are dramatic and engaging. *Arachne, the Spider Woman* is all about the consequences of reckless pride. It tells the story of what happens when Arachne, a mere mortal, challenges a goddess, Athena, to a weaving competition and how she gets turned into a spider as a punishment. 'Poor Arachne. How she wished she had not been such a show-off, and so rude to the goddess Athena!' Great stuff!

Karen Wallace

■ Apart from Arachne, the other stories in the collection are *Icarus, the Boy Who Could Fly*; *Perseus and the Monstrous Medusa*; *The Secret of Pandora's Box*; *Odysseus and the Wooden Horse* and *King Midas's Gold Fingers*.

* * * * * * *

FIRST THOUSAND WORDS series
Heather Amery, illustrated by Stephen Cartwright

From the simplicity of the **First Hundred Words Sticker Book** series to the slightly more advanced **First Thousand Words**, these books are wonderful introductions to other languages. With Stephen Cartwright's warm and gentle illustrations, they show the world around us, and have a story that can be worked out from the images. Around each page, objects are picked out and labelled in whichever language the book particularly focuses on.

The format, with lots of things on each page to look at and talk about, means that foreign vocabulary can be absorbed quite easily, often without the child realising they are 'learning' anything. The series is now fairly staggering in its breadth, with not only the basic European languages available, but others from further afield, too, such as Arabic, Chinese, Russian and Japanese.

Leonie Flynn

THE FISH IN ROOM 11
Heather Dyer, illustrated by Peter Bailey

This big-hearted fishy tale features the unusual Eliza Flot and her family; unusual because they happen to be mermaids. Discovered on the beach and befriended by Toby, a pyjama-clad foundling who lives in a run-down seaside hotel, a plan is hatched to hide them in Room 11. But the hotel owner cottons on to their identity and before long devises a plan of his own – one featuring the media and lots of cash for himself... Can Toby keep the Flots safe, and maybe even uncover the truth of his own origins? Imaginative, charming and quirky.

Catherine Robinson

* * * * * * *

FLAT STANLEY
Jeff Brown, illustrated by Scott Nash

One night Stanley is squashed flat by a large bulletin board that falls on his bed. And by flat I mean totally flat. At first he's a bit miserable, but then begins to realise how great being flat can be – he can slide under doors, find things that have fallen down gratings, post himself in an envelope, become a kite! He has such fun that his brother Arthur even tries to get squashed flat, too! Through his simply told stories, Stanley regains his roundness – only to be squashed flat again... The stories are over 40 years old, yet have lost none of their appeal, and are perfect for children finding their independence as readers.

Leonie Flynn

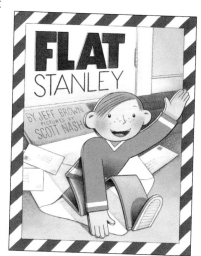

■ Further titles in the series include *Flat Stanley; Stanley, Flat Again; Invisible Stanley* and *Stanley in Space*.

FLOWER FAIRIES series
Cicely Mary Barker

This is a classic series that, despite having been merchandised almost out of all recognition, retains its charm. Definitely one for the girls, your favourite flower fairy says much about you (for the record, I love the tomboyish tree fairies best!). Each fairy has her own distinctive character: some regal, some waif-like and some plump little babies, barely out of the nursery; and all are dressed in the livery of their flower. Forget the doggerel that accompanies each plate and just enjoy the beautiful evocation of gardens and wayside hedgerows.

Laura Hutchings

■ There is a hardcover *Flower Fairies Complete Collection*, which has all the original books (*Spring, Summer, Autumn, Winter, Wayside, Garden Alphabet* and *Trees*). There are spin-off titles, too, with modernised text, such as *Flower Fairies Magical Moonlight Feast* and *Primrose's Woodland Adventure*.

* * * * * * *

FRED Posy Simmonds

This is the secret life of Fred the cat, told in comic-strip form. The story begins with Fred's death. He was dearly loved by his owners Sophie and Nick, and they think back fondly about how their lazy pet liked sleeping and doing wees on Mrs Spedding's flowers. That night they are woken by a chorus of 'meeows', and sneak out to find that all the cats in the vicinity are attending a midnight wake for Fred. It turns out that Fred is not the laziest cat in the world but the most famous cat in the world: he's been leading a double life, and at night would become an Elvis Presley among cats, singing with his band, The Heavy Saucers. Funny and shrewd, and touchingly drawn in soft colours, *Fred* will enchant everyone.

Caroline Pitcher

GEORGE SPEAKS
Dick King-Smith

Seven-year-old Laura longs for a baby brother; but though George, with his round face and squashy nose, looks normal enough it soon becomes clear that he is not at all the little boy she had expected. When he's just four weeks old, George begins to talk. George insists that his ability must remain a secret between the two of them and soon his understanding of all that is being said around him turns out to be rather exciting. He begins to wink and share jokes with Laura and his mathematical skills are well developed, too! At six weeks he reveals his skill to the family and a lively story begins. This is a good introduction to the work of Dick King-Smith, a writer both entertaining and accessible to beginner readers.

Wendy Cooling

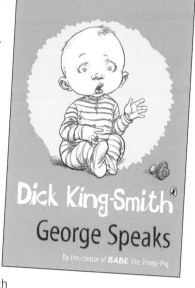

Dick King-Smith
George Speaks
By the creator of *BABE* the Sheep-Pig

* * * * * * *

GEORGE'S MARVELLOUS MEDICINE
Roald Dahl, illustrated by Quentin Blake

Take a vile, witchy old woman and an eight-year-old boy, add to the mix a succession of bizarre ingredients from flea powder to glossy brown paint, then bring to the boil and you have the recipe for a twisted and wickedly funny story. When George is left alone with his horrible grandmother, who likes nothing better than tormenting her young grandson (although eating lettuce leaves topped with live slugs comes a close second), he dreams up an unexpected way to 'cure' her. What if he replaced her daily medicine with a marvellous tonic to transform her into a nice old lady? Wildly inventive and dangerously hilarious, this is a book with real child appeal and a fantastic introduction to the world of Roald Dahl.

Katie Jennings

THE GHOST OF ABLE MABEL
Penny Dolan, illustrated by Philip Hopman

Both funny and thrilling, this spooky twist on the David and Goliath theme is a terrific book to read aloud and has just the right ingredients for a beginning reader to keep persevering until the end. Young Sam Sprockett is determined to find the gold that once belonged to his grandad and was stolen by the terrifying Able Sea-Cook Mabel, power-pirate extraordinaire. But how can a little lad get the better of Mabel's even more terrifying *ghost*? The illustrations aptly echo the atmospheric but humorous quality of the writing.

Patricia Elliott

* * * * * * *

THE GIGGLER TREATMENT Roddy Doyle

You get the Giggler Treatment if you are mean or unfair to children, or tell them lies – the punishment is to step in dog poo. In this case, the Gigglers (furry, colour-changing creatures) think Mr Mack has unfairly chastised his children, and he is about to get the treatment when they realise they have made a mistake. What follows is a madcap race against the clock involving a talking seagull, a millionaire dog and, of course, piles of poo. There are detours, red herrings and many facets to this story, which is a sheer delight and a huge favourite in our house.

Jane Churchill

■ Get your hands on the CD, too. It's brilliantly read by Tommy Tiernan, and bears listening to again and again. The sequels *Rover Saves Christmas* and *The Meanwhile Adventures* are just as zany.

* * * * * * *

GOBBOLINO, THE WITCH'S CAT
Ursula Moray Williams

No witch wants Gobbolino, with his one white paw and beautiful blue eyes, so he's abandoned as a kitten and left to fend for himself. All Gobbolino wants is to be a kitchen cat, curled by the fire, belonging to a loving family. But it's hard for a witch's cat to forget its magic past, and Gobbolino's kind heart soon gets him into trouble – and sometimes danger, too – on his quest to find the right home. Fairy tale, fable, adventure story – with a satisfyingly happy ending – this delightful classic is a joy to read aloud.

Patricia Elliott

THE GOOSE PIMPLE BAY SAGAS
Karen Wallace, illustrated by Nigel Baines

Young readers will love the humorous characters and situations in *Ma Moosejaw Means Business*, a very funny Viking quest with a twist. Fearsome Ma Moosejaw wants to retire and visit the far North, but her sons, weedy Whiff Erik and mean Spike Carbuncle, are too useless to be left alone. She decides they must each find a bride before the next full moon. Whoever brings back the best bride gets to rule Goose Pimple Bay, while the other will be banished to the forest for ever. Amazingly, the dopey duo both find their true love, but Spike Carbuncle's feisty girl, Fangtrude, ensures the ending is not *exactly* what Ma Moosejaw had planned!

Mike Bostock

> ■ There are three more **Goose Pimple Bay Sagas** to enjoy. Move on to *Whiff Erik and the Great Green Thing* next, or try one of the titles in Karen Wallace's other historical fiction series, **The Crunchbone Castle Chronicles**.

* * * * * *

GREEK TALES series
Terry Deary, illustrated by Helen Flook

Terry Deary is a genius. Famous for his **Horrible Histories**, it's worth knowing that he also writes these stories for younger readers set in historical times. So far we have **Tudor Tales**, **Egyptian Tales** and now **Greek Tales**, all of which are funny, use real history brilliantly as a backdrop and yet have exciting storylines, enhanced by Helen Flook's perfectly pitched illustrations.

The Tortoise and the Dare is about brother and sister Cypselis and Elena, a dare (that if lost will mean the sister's enslavement) and a race. The race just happens to be part of the Olympics in 776 BC, so along the way we learn about the Games, about Greek life (including the way women were treated) and yet also laugh at the squabbling siblings – as well as hoping that Cypselis wins!

Leonie Flynn

> ■ Look out for the rest of Terry Deary's **Greek Tales**. Titles in the series are: *The Boy Who Cried Horse*; *The Town Mouse and the Spartan House* and *The Lion's Slave*.

Series Fiction

There comes a point in a child's reading life when what they want more than anything is security. Just as toddlers clamour to have the same story read and reread to them, some young readers need to know that the formula of a book they've loved will be repeated in the next volume. This is where series fiction comes into its own, delivering – time after time – the comfort of the familiar and the reassurance of well-loved names and situations.

Luckily for all of them, publishers are aware of the need and have catered for it. Series fiction at this level is often targeted at either boys or girls (see our feature on p.296) but there is plenty out there that is non-gender specific – take your child to a bookshop or library and see what appeals. Here are some of our suggestions:

Some of the Series Fiction Recommended in the *UFBG*

Happy Families by Allan Ahlberg et al (*UFBG* 241)

Clarice Bean by Lauren Child (*UFBG* 217)

The Last Polar Bears / Gold Diggers / Castaways / Cowboys by Harry Horse (*UFBG* 252)

Horrid Henry by Francesca Simon (*UFBG* 242)

Flat Stanley by Jeff Brown (*UFBG* 235)

Seriously Silly Stories by Laurence Anholt (*UFBG* 283)

Magical Children by Sally Gardner (*UFBG* 259)

Astrosaurs by Steve Cole (*UFBG* 210)

Captain Underpants by Dav Pilkey (*UFBG* 216)

Judy Moody by Megan McDonald (*UFBG* 250)

The Worst Witch by Jill Murphy (*UFBG* 304)

Rainbow Magic by Daisy Meadows (*UFBG* 280)

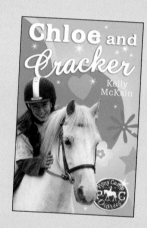

And Some Series Fiction Not in the *UFBG*

Geronimo Stilton by Geronimo Stilton

Not Quite a Mermaid by Linda Chapman

Pony Camp Diaries by Kelly McKain

Pony Mad Princess by Diane Kimpton

Nina Fairy Ballerina by Anna Wilson

World of Wishes by Carol Barton

Magic Kitten by Sue Bentley

Brambly Hedge by Jill Barklem

Sheltie by Peter Clover

Magic Treehouse by Mary Pope Osborne

HAPPY FAMILIES series
Allan Ahlberg, various illustrators

Originally designed as books for beginner readers, these little gems make wonderful read-alouds for three-to-fives, too. Each one tells a story about a particular family. The deceptively simple texts are packed with humour and a full range of human idiosyncrasy, and the brilliant illustrations are by some of the best picture-book artists of the last 30 years – André Amstutz, Colin McNaughton, Faith Jaques and the sadly missed and irreplaceable Janet Ahlberg. Perennial favourites are *Mrs Plug the Plumber*, *Mr Tick the Teacher*, *Miss Brick the Builders' Baby* and *Master Money the Millionaire*, but they're all terrific.

Tony Bradman

* * * * * *

HEDGEHOGS DON'T EAT HAMBURGERS
Vivian French, illustrated by Chris Fisher

There are two good, quite-short stories in this little book, both featuring Hector the hedgehog and his friends and enemies. The first begins with a search for hamburgers, something that hedgehogs just don't eat, then turns into a traditional-sounding tale as Hector and his friends outwit a fox who fancies them for supper. The second involves singing naughty songs, being overheard and dealing with an encounter with a badger. The book is very well designed for beginner readers – good illustrations on every page, clear, quite large print and lots of white space – and Vivian French writes with rhythm and humour, as well as using repetition to make the stories easy to read.

Wendy Cooling

HE'S NOT MY DOG! Dyan Sheldon

This delightful, thoughtful, touching story tells of a black-and-white mutt with a sad face, who sits outside the newsagent's and wants to come home with Andre. 'He's not my dog,' Andre tells everybody. They don't believe him and neither do we.

He's Not My Dog! is a story a child will eventually want to read alone. It has simple line drawings, and the heart-warming narrative is written with everyday details in clear language that reads aloud well.

Caroline Pitcher

* * * * * * *

HORRID HENRY series
Francesca Simon, illustrated by Tony Ross

Henry is the sort of boy I hope never to meet – though, in fact, I probably have met him in a supermarket and also on a train... So imagine my surprise when I discovered that I liked these books. How can such a horrible boy be so endearing? And how can his apparently much nicer friends be utterly creepy? I don't know – but I do think there's magic in Francesca Simon's pen.

These stories are perfect for newly independent readers, particularly boys. Luckily, there are lots of books featuring Henry to reread whilst avidly awaiting the next in the series.

Nicola Morgan

■ Further titles include *Horrid Henry's Underpants*; *Horrid Henry's Nits*; *Horrid Henry and the Tooth Fairy*; *Horrid Henry and the Football Fiend*; *Horrid Henry's Stinkbomb* and *Horrid Henry's Jokebook*.

* * * * * * *

HOT DOG HARRIS
Rose Impey, illustrated by Shoo Rayner

Hot Dog Harris is so small he can squeeze into the tiniest spaces and the Harris family has to be careful not to sit on him or hoover him up by mistake. But when one day Hot Dog escapes outside, he quickly discovers that life outdoors is far more dangerous still. This is one in a series of hilarious **Colour Crackers** storybooks, each inspired by true facts about animal 'record breakers'. The straightforward, chatty text; comical full-colour illustrations and terrible jokes at the end of each book are ideal for children who are just starting to read for themselves.

Kathryn Ross

HOW THE WHALE BECAME
Ted Hughes, illustrated by Jackie Morris

'Long ago when the world was brand new, before animals or birds, the sun rose into the sky and brought the first day...' So begins this lyrical and humorous collection of creation stories. Ted Hughes' explanations of the development of animals and their particular characteristics are creative, funny and sometimes sad; they are stories he read to his own children and they are a joy to read aloud still. The story of the whale who grew up in God's vegetable garden only to be banished when he became so large that he crushed the carrots, is my favourite. Jackie Morris' splendid illustrations really do capture the magical quality of the stories. There are small paperback editions, but the full-colour, large picture book is a thing of beauty.

Wendy Cooling

* * * * * * *

HOW TO LIVE FOREVER
Colin Thompson

This book is proof that picture books are for ever, and can be enjoyed by people of any age. Very young children can pick this up and be fascinated by the complex pen-and-ink pictures of a vast library, with half-hidden objects amongst the shelves and a boy walking through a mysterious world structured from books. Older children will enjoy the visual puns, the rows of books all with invented titles that are almost the same as ones we know, and adults will just be swept along by everything. There is a story, and a message, but to me they are incidental, as the point of *How to Live Forever* is its delight in books, in libraries and in the joys of visual discovery.

Leonie Flynn

HOW TO WRITE REALLY BADLY
Anne Fine

Chester Howard (or is that Howard Chester?) has been to a lot of schools in his time, but none quite as gruesome as Walbottle Manor (Mixed). It's not that the teachers are mean, or the other pupils are nasty bullies, or that the work is hard – it's just that it's all too *nice*. All friendly, all nauseatingly *nice all the time*. Worst of all, Chester (or is that Howard?) is stuck sitting next to the distracting Joe Gardener, who Howard (Chester?) thinks isn't too bright. But when he starts helping Joe, he finds out that Joe has some amazing talents, even if (as Chester points out) his writing looks like a troupe of drug-crazed centipedes in leaking ink boots have just held a barn dance in his workbooks...

This is a challenging read, but it's wonderfully funny and upbeat, with an encouraging ending sure to leave a smile on your face.

Daniel Hahn

* * * * * * *

THE HUNDRED-MILE-AN-HOUR DOG
Jeremy Strong

An ideal book to get those boys reading. Strong is noted for humour and lightness of touch and this story certainly has both. Streaker is not an ordinary dog but is likened to a rocket on four legs, so walking her is not something people are queuing up to do. Trevor has made a bet that he can train her to walk at heel and behave well by the end of the summer holidays – a huge challenge, but one that can be met with a little female help.

This book won the Children's Book Award, a prize for which children are the judges. There are many great Strong titles to move on to, including a sequel to this one, *The Return of the Hundred-Mile-An-Hour Dog*.

Wendy Cooling

THE ICE-CREAM MACHINE
Julie Bertagna

Wayne and Wendy have the very worst parents in the world; parents who have a seemingly endless stream of get-rich-quick schemes, each one madder than the last. Having failed in their attempt at goat farming – and been left with a naughty pet goat Gina – the parents decide to buy a cranky old ice-cream van called Macaroni. Of course, Macaroni is no ordinary ice-cream van, as the family discover all too soon. When Macaroni goes missing the children will stop at nothing to get him back again...

This is an original and very funny book that will exercise the imagination, and newly fluent readers will enjoy discovering it for themselves.

Eileen Armstrong

* * * * * * *

IN SPECTACULAR CROSS-SECTION
series Stephen Biesty

If your child likes to spend hours poring over incredibly detailed pictures, these books are ideal. They were at the forefront of the cross-section craze, and are still the best of their kind. Biesty's extremely accurate, meticulously researched images are laid out with explanatory text by Stewart Ross, each complementing the other. What gives these books the edge is the drawing style – all the illustrations are somehow endearing, possibly because Biesty draws everything freehand! The *Egypt* title contains such things as a quarry, a palace and the spectacular temple at Karnak.

Leonie Flynn

■ Other books in the series include *Greece* and *Rome*.

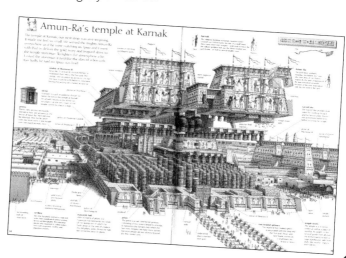

Amun-Ra's temple at Karnak

Help! My Child Doesn't Like Reading!

There may be all sorts of reasons why your child is not a reader, explains **Nicola Morgan**, and all sorts of ways you might help to transform a reluctant reader into a bookworm.

Some children take to reading with ease, consuming books like food, always hungry for more. Other children may not be so eager, but they'll read, happily making time for the latest **Horrid Henry** or **Rainbow Magic**, with reading as part of their lives but not overwhelmingly important. But not all children enjoy books, and those who don't can often be a cause for anxiety – as, after all, the enjoyment of reading makes learning easier. So, if your child really does not like reading, try to work out why.

The cause will be amongst the following:

- Your child is actually *afraid* of reading because he or she thinks it's difficult.
- Your child has not yet found the right book(s).
- You don't like reading. It's not a crime, so don't feel guilty. But children take cues from the adults around them. Have you unconsciously given the message that reading is difficult or boring? Does your child see you enjoying reading?
- Perhaps he or she simply doesn't like 'made-up stories'? Some people, often boys and men, don't 'get' fiction because it doesn't feel real. But non fiction could really inspire your child (see p.286).
- Of course, your child *may* have a reading problem (see p.254 and p.262) in which case be very sympathetic because no one enjoys doing something difficult and frustrating.

Some solutions:

- Remember: reading should be for pleasure. Books are like strawberries – we eat them because they're delicious, forgetting that they are also good for us; not like steamed spinach, which we eat only because it's good for us. Let children read the books they enjoy, not the ones you think will improve them.

- Help your child associate reading with feeling good. For example, being cosy with a caring adult who has taken time to read together is a great way to grow a love of books. If reading is always associated with discomfort, failure and stress, it will always be disliked.

- Think about topics your child might enjoy. Just as valuable as storybooks are non-fiction books about favourite sports or hobbies, or about fascinating or disgusting subjects, and books with intricate diagrams or pop-ups. Magazines provide reading practice, too, and can lead on to books.

- Create an environment where reading is valued, fun and a top choice rather than a last resort to satisfy a teacher. Read in the garden, in bed, on holiday, on trains. Turn the TV off during the day and well before bedtime and REFUSE to have a TV in your child's bedroom. Make space and time for deeper pleasure.

Audiobooks

Stories were originally told aloud, not written, and hearing a story is as valuable as reading it. If introduced to stories through audiobooks, children are likely to grow to love them and then want to experience the written text, too. For children who really find reading difficult, they are a brilliant way of not missing out on all the developmental opportunities that come from books. Audiobooks also allow children to hear stories that might be too long or advanced for them to read themselves (but make sure the content is suitable).

Finally, be patient – reading is not something you can or should force. Loving books is a lifelong pleasure and your child may come to that pleasure much later. ●

THE INDOOR PIRATES
Jeremy Strong, illustrated by Nick Sharratt

Bald Ben, Lumpy Lawson, twins Polly and Molly, and Captain Blackpatch are pirates. Bad pirates. Oh, not bad as in wicked (though they are as villainous a crew as ever there was), but bad at being pirates – because they hate the sea! Instead of life on the ocean waves, they live in a nice house, which has its own problems, such as the electricity bill... which they can't pay! So, they need treasure – quickly – and then the mayhem really begins.

All Jeremy Strong's stories are very funny, and he has the knack of making children giggle whilst they eagerly turn the pages to find out What Happens Next. *The Indoor Pirates* is a great introduction to his books, and there is a sequel in which the crew has to brave the horrors of travelling by boat: *The Indoor Pirates on Treasure Island.*

Leonie Flynn

* * * * * * *

IS A BLUE WHALE THE BIGGEST THING THERE IS?
Robert E. Wells

What a great book! The answer to the question is 'no'. I knew that, of course. But I didn't know how utterly miniscule a blue whale is compared, say, to Mount Everest. If you stacked a massive tower of really big jars each containing 100 blue whales on top of Mount Everest, it would look quite tiny.

This book really works. A difficult concept – space, the universe and everything – is neatly stripped down and simply explained so that you can almost understand it. The clear, funny illustrations show you the relative sizes of whales, mountains, the Earth, the Sun, the Milky Way, galaxies, space and THE UNIVERSE. Although, never having seen the universe, a blue whale still looks pretty big to me.

Kaye Umansky

IT WAS A DARK AND STORMY NIGHT

Allan Ahlberg, illustrated by Janet Ahlberg

Yet again the Ahlbergs manage to give the familiar a twist of their own. Antonio, aged eight, has to keep his brigand kidnappers happy by telling them stories. Constant interruptions, particularly from the chief, mean he has to keep changing the story, until somehow he can escape. Perfect for reading aloud, but young readers will also love tackling it alone – maybe with a little help in working it all out. The strong author's voice is well matched by Janet Ahlberg's rich, detailed pictures filled with character in both tiny vignettes and detailed, full pages.

Liz Attenborough

* * * * * * *

JACK STALWART: THE ESCAPE OF THE DEADLY DINOSAUR

Elizabeth Singer Hunt

Jack Stalwart's brother Max is missing. Max was a secret agent working for the Global Protection Force and Jack is recruited by them, too. He ends up travelling around the globe solving crimes and hunting for his missing brother. Luckily for Jack, he can travel to each adventure in an instant, and is returned only a few real-time moments after he left, so his family are none the wiser!

Each book takes Jack to a different country, and the solid reality of each place is the grounding for the fantastical stories. Packed with Bond-like gadgets, they're fast and exciting – just right for boys not quite ready for Alex Rider, and with eight titles so far in the series, they'll entertain them for a good while, too!

Leonie Flynn

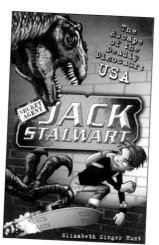

■ Jack's adventures continue in *The Mystery of the Mona Lisa; Search for the Sunken Treasure; Secret of the Sacred Temple* and *Pursuit of the Ivory Poachers*.

THE JESSAME STORIES Julia Jarman

This is a collection of short stories about the everyday life of Jessame Aduke Olusanya, a small girl living with a close-knit family in the East End of London. We read about how Jessame loves to visit the Museum of Childhood, but always dashes round the drive in a big loop instead of going straight through the door. And how she adores the visit of her uncle, but hides when she hears his familiar knock, waiting for him to say, 'Where is my Little Flower?' before leaping out at him.

There is something incredibly real about these stories, which I think is in the fine detail that feels like it has been taken straight out of someone's life (and if you read the dedication, it looks like it has).

Susan Reuben

* * * * * *

JUDY MOODY series
Megan McDonald, illustrated by
Peter Reynolds

Hurrah – a book about a girl, and not a fairy or pink cover in sight! The humour is so spot-on and the characters so true-to-life that even boys count themselves fans of lovable, bossy Judy Moody. Caught up in the comical mishaps of Judy, her little 'bother' and her friends, readers will absorb historical and scientific facts and new vocabulary without even noticing.

Peter Reynolds' amusing line drawings break up the text, and newly fluent readers will feel proud to read a chunky book all by themselves. It's fun to read aloud, too. First in a series of six – and don't forget to try the books about Judy's little brother, *Stink* (*UFBG* 290).

Madelyn Travis

■ Further titles include *Judy Moody Declares Independence*; *Judy Moody: Around the World in 8½ Days*; *Judy Moody Gets Famous*; *Judy Moody M.D.: The Doctor Is In*; *Judy Moody Predicts the Future* and *Judy Moody Saves the World!*

THE KING OF CAPRI
Jeanette Winterson, illustrated by Jane Ray

The King of Capri, with its folk-tale elements, is all wit and wonder. Its eponymous hero – greedy, indulgent and selfish – faces the first real challenge of his life when a stormy wild wind sweeps away all his treasures and deposits them in a poor washerwoman's yard in neighbouring Naples. Once destitute, he also loses his servants and his false friends. A voyage to self-knowledge, wisdom and a jewel of a wife awaits him. Jane Ray catches the tale's Mediterranean warmth and setting through decorative means: detailed painting and collage, rich patterning, luminous jewel-like colour, and exuberant dib-dabs of gold paint.

Jane Doonan

* * * * * * *

KITTY AND FRIENDS series
Bel Mooney

Kitty is an irrepressible tomboy with an 'oh so perfect' brother. In the first title, *I Don't Want To!*, the grown-ups keep telling her what to do, and it's rarely to her liking. From brushing her teeth to eating her veggies and tidying her room, Kitty has to find her own inventive ways to deal with the unreasonable demands made on her.

This is a great series for newly fluent readers – there are 12 titles, so once they have got to know and love Kitty, they can build their confidence by reading them all.

Susan Reuben

■ Other titles include *It's Not Fair!*; *I Can't Find It!*; *Why Not?*; *Why Me?*; *It's Not My Fault*; *I'm Scared!* and *But You Promised!*

* * * * * * *

LADY LONG LEGS Jan Mark

Outwardly the story of a new girl standing up for herself against petty nastiness, *Lady Long Legs* deftly draws the reader into valuable lessons about being different, asking questions, being reasonable, decency, bravery, friendship. There's real warmth here, and the feeling that bullying is not simple but can always be dealt with. Moreover, I will never look at a rubber glove and frozen peas in the same way again. May the Hand of Peace be upon you…

Nicola Morgan

THE LAST POLAR BEARS / THE LAST GOLD DIGGERS / THE LAST COWBOYS / THE LAST CASTAWAYS Harry Horse

A journey to the Arctic, a trip around America's Wild West, a trek through the Australian bush and a disastrous sea voyage: these are the settings for Harry Horse's original and endearing adventure stories. In each book, Grandfather, accompanied by his dog Roo, sets out on a quest. Inevitably, by the last third of the book things are looking grim, and then help arrives. The narrative template quickly becomes familiar and young readers can feel secure while Horse introduces new characters and memorable encounters with the indigenous wildlife. The cartoon-like illustrations are chock full of humorous detail – perfect for looking at again and again.

Laura Hutchings

* * * * * * *

THE LEGEND OF SPUD MURPHY
Eoin Colfer

The Legend of Spud Murphy is one of my absolute favourites for this age range. Spud Murphy is a battle-axe librarian, who's forgotten that books are for enjoying. Marty and Will are two brothers who have never discovered that books are for enjoying. They all battle it out in the hallowed library, where children must be QUIET and STILL.

Marty and Will appear again, in the amusingly spooky *The Legend of Captain Crow's Teeth*, another small masterpiece which wonderfully depicts the tangled behaviour of brothers – Colfer is writing about what he knows, as the second of five boys himself. More importantly, he's a consummate storyteller who knows how to tell a simple story and make it engrossing.

Nicola Morgan

LILY QUENCH AND THE DRAGON OF ASHBY Natalie Jane Prior

As a child, I, like many little girls, detested all things pink and sparkly and was frustrated by the lack of feisty female adventurers. Fortunately for girls like me, the **Lily Quench** series now comes to the rescue. Lily is the spirited and independent heroine of this thrilling and often comic book. She is the only surviving Quench – the last in a long line of dragon slayers. However, Lily discovers that Queen Dragon is not a foe but in fact her greatest friend, and together they embark on fantastic adventures and fight to overthrow the oppressive regime of the Black Count. These stories are perfect for children who want dragons and adventure – and, despite a female central character, boys will love them, too.

Helen Norris

■ Lily's adventures continue in *Lily Quench and the Black Mountains*, in which Lily has yet again to prove her bravery.

* * * * * * *

LITTLENOSE THE HUNTER
John Grant, illustrated by Ross Collins

Littlenose is just like any other small boy who gets into scrapes, except Littlenose's scrapes tend to involve forest fires, rhinoceros traps, angry mountain lions or a visit to the local witch doctor. Littlenose's adventures take place 50,000 years ago, when people wore furs, hunted animals and lived in caves. Whether he's playing with his pet mammoth Two-Eyes, holidaying with his wild uncle Redhead or trying to impress the rest of the tribe with his tracking skills, Littlenose is never far from fun, and trouble. John Grant has written a companion volume, *Littlenose the Hero*. Perfect stories for little savages!

Sarah Frost Mellor

Worried? What You Should and Shouldn't Worry About

Some children have genuine difficulties learning to read, but most cases of parental anxiety in this area are altogether unfounded. **Nicola Morgan** distinguishes between what does and doesn't constitute a cause for legitimate concern...

Parents often worry about their child's reading progress. Sometimes there is cause for concern; more often there isn't. Two things make it difficult to decide: first, children progress at different speeds, for different reasons, so we can't say that all children *should* take a set number of months or years to acquire a particular skill. Second, many signs of difficulty are actually things that virtually all children do at first. For example, most four-to-seven-year-olds confuse 'b' and 'd', yet most are not dyslexic and soon stop confusing letters; but *persistently* confusing 'b' and 'd', in combination with other symptoms, is a sign of dyslexic-type difficulties.

Sometimes reading problems are linked with a separate issue, such as hyperactivity, speech difficulty, vision problems or dyspraxia. The Literacy Trust webpage at the end of this article will direct you to more information if you suspect one of these, or you can ask your GP for advice.

If your child *often* shows two or more of the following symptoms, despite good 'formal' education for one to two years, discuss it with the teacher and ask for further investigation. If your concerns are very severe earlier than this, also ask for investigation.

- Often confuses b / d, n / u, m / w, p / q
- Tends to write backwards or mirror-write
- Cannot learn or remember simple spellings
- Cannot learn or remember which letters make which sounds
- Cannot follow instructions with two or more parts
- Is highly disorganised and / or clumsy – e.g. has difficulty with cutlery, despite help
- Has great difficulty with sequences – e.g. days of week, months
- Has extremely poor pencil control
- Cannot read simple made-up words – e.g. ped, yad, dop
- Has a close relative (parent, sibling, grandparent) who finds / found reading / spelling difficult

There's no room to go into further detail here. However, do follow these tips:

- Trust your instinct – but beware of drawing comparisons with a friend's child, which can be misleading, irrelevant and unhelpful.
- If worried, raise your concerns – but DON'T let your child sense them.
- If there is a problem, early intervention is important – but it's never too late.
- Arm yourself with knowledge – but from a variety of sources, not just one company with a product to sell.
- Remember: many brilliantly successful people have reading and / or spelling difficulties.
- Keep your child's confidence high. Confidence is the best gift you can give.
- All problems improve with patience and appropriate help. Some disappear altogether.
- All children, whatever their reading level, have strengths, skills and value. Nurture them!

These organisations offer further help:

- The Literacy Trust, especially this page:
  http://www.literacytrust.org.uk/links/special.html
- The British Dyslexia Association: **www.bdadyslexia.org.uk**; helpline: 0118 966 8271
- The Dyslexia Institute: **www.dyslexiaaction.org.uk**
- The Child Literacy Centre: **www.childliteracy.com**

Caution: because there are many types of problem, with many causes, there is no single remedy. Be cautious if someone offers a simple solution to all reading problems. ●

LITTLE PRINCESSES series
Katie Chase

This series of girl-oriented books takes its heroine – and its reader – to different cultures, some real, some mythic. Rosie lives in her great-aunt Rosamund's castle in Scotland. Her great-aunt is away travelling, but before leaving she told Rosie that around the castle there are pictures of various little princesses, and that to each in turn she should curtsey and say hello. By magic she will then be transported to the real princess, and once there will help the princess sort out some trouble or problem. First in the series is *The Whispering Princess*, in which Rosie has to help the Persian princess Azara defeat the wicked genie who has imprisoned her father, stolen her voice and taken over the kingdom.

■ More **Little Princesses** include: *The Cloud Princess* (ancient Rome); *The Silk Princess* (India); *The Fairy Tale Princess* (medieval England) and *The Peach Blossom Princess* (Japan).

   Short chapters make these ideal bedtime stories for younger girls, and perfect – if formulaic – fantasy fodder for older ones, especially if they like role-play and dressing up.

Leonie Flynn

* * * * * * *

LITTLE SWAN series
Adèle Geras

A must for every young would-be ballet dancer, several of these **Little Swan** stories have now been reissued in one book. Their simple but compelling plots, told in six chapters, feature the ups and downs of sparky eight-year-old Louisa, or 'Weezer', who is determined to be a famous ballet dancer when she grows up. Told with humour, gentleness and warmth, each story works within the confines of a young child's world – family and friends, school, ballet class, the first show – yet contains enough information about the grown-up world of ballet to satisfy any small dancer.

Patricia Elliott

■ Follow Louisa's hopes and dreams in the rest of the books in the series: *Louisa's Secret*; *Louisa in the Wings*; *A Rival for Louisa*; *Louisa on Screen* and *Good Luck, Louisa*.

LITTLE WOLF series
Ian Whybrow, illustrated by Tony Ross

Ian Whybrow's **Little Wolf** books have been described as 'foolproof' and this would seem to be particularly true where boys are concerned. Broken up into bite-sized pieces of text, with a continuous narrative binding them together, the pages are laden with Tony Ross' excellent drawings, jokey cultural references and wordplay. Little Wolf has to fight against family expectations because he just isn't bad enough, and in doing so, he has one adventure after another. My favourite is *Little Wolf's Book of Badness*, the first book, where he is sent away to school to get his Bad badge and ends up joining the cub scouts because they have 'loads of badges'!

■ Titles include *Little Wolf's Book of Daring Deeds*; *Little Wolf's Haunted Hall for Small Horrors*; *Little Wolf, Terror of the Shivery Sea*; *Little Wolf, Forest Detective* and *Little Wolf's Big Book of Spooks and Clues*.

Laura Hutchings

* * * * * * *

LIZZIE ZIPMOUTH
Jacqueline Wilson

Lizzie likes living with her mum even if their flat is a bit on the pokey, shabby side. So when her mum announces they're moving in with Sam and his two sons Lizzie simply refuses to speak. It's easy to see why: Lizzie's experiences with previous stepdads have been far from happy ones. Nothing in the world can persuade Lizzie to speak again, even though Sam and her new stepbrothers prove to be very friendly. Nothing, that is, until she meets her match in Great Gran. Gradually the two form a strong friendship and come to mean more to each other than either could have expected...

Jacqueline Wilson offers her readers ways of coping in stressful family situations, and lightens up her narratives with flashes of genuinely funny humour.

Eileen Armstrong

LOUDMOUTH LOUIS Anne Fine

Louis talks so much that when he decides to do a sponsored silence to raise money for a new school library, everyone just laughs. Only his mum offers him some sound advice, telling him to listen carefully to things so he will become interested in them and won't need to talk as much. But being such a loudmouth, that's easier said than done...

Anne Fine has a sharp ear for dialogue and an eye for realistic detail. If you've got a child that won't stop talking, try getting them to read this!

Eileen Armstrong

* * * * * * *

LUKE LANCELOT AND THE GOLDEN SHIELD Giles Andreae

At the top of the age range covered by this guide, this is a fabulous story of three children (Luke, Gwinnie and Arthur) whose interest in the King Arthur legends becomes startlingly realised when Arthur gets a sword for his birthday and, through the auspices of Merlin himself, they all end up living their playtime adventures for real.

With evil witches, capture, escape, jousts, life-or-death situations and dragons, this is a wild adventure that will appeal to children enthralled by myth and yet who want something as fast as a computer game.

Leonie Flynn

> ■ There's also a sequel, *Luke Lancelot and the Treasure of the Kings.*

* * * * * * *

THE MAGIC FINGER
Roald Dahl, illustrated by Quentin Blake

Our eight-year-old narrator has a magic finger that can be pointed when she gets cross to change annoying things. Hence the Gregg family are stopped from their duck-shooting expedition by being turned into ducks themselves, as a family of large ducks turns the tables and take over their farmhouse.

This story for younger readers carries all the usual Dahl hallmarks, including extravagantly horrible villains, a brave and right-thinking hero and a satisfying revenge.

Liz Attenborough

MAGIC PONY CAROUSEL series
Poppy Shire, illustrated by Strawberrie Donnelly

I can hear the parental groans at yet another series of pink sparkly books! But, though these kind of stories hardly break new ground in children's literature, they are useful to some kids' reading development (see our feature on p.240). The Magic Pony Carousel of these stories is a fairground carousel, one that sometimes transports the rider, along with the pony she's riding, to another place, where she'll have to help someone who's in trouble. Oh, and probably get to wear lovely clothes and talk to her Magic Carousel Pony (who of course can talk back), too.

Leonie Flynn

* * * * * * *

■ *Sparkle* starts the series off, with pony Sparkle taking her rider to a circus. Some of the other carousel pony stories are *Star* (a Wild West cowgirl's pony); *Brightheart* (who belongs to a medieval princess); *Crystal* (a mountain adventure); *Jewel* (an adventure with highwaymen) and *Flame* (Arabia!).

MAGICAL CHILDREN series
Sally Gardner

This is a series about children who, for some reason or other, become empowered with magical gifts. Children love the idea of being special. These books let them imagine being very special indeed. Whether it's strength, flying, invisibility or skill, the results are often hilarious but never over the top – this is not slapstick: it's more grounded and subtle. There are plenty of adults around and many of them are entirely unmagical – the worst utterly lack imagination and warmth though the best have the sort of patience and wisdom that many of us would aspire to. But the important thing is that the children inhabit a richer, more meaningful world. They have real magic: the creativity of the imagination.

Nicola Morgan

■ The series starts with *The Strongest Girl in the World* and continues with *The Boy Who Could Fly*; *The Invisible Boy*; *The Smallest Girl Ever* and *The Boy With the Magic Numbers*.

The Boy With the Lightning Feet

sally gardner

MARCIA WILLIAMS' COMIC STRIPS
Marcia Williams

Whether they're into legends like 'King Arthur' or 'Robin Hood', or searching for the storylines of Dickens and Shakespeare, or after information about God's Creation, Greek myths or inventors, children will find everything they are looking for and more in these accessible, absorbing and entertaining reads.

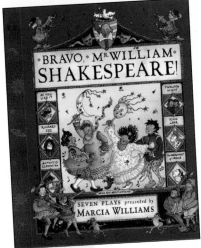

Williams cleverly condenses the classics, packing all the action and excitement of the originals into just a few pages of colourful and intricate comic strips. Very young readers will enjoy spotting tiny, humorous details, like a more intellectually demanding *Where's Wally?* (*UFBG* 298), while older readers will glean oodles of historical information from reading the speech bubbles and cartoon captions and hunting for the witty asides from the supporting characters.

Eileen Armstrong

* * * * * * *

MARVIN REDPOST
Louis Sachar

Louis Sachar is a wonderful writer – witty and incredibly observant – who cares about what children read and learn. Marvin Redpost is a truly decent boy with all the fears and misunderstandings of a normal child, though he is not always helped by the things his friends say and do. The adults in his life are decent and wise but don't entirely understand children, so Marvin and his friends have to work things out for themselves... and make some mistakes along the way. These short, funny stories are perfect for newly confident readers, especially boys.

Nicola Morgan

■ Other **Marvin Redpost** titles to enjoy include: *Why Pick on Me; Kidnapped at Birth; Super Fast; Out of Control* and *A Magic Crystal*.

MASAI AND I
Virginia Kroll, illustrated by Nancy Carpenter

Linda learns about the Masai at school and feels 'the tingle of kinship' flowing through her veins. Virginia Kroll's story is told in a wonderfully exultant voice. It celebrates both Linda's inner-city family life and the ways of the tall, proud Masai, alternating seamlessly between the two cultures.

Masai and I is a joy to read aloud, especially the passage about the African night, when 'the low, white moon glowed yellow and rose straight above, until whole flocks of flashing fireflies turned streets into lanterns'. Nancy Carpenter's illustrations are stunning. This is an exceptional story of difference, of harmony and of love.

Caroline Pitcher

* * * * * * *

MEERKAT MAIL   Emily Gravett

Emily Gravett arrived on the children's book scene like a meteor, winning the Kate Greenaway medal for *Wolves* (*UFBG* 195). *Meerkat Mail* is an equally sophisticated, detailed story about Sunny, an adventurous meerkat. Fed up with the close family structure of his meerkat community, he leaves home for more interesting parts. He sends back rather upbeat postcards, which don't quite accurately reflect his true experiences. Finding that life on his own is not as much fun as he anticipated, gradually he realises there is no place like home.

This story is for every child who has headed down the front path with a suitcase. It gives lots of scope to explore fears as independence beckons.

Sonia Benster

Children With Reading Difficulties

It may be that your child does have real obstacles to learning to read. But if so, don't despair – there's a lot that you and your child's school can do to make the process easier. Here is some practical advice from **Nicola Morgan**...

Knowing that your child has reading difficulties is horribly stressful. It's particularly distressing when you see other children learn without effort. Worst of all is when you realise that your child also senses a problem and starts to lose confidence.

I've talked about things you should and shouldn't worry about on p.254. If you haven't already, do read that now. For this piece, I am assuming that you have established that your child does have a specific problem with reading and / or writing.

What the school should do:

- Arrange an assessment to analyse the problem. In order to help, a teacher needs to know whether the problem is auditory or visual, whether it's in sequencing, the exact state of all areas of weakness and strength. Sometimes the cause is relevant – for example, a temporary hearing deficit caused by ear infections at the time when contemporaries were learning to blend sounds can cause a temporary delay in reading.
- Arrange and inform you about the programme of help. How will the school manage your child's specific need? Will extra teaching be one-to-one or in a small group?
- Keep you informed about progress.
- Understand and manage the emotional and behavioural issues for a child who finds schoolwork difficult.
- Be emotionally supportive, to you and your child.

What you can to do help:

- Boost your child's confidence by focusing on strengths.
- Reward and praise effort and all successes.
- Don't expect too much – this will be a slow process, but your child will move forward (though not necessarily regularly).
- Give your child tasks you know he or she can do – success breeds confidence and confidence breeds more success.
- Be very sensitive if a younger sibling is more advanced.
- Choose a range of library books that are easy – even if your child has read them many times. Then let your child pick from that range.
- Investigate Toe-by-Toe (**www.toe-by-toe.co.uk**). This is a popular, low-cost programme written for untrained adults to use with a child.
- Keep things in perspective: although it's difficult, it's not the end of the world. Many highly successful people, for example in business or the creative world, and happy and fulfilled people in all walks of life, have or have had reading problems. Although some difficulties never entirely disappear, there are many ways for your child to develop into a successful and happy adult, and even a happy and successful reader. Some people even believe that such problems bring an extra strength, an edge over those who found it all so easy.

To sum up:
Be informed, kind, and positive. And ask for help. ●

Further Help

- Your GP
- The Literacy Trust, especially this page: **http://www.literacytrust.org.uk/links/special.html**
- The British Dyslexia Association: **www.bdadyslexia.org.uk**; helpline: 0118 966 8271
- The Dyslexia Institute: **www.dyslexiaaction.org.uk**
- The Child Literacy Centre: **www.childliteracy.com**
- There's also a very useful factsheet on 'Specific Learning Difficulties' in the 'Mental Health and Growing Up' section of The Royal College of Psychiatrists website: **www.rcpsych.ac.uk**

MERMAID S.O.S. series
Gillian Shields, illustrated by Helen Turner

The first six of these books tell of six young mermaids who are charged with collecting that year's crop of magic crystals – the crystals that ensure the health and security of all the creatures and plants that live in the sea. Of course, they are delighted to show how brave they are, but little do they know quite how brave they'll have to be. Each book tells a different mermaid's story. Simply told yet delightful, these stories are about friendship, courage and the importance of the environment. There's an evil, witch-like mermaid who's determined to hinder all their efforts, a cast of sea creatures – and a second series in which the mermaids have to find the stolen snow diamonds and stop the ice-caps from melting.
Leonie Flynn

■ Also in **The Magic Crystal** series: *Misty to the Rescue*; *Ellie and the Secret Potion*; *Holly Takes a Risk*; *Scarlett's New Friend* and *Lucy and the Magic Crystal*. The **Snow Diamond** series starts with *Amber's First Task*.

* * * * * *

MILLY-MOLLY-MANDY STORIES
Joyce Lankester Brisley

Millicent Margaret Amanda – Milly-Molly-Mandy to her friends and family – lives with her mother and father, uncle and aunty and grandmother and grandfather in a nice white cottage with a thatched roof. She wears pink and white cotton frocks in summer and red serge in winter. Her adventures are domestic: a day at the seaside, a trip to the photographer, picking mushrooms, fishing for minnows, being given her own bedroom; but they're characterised by a faith in family, community and friendship which makes them wonderful both for independent reading and for reading aloud.
Antonia Honeywell

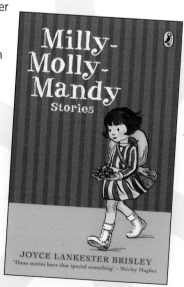

MIRANDA THE EXPLORER
James Mayhew

Miranda's adventure in a balloon takes her all round the world and gives her just a glimpse of all the great things to be seen – the Taj Mahal, the Great Wall of China, the Eiffel Tower, Mount Everest and more. She meets people and talks to them wherever she goes, making this book an exciting introduction to the world and the rich variety of people and places to be discovered in it. A book to touch the imagination of readers from five upwards. Look out also for *Miranda the Castaway*, Miranda's first adventure in which she must learn to survive alone on a desert island – perfect for anyone interested in simple technology!

Wendy Cooling

* * * * * * *

MR MAJEIKA series
Humphrey Carpenter

Mr Majeika is a primary school teacher, but he's not like any teacher you've ever met – and when he flies in through the window on a magic carpet, the children in Class 3 know instantly it's going to be an extraordinary term, where anything at all could happen. Although longer than the average book for emergent readers, the simple story style, laugh-out-loud funny incidents and scribbly black-and-white sketches mean that every child will power through the pages and build reading confidence, ready for the next in the series. They'll definitely wish there was a Mr Majeika in their school.

Eileen Armstrong

> ■ Titles include:
> *Mr Majeika and the Haunted Hotel*; *Mr Majeika and the Ghost Train*; *Mr Majeika and the Music Teacher*; *Mr Majeika Vanishes*; *Mr Majeika on the Internet*; *Mr Majeika and the Lost Spell Book* and *Mr Majeika and the School Trip*.

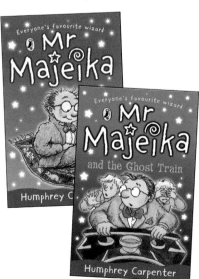

MOUSE NOSES ON TOAST
Daren King, illustrated by David Roberts

Paul Mouse is a mouse like any other. Except that unlike normal mice, poor Paul is allergic to cheese. But this allergy soon becomes the least of his worries, when he learns that the human restaurant above them has taken to serving a most horrible delicacy: mouse noses on toast! It's up to Paul and his friends – Sandra (a Christmas tree angel), Larry (a hippy mouse), Rowley Barker Hobbs (a shaggy dog) and the Tinby (just don't ask) to put a stop to this practice. Their various well-meaning schemes make for a lively story, with the offbeat humour of King's writing perfectly set off against Roberts' quirky artwork.

Daniel Hahn

* * * * * * *

MONSTER AND FROG
Rose Impey, illustrated by Russell Ayto

Monster and Frog are friends, and they have adventures. With no more than about two simple sentences per page and bright, stylised illustrations that perfectly embody lugubrious, timid Monster and excitable, energetic Frog, each book can be read aloud or read alone and is perfect for giving unsteady readers confidence.

Leonie Flynn

■ There are eight titles in the series, from the first, *Monster and Frog and the Big Adventure*, to *Monster and Frog and the Terrible Toothache*.

* * * * * * *

THE MONSTER IN THE MIRROR
Jean Ure, illustrated by Doffy Weir

Stretch is a cat, and king of the house. Woffle is a dog – he's a bit nervous, scares easily, but so long as everyone lets him go about his business woffling around the garden, he's happy enough. Then a little kitten arrives; but this is not a lovely fluffy little kitten, it's a fierce kitten with teeth and claws, and poor Woffles is terrified... Yes, Stretch is going to have to teach that little monster a lesson...

A pacy early reader with a very satisfying twist, and Doffy Weir's illustrations give the animals real character.

Daniel Hahn

MOOMIN series
Tove Jansson

Translated into numerous languages from the original Finnish, the **Moomin** books won Tove Jansson the prestigious Hans Christian Andersen Award for her contribution to children's literature. Jansson's fantastical characters – Moomintroll, his family and friends in the enchanted Moominvalley – originated in a weekly comic strip for adults. While on vacation on her isolated island, Jansson began to spin the whimsical account of the Moomins' summer adventures and the discovery of the magical Hobgoblin's Hat, which transforms anything put inside it... The seemingly simple yet emotionally precise storytelling makes this series a true masterpiece, which will mesmerise first readers.

Noga Applebaum

MS WIZ series
Terence Blacker, illustrated by Tony Ross

My daughter discovered the Ms Wiz books in 1995. These are fast-paced adventures written in short chapters with a lovely sense of humour.

> ■ Titles include *Ms Wiz Mayhem*; *Ms Wiz Spells Trouble*; *In Control, Ms Wiz* and *Ms Wiz in Hollywood*.

With her black nail polish, magic rat and special powers, Ms Wiz is no ordinary Year 3 teacher. She arrives at St Barnabas to help the children with all sorts of problems and can handle anyone from Dracula (or is he the school inspector?) to a fashion designer and even the prime minister. As the series has developed, the children have progressed to Year 5, Ms Wiz has had her own baby, the Wiz Kid, and the stories have become even wilder. Ms Wiz is a 'paranormal operative' who goes wherever magic is needed. She certainly did the trick in my home and contributed to my daughter becoming an avid reader.

Sarah Manson

THE MUMMY FAMILY series
Tony Bradman, illustrated by Martin Chatterton

The Mummy family are... mummies, of the ancient Egyptian, wrapped-in-bandages sort. Two parents (Daddy Mummy and Mummy Mummy), two kids (Sis and Tut) and a cat-mummy live in a pyramid in the Land of Sand. Beginning with *The Magnificent Mummies*, other titles in the series include *The Mummy Family Find Fame* (in which the family compete on a reality TV show) and *The Surprise Party* (in which a party for the grandparent Mummies' 5,000th wedding anniversary almost goes horribly wrong...) The illustrations are full of witty details to spot, and the simple and lively texts (in good short chapters with speech bubbles) are packed with jokes and puns to entertain new readers.

Daniel Hahn

* * * * * *

MY NAUGHTY LITTLE SISTER
Dorothy Edwards, illustrated by Shirley Hughes

Originally written in the early 1950s for *Listen With Mother*, the BBC radio programme, these stories were inspired by the author's recollections of her own childhood and some aspects could now be viewed as old fashioned – as can some of the language! But their timelessness more than compensates for the anachronisms. First experiences and significant childhood events are described with humour and affection, and Shirley Hughes' warm, nostalgic illustrations add an extra enjoyable dimension. We never discover My Naughty Little Sister's name, but we all know somebody just like her – perhaps my own little sister, or maybe even me!

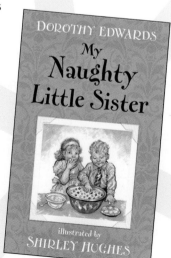

Catherine Robinson

MY SECRET UNICORN series
Linda Chapman

Most of the time, Twilight looks just like any other small grey pony – but when Lauren says the Turning Spell, he changes into a unicorn with the power to fly. Naturally, there are other secret unicorns like Twilight all around the world, and each has to find a human friend to help them use their magic to do good and help people. This long-running series works so well because it combines wish-fulfilment fantasy with real-life relationship issues that any horse-loving girl can relate to. Linda Chapman never patronises her readers and her passion for ponies shines through in a collection of satisfying, sparkly stories.

Steve Cole

■ Titles include:
Moonlight Journey; *Rising Star*; *Snowy Dreams*; *Friends Forever*; *Stronger than Magic*; *A Winter Wish*; *A Touch of Magic*; *Dreams Come True* and *Starlight Surprise*.

* * * * * * *

MYTHS AND LEGENDS
Geraldine McCaughrean

There are many versions of the world's myths and legends around for children, but none are better than Geraldine McCaughrean's. There are her classic *The Orchard Book of Roman Myths* (Romulus and Remus, Venus, Mars and so on) and *The Orchard Book of Greek Myths* (Icarus, Theseus, Odysseus, Jason and so on). Then look out for *100 World Myths and Legends*, which contains stories from all around the world.

McCaughrean has written paperbacks suitable for those starting to read independently – stories from the Greek and Roman myths such as *Perseus and the Gorgon*, *Medusa* and *City of Dreams*. And there are also themed collections: *The Book of Starry Tales*, all centred around the stars, *Stories from the Ballet* and *The Book of Love and Friendship*.

Leonie Flynn

Fairy Tales

Yes, fairy tales are wonderful, enchanting – but they're not all as pretty and safe and benign as you might expect, as **Adèle Geras** explains...

Fairy tales should come with a health warning. They're not the fluffy, cuddly, pretty narratives some people imagine. Most were not written for children, but have their origins in tales told by women to other women. The stories of Perrault, in the 17th century, were written for educated, sophisticated people and have been passed down with their content often diluted, sanitised and made palatable for a young audience.

Many children meet fairy tales for the first time in Disney films and – excellent though some of these are (especially the earlier ones: *Snow White*, *Sleeping Beauty*, *Cinderella* etc.) – there's no substitute for a story told or read to a child by a trusted adult.

Because these stories are so strong, so full of things that stick, burr-like, to the imagination, it's as well to be on your guard when choosing versions for younger children. For instance, Louise Brierley illustrated a collection I wrote, called *Beauty and the Beast and Other Stories* (now out of print) with the most outstanding pictures, but some of them would certainly produce nightmares in the very young... They were chilling and spooky in the extreme, which was only to be expected considering some of the stories they were illustrating: 'Bluebeard', 'The Tinderbox' and 'Hansel and Gretel', for example.

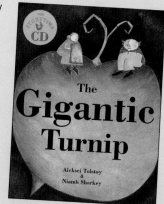

For the under-sevens, I'd steer clear of anything where someone meets (and has to meet, for the purposes of the story) a really gruesome death. Thus, avoid 'Hansel and Gretel', 'Bluebeard', and possibly also 'Little Red Riding Hood' in the case of very sensitive children. There are still many other tales for the very young, though even these have their dark side. I've never felt entirely at ease with the 'Three Billygoats Gruff'. That troll is worrying. 'Cinderella'

is fine, because chopping off toes to fit into the glass slipper is no longer a part of the story we tell. 'Sleeping Beauty' is OK, because somehow children understand very early on that the prince is going to wake 'Sleeping Beauty' in the end with a loving kiss and all will be well. There are lots of others… 'The Gingerbread Man', 'The Elves and the Shoemaker', 'Chicken Licken', 'Puss in Boots', 'Goldilocks and the Three Bears' and so on. Look out also for versions of Hans Andersen stories. 'The Ugly Duckling', 'Thumbelina' and 'The Princess and the Pea' are suitable for children of six or so… but keep away from 'The Snow Queen' and 'The Tinderbox'.

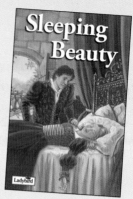

Rose Impey has retold stories for the younger reader / listener in *The Orchard Book of Fairy Tales*, which has lovely illustrations by Ian Beck. Her easy, friendly style is just right for this age group. Berlie Doherty's collection *Fairy Tales*, beautifully illustrated by Jane Ray, is a treasure for readers of any age, though it does include 'Hansel and Gretel'. You may have to do a bit of on-the-spot editing as you read… Just leap over and leave out anything you suspect your child can't deal with. My mother always covered up the fox in Beatrix Potter's *Jemima Puddle-Duck* because I was so terrified of him: I found the jacket, the smoothness, the foxiness of him quite horrifying.

Single stories are available in many forms. Something lavish, like Christian Birmingham's gorgeous version of 'Sleeping Beauty' for which I provided the words, makes a good present, but I've yet to meet the child who is not completely entranced by what are now called the Ladybird Tales. ▶

Some Fairy Tales in the *UFBG*

Fairy Tales illustrated by Jan Pieńkowski, translated by David Walser (*UFBG* 101)

The Gigantic Turnip by Aleksei Tolstoy, illustrated by Niamh Sharkey (*UFBG* 105)

The Princess and the Pea by Lauren Child, photographs by Polly Borland (*UFBG* 159)

Fairy Tales by Sarah Hayes, illustrated by P.J. Lynch (*UFBG* 100)

Years ago, my children adored *The Elves and the Shoemaker* with its rather hideous, 1950s-style pictures, but these stories now have new illustrations and look much better. They're amazingly good value for money and you can collect the set... There are lots in the series. *The Magic Porridge Pot* and *The Great Big Enormous Turnip* were also great favourites.

Try also Usborne's **First Stories**, which include *Rumplestiltskin* and *The Three Little Pigs*. Watch out for anything illustrated by Ian Beck... He's done a delightful 'Ugly Duckling', for instance. There's no rush to read the more hard-hitting stuff. Children should be ready for the more harrowing Andersen tales (like 'The Little Mermaid'), for Perrault and even for the Brothers Grimm when they're about ten. Fairy tales speak to our human nature, and we respond to them as generations of others have done, with wonder and horror and delight. And recognition. ●

Classic Fairy Tales Given a Twist

The Pea and the Princess by Mini Grey (*UFBG* 156)

Seriously Silly Stories by Laurence Anholt (*UFBG* 283)

The Three Little Wolves and the Big Bad Pig by Eugene Trivizas, illustrated by Helen Oxenbury (*UFBG* 185)

The Stinky Cheese Man by Jon Scieszka, illustrated by Lane Smith (*UFBG* 290)

Modern Fairy Tales

The Emperor of Absurdia by Chris Riddell (*UFBG* 100)

The King of Capri by Jeanette Winterson, illustrated by Jane Ray (*UFBG* 251)

The Selfish Giant by Oscar Wilde (*UFBG* 283)

Other Collections to Look Out For

The Hutchinson Treasury of Fairy Tales by various

The Barefoot Book of Fairy Tales by Malachy Doyle, illustrated by Nicoletta Ceccoli

Andersen Fairy Tales translated by Anthea Bell, illustrated by Lisbeth Zwerger

NAUGHTY AMELIA JANE
Enid Blyton

This is a classic collection from the prolific pen of Enid Blyton. Amelia Jane is the naughtiest toy in the toy cupboard. In each chapter, she thinks up a new way to tease and terrify the other toys: she snips off pink rabbit's tail, scares the toys by pretending to be a cat, and pushes the brown teddy bear into a pool of water. But even though Amelia Jane is the largest of the toys, the others are quite good at teaching her a lesson. Whenever she gets her comeuppance, she promises to be good in future… but her resolution is always short-lived!

There are three collections of Amelia Jane stories to enjoy.

Susan Reuben

* * * * * * *

NICHOLAS series
René Goscinny, illustrated by
Jean-Jacques Sempé

This is a series of five books following the adventures of Nicholas, a highly imaginative young French boy who always tries to do the right thing, but ends up wreaking havoc. Told by Nicholas himself, who doesn't always realise the mess he's making of things, the books are not only hilarious but also celebrate the triumph of this clever child over the slow-witted adults around him. Translated four decades after their original publication, these books are gems waiting to be discovered by English-speaking readers. The new editions are also a joy both to look at and to handle. Short chapters, each focusing on a particular adventure and accompanied by funny cartoons, ensure their appeal to young readers.

Ariel Kahn

THE NIGHT OF THE UNICORN
Jenny Nimmo, illustrated by Terry Milne

Jenny Nimmo's books always tingle with wonder and the possibility of magic. In this, a night of shooting stars sparks unexpected events: the disappearance of Amber's hen; the coming of a strange, white horse with a mark on its forehead; Amber's friendship with Luke, a lonely boy with a secret wish. Blurry, nicely old-fashioned illustrations suit the reassuring feel of the narrative. Two parallel storylines – Amber's and Hennie's – and a large character cast make this one for the top of the age range. Nimmo's exquisite shorter books, *The Stone Mouse*, *Toby in the Dark* and *The Owl Tree* (below) are also well worth seeking out.

Patricia Elliott

* * * * * *

THE OWL TREE
Jenny Nimmo, illustrated by Anthony Lewis

While many young fiction titles are full of cartoons and jokes and frippery, Jenny Nimmo has written a clutch of brilliant, quiet, thoughtful storybooks – several, as this one is, prize winners. This is a novel about a magical person-like tree that is beloved by Joe's granny and scorned by Granny's neighbour. Can Joe discover its secrets and save it from destruction – even though he is too afraid to climb it?

Wholly accessible, with short chapters and generous black-and-white illustrations, this may be part of your children's Guided Reading programme at school. Buy it for them if not, as it shouldn't be missed.

Jon Appleton

Everybody's Favourite...

THE OWL WHO WAS AFRAID OF THE DARK

Jill Tomlinson, illustrated by Paul Howard

Children who fear darkness will find comfort in the tale of an owlet who learns to enjoy the dark. The gentle illustrations in soft, deep colours, emphasise the positive aspects of night-time as the little owl learns about the night's beauty, its exciting difference from the daytime and the things that can be done or seen only at night: a dazzling display of fireworks is reflected in the owls' eyes; an astronomer reveals the stars through his telescope and a cat shows him a sleeping town in the moonlight. The text and illustrations unite in perfect harmony to tell this reassuring tale.

Gill Vickery

One of the best-loved bedtime stories ever written, this book has soothed countless children and delighted their tired parents. The little owl Plop is afraid of the dark, a problem for owls and a problem for many children, too. Plop learns to see the dark through new eyes and so does the reader. It's a cocooning story, the sort of story to read in the dark, wrapped up cosily before a goodnight kiss. A must-have book for every bedroom.

Nicola Morgan

Everybody's Favourite...

PADDINGTON BEAR
Michael Bond, illustrated by Peggy Fortnum

Not quite as old as Pooh, but just as recognisable, Paddington Bear is a true classic of children's literature – ageless and hugely enjoyable. The marmalade-loving bear from Darkest Peru has been part of children's lives for almost 50 years, for very good reason. He is polite, yet assertive. He is a quick learner who uses his initiative, often with highly surprising results. He is very funny. He has an iconic sense of style. His many adventures make for a long-term relationship with his readers. And he's a great role model, although we might suggest that under your hat is a better place for keeping secrets than for marmalade sandwiches.

Antonia Honeywell

MICHAEL BOND
A BEAR CALLED
PADDINGTON

The original story of the bear from Darkest Peru.

illustrated by PEGGY FORTNUM

Children often ask me what I read when I was a boy and I always smile and say Paddington Bear. This usually brings forth a ripple of amused solidarity, because the hapless bear from Peru is clearly just as accessible now as he was 45 years ago. It would be true to say that the Brown family who adopt Paddington, with their cosy suburban life and housekeeper, are a little outdated, but the bear himself is timeless. The situations and scrapes he gets himself into (and out of) are all managed with precise humour and a writing style as smooth as chocolate. They are wonderful to read aloud to children, especially at night with a mug of cocoa!

Chris d'Lacey

PIRATE DIARY and CASTLE DIARY
Richard Platt, illustrated by Chris Riddell

I'm a big fan of these books because I'm a big fan of anything that keeps boys reading. Boys often prefer factual books and these fuel that need, while still offering good prose and food for the imagination. Through the fictional diaries of young Tobias Burgess (*Castle Diary*) and Jake Carpenter (*Pirate Diary*), we learn about the life of a 13th-century pageboy and 18th-century cabin boy, respectively. After the diary comes the usual paraphernalia of non fiction, with explanations, sources, glossary and index. The latest in the series takes the reader back to 1465 BC with *Egyptian Diary*. All of these books are perfect for confident young readers hungry for facts and adventure.

Nicola Morgan

* * * * * * *

POLLY'S RUNNING AWAY BOOK
Frances Thomas, illustrated by Sally Gardner

Polly's fed up. Her mum cooks too much broccoli, her hamster's missing, there's no money for holidays and she's about to get a baby brother – which she does not want! Funny, grumpy and delightfully cynical, Polly doesn't actually run away, though she thinks about it very hard, and even tries to keep a store of food for when she does... but the sandwiches go mouldy. Of course, in the end everything works out just fine, and Polly finds her hamster and actually likes the new baby. Though she never gets to like broccoli.

Quirkily written and brilliantly illustrated with a mixture of drawings and collage, this is funny, thoughtful and warm.

Leonie Flynn

Poetry

Poet and Children's Laureate **Michael Rosen** shares his thoughts about what makes poetry special, and why we should all (and not just children) be reading more of it.

Poems are special ways of saying things. We are most used to poems that use rhyme and rhythm. This kind of poem has used the sounds of language to create a soundtrack. Unlike in a movie, where you can separate what people are saying from the music, in poetry it's the very words themselves that make this soundtrack. So something mysterious happens: even as we think we understand the words of the poem, the music those words make is having an effect, too.

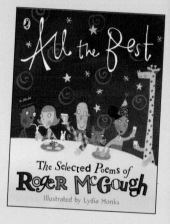

Poems are a kind of humanly made magic and offer children a way of looking at the language they know in what I'd call a 'physical' way. That's to say they draw attention to the material making of words (sounds, rhythms, tones, pitch, cadence and so on). I think this is especially attractive to children who are surrounded by words that are too unfamiliar to mean much and yet still have their physical qualities. Poetry allows children to play with this physical side and enjoy the surprising meanings that may result from the play... ploy... ply... (*that* sort of thing!).

Some poems offer highly compressed ways of saying things. Prose stories often rely on an elongated sequence of events with a clear outcome. Poems don't have to do this. They can be much more suggestive, with gaps and inconclusive parts. This means that they can invite the reader to fill in and make guesses about what might be going on. This kind of poem is great for getting children to slow down, reread, contemplate and speculate and not be worried about whether there is a right and wrong way of understanding.

Poems often work by juxtaposition. That's to say, images or ideas (or both) are given to us side by side in ways that we might not expect. An obvious way of doing this is through simile ('I wandered lonely as a cloud') but it can also happen less obviously by association. Simply writing about, say, a frown and a bird in the same line of poetry will encourage the mind to try and find some connection. The 'movement' of a poem may well involve an unwritten, non-explicit dance of associations between images. This side of our minds is not often explored in schools, and yet there's very good evidence to suggest that this process is a major part of how we think and feel.

Poetry often scavenges language. It borrows and steals phrases and sounds from wherever it can in order to surprise us. It's often been said that poetry can make the familiar unfamiliar and the unfamiliar familiar. It has many ways of doing this, but one of the ways is that it grabs a phrase from one context and puts it into another. This creates new meanings, which may make us laugh or cry or gasp. When Mercutio is dying in *Romeo and Juliet*, he says to Romeo, 'ask for me tomorrow, and you shall find me a grave man'. This is a 'poetic' moment as it compresses humour and tragedy into the one word 'grave'. This kind of double quality (sometimes it can be more than double) helps children to see that part of what we are saying is how we are saying it. It encourages us to think along several lines at the same time. To investigate such matters is to invite curiosity in the thing that appears to be so familiar as to be beyond curiosity: the language we use to express ourselves in.

Poems offer us excellent platforms for creating new imaginative acts, whether that's through making more poems, or through making things in other media: dance, music, pottery, cartoons, drama, mime, story, photography or whatever. Poems don't have to be interrogated and reduced to conclusive interpretations. They can be treated as openings not closings. If we're genuinely interested in the idea of helping children discover that they can be creators and interpreters, people who can transform experiences into something new, then poetry provides an excellent framework for this to happen.

I don't think there is much evidence to suggest that reading or writing poetry makes us better people. What it does is give us a chance to stop the flow and reflect. This aspect of education is undervalued and yet it's something that makes life possible. We should be giving children resources that will enable them to spend time reflecting. Poetry is one of those resources. ●

Poetry Collections to Look Out For

All the Best: Selected Poems of Roger McGough

All the Colours of the Earth ed. Wendy Cooling, illustrated by Sheila Moxley

A Book of Nonsense by Edward Lear

A Child's Garden of Verses by Robert L. Stevenson

Gargling with Jelly by Brian Patten

Heard it in the Playground by Allan Ahlberg

Mustard, Custard, Grumble Belly and Gravy by Michael Rosen

The Owl and the Pussycat by Edward Lear, illustrated by Ian Beck

Please Mrs Butler by Allan Ahlberg

The Puffin Book of Fantastic First Poems by June Crebbin

PRINCESS MIRROR-BELLE
Julia Donaldson, illustrated by Lydia Monks

● ● ●

Ellen is a perfectly ordinary girl, until one day she looks in a mirror, and instead of her own reflection she sees someone who looks just like her called Princess Mirror-Belle. Mirror-Belle proceeds to climb into Ellen's world and get up to all sorts of mischief, but just as things are becoming a bit sticky, she disappears back into the nearest mirror, leaving Ellen to face the consequences.

This is a series of short stories for confident readers, with each chapter describing a new adventure. Lydia Monks' witty illustrations appear throughout. Ellen and Mirror-Belle's adventures continue in *Princess Mirror-Belle and the Magic Shoes*.

Susan Reuben

* * * * * * *

RAINBOW MAGIC series
Daisy Meadows

● ●

Safe, undemanding and unashamedly a girls' read, **Rainbow Magic** is the kind of series that can find itself dismissed as being enjoyable but not entirely worthy reading matter. But with millions of copies sold, it is clearly a series to get children reading – and more importantly, to *keep* them reading (if only to collect the 'lost item' in each book that enables the successful outcome of the story). Already running to 30+ titles, to which more are constantly being added, there are enough stories about sparkling fairies and nasty goblins to satisfy the most voracious appetite and help develop a positive reading habit. There are also themed mini-series within the overall **Rainbow Magic** brand, such as 'Weather Fairies' and 'Pet Fairies', all of which have their own particular sparkle. Buy one for just the right child and watch her collect them all!

Philippa Milnes-Smith

THE REAL TILLY BEANY
Annie Dalton, illustrated by Kate Sheppard

Who can resist the entrancing Tilly Beany? Miss Hinchin, her unimaginative, dour-faced teacher, perhaps, but not me. These beguiling, funny books made my younger son giggle with glee when we first read them. Tilly Beany has all the doubts and fears of any ordinary five-year-old, but with the aid of her extraordinary imagination, her feisty nature and the loving support of her long-suffering family, she is ready to take on the world. The short, linked stories in each book are illustrated with Kate Sheppard's scratchy line drawings that convey just the right mixture of chirpiness and charm.

Patricia Elliott

* * * * * * *

REVOLTING RHYMES
Roald Dahl, illustrated by Quentin Blake

'Cinderella', 'Red Riding Hood', 'The Three Little Pigs', 'Jack and the Beanstalk'... So far, so familiar. But if you know anything about Roald Dahl you'll know that these tales will be different from any other versions around – offbeat, spiky, sometimes gruesome, always subversive and always funny. An ending where Cinderella marries a jam-maker instead of the prince; a world where Red Riding Hood carries a pistol and the wolf threatens the three little pigs' brick house with dynamite... Each rhyme is a glorious, read-aloud riot, and the changes to the familiar versions will delight readers young and old, and as if this weren't enough you have pictures from Dahl's regular collaborator, the peerless Quentin Blake, too.

Daniel Hahn

RONNIE'S TREASURE HUNT
Pippa Goodhart, illustrated by Deborah Allwright

Ronnie finds a rocket parked in his road, and some not-very-bright-pirates (rockets + pirates = favourites with many children). The pirates are hoping to steal the treasure from the skies, which Ronnie knows are the stars, the Sun and the Moon. They kidnap him to be their cabin boy and fly high after the 'twinklers'. The pirates don't find the treasure they're hoping for, but Ronnie does meet an alien and in the end everyone gets more than they expected, especially Ronnie's put-upon mum. This is a cheerful chapter book with sumptuous colour illustrations, in which the child ultimately wins through.

Caroline Pitcher

* * * * * * *

THE SAD BOOK
Michael Rosen, illustrated by Quentin Blake

How do you define sadness? It's so hard to talk about although we've all experienced it; we can't find the words. In order to define sadness, you have to really think about it, and few of us can do that, because it hurts.

But Michael Rosen has managed it. He lost his son Eddie in shocking circumstances, and this honest, deeply personal book is a reflection on the way he tries – and often fails – to cope with this. A lot of people felt they knew Eddie, who regularly featured in his dad's early poems. He was the funniest kid. It was a terrible loss.

It must have taken a lot of strength to write this. It's truthful, poignant and it doesn't pull punches. But it's funny, too. There are little human touches that lift the mood. Cheerful things going on in Quentin Blake's wonderful artwork that make you smile. It's a brave, lovely, sensitive book, and the ending broke my heart. Read it when you're feeling sad. It might help.

Kaye Umansky

THE SELFISH GIANT
Oscar Wilde, illustrated by Michael Foreman

When the Selfish Giant builds a high wall around his beautiful garden to keep the children out, he wonders why it's eternal winter outside and spring never arrives. Then he happens to meet a very special little boy, and his heart is softened... Written in language that is both simple and powerful, Oscar Wilde's delicately crafted story not only appeals to young readers on an immediate level, but also exists as an imaginative moral tale with a life-affirming message. Touching, uplifting and honest – it is a true classic. But be warned: tissues may be necessary for the ending!

Catherine Robinson

SERIOUSLY SILLY STORIES
Laurence Anholt, illustrated by Arthur Robins

Sparky twists on traditional fairy tales just don't come any better or more hilarious than this. The titles alone are guaranteed to tempt reading – 'Shampoozel?' 'Eco-Wolf and the Three Pigs?' Read all about Cinderboy's winning goal and Snow White's shock singing appearance on *Top of the Pops* with the Aliens. These are tales irreverently turned upside down, back to front and inside out. The scribbly line drawings are pure genius, bringing the wacky characters to life and adding hugely to the silly, slapstick humour. Short sentences and simple language make these stories perfect for beginner readers.

Eileen Armstrong

> ■ Or try the same partnership's *Seriously Silly Rhymes*, which gives the same imaginative treatment to familiar, well-loved nursery rhymes.

Everybody's Favourite...

THE SHEEP-PIG
Dick King-Smith

When Farmer Hogget wins a piglet at a local fair, his wife looks forward to bacon and ham for Christmas. Babe, however, is determined to become a working animal, like his foster-mother Fly, the sheep dog. By being polite to the sheep, Babe secures their co-operation and Hogget enters him into the Grand Challenge Sheep Dog Trials. This enchanting, aspirational tale has all the hallmarks of a classic. There are adventures and setbacks along the way, and the climax of the story, Babe's performance in the trials, is genuinely moving. This is a book that will be read again and again.

Laura Hutchings

Dick King-Smith
The Sheep-Pig
The book which inspired the blockbuster film *BABE*

This is the story of how an orphaned pig, Babe, is destined for the butcher's block but goes on to become a champion sheep herder. Published in 1983, it became an immediate bestseller and went on to win the Guardian Children's Fiction Prize. The story is funny, endearing, exciting and moving. But above all it is real. Dick King-Smith was a farmer. He knows his people and his animals. This knowledge, coupled with a wonderful gift for dialogue and characterisation, informs all of his books. Meanwhile, themes like decency, kindness and courtesy are woven imperceptibly into the narrative. Like Babe at his moment of triumph, *The Sheep-Pig* gets 'a hundred out of a hundred'.

Karen Wallace

SOPHIE'S ADVENTURES Dick King-Smith

There are three stories in this substantial chapter book for good readers. Sophie is an unusual and determined girl who wants to grow up to be a farmer. She starts small by looking after a snail, graduates through cats and kittens, a puppy and a rabbit, then goes on to have horse-riding lessons. Sophie is always very clear about her goals, which include earmarking a boy at school as an ideal future husband, because he lives on a farm.

Liz Attenborough

> ■ There are three more stories about the feisty heroine in *Sophie's Further Adventures*.

* * * * * * *

THE SPIDER AND THE FLY
Based on the poem by Mary Howitt, illustrated by Tony DiTerlizzi

This book introduces readers of six and above to the sophisticated art of *Spiderwick Chronicles* illustrator Tony DiTerlizzi and to Mary Howitt's cautionary narrative poem of 1829, in which a charismatic spider flatters a fly to death. The evocative, read-aloud text is set in a haunted dolls' house, inside a Gothic mansion inspired by classic horror films. The wide-eyed flapper-girl fly, who falls for the corpulent spider's charm, looks like a Hollywood ingénue, though children will enjoy knowing better.

Geraldine Brennan

* * * * * * *

SPIDER MCDREW
Alan Durant, illustrated by Martin Chatterton

With his uncontrollable hair, odd socks and wandering concentration, everyone says Spider McDrew's a lost cause. Whatever he's involved in, things always go wrong: he scores goals for opposing teams and brings a cow to school. But somehow things end up right in the end – like the time he suddenly, heroically remembers *all* the lines – but of someone else's part – in the Christmas play!

These short, jaunty stories make you feel just that bit better about being the clumsiest, dreamiest, least confident one.

Helen Simmons

Don't Forget Non Fiction

Non fiction is just as important and enjoyable as fiction, and can be a great way of getting reluctant readers interested in books – especially boys, suggests **Nicola Morgan**.

We do tend to forget non fiction when we're talking about the pleasures of reading. Sometimes we seem not to regard it as real reading. When I ask adults if they're keen readers, I often get the answer, 'No, not really. But I do like biographies – oh, and history, too…' I think we have to fight against this attitude. It's the quality of the writing that's important, not what it's about. There is no reason for viewing good non fiction as any less important than good fiction.

If we send a message to children that we don't think their chosen reading material counts, we will put them off reading altogether. This is crucial when we add two facts together: first, that boys more often tend to be reluctant readers and to have reading difficulties than girls, and second, that boys (and men) more often prefer reading non fiction.

With books for the very young, it's often hard to say which of the two categories a book falls into. And there's no point in trying to differentiate – they're all books, they all contain words (well, usually), and they all teach young children something about the world. But as children move on from picture books, the difference becomes a little clearer (though it's sometimes still not absolute). Children's preferences by that time have begun to become clear as well. Your child may be very interested in machines / cars / lifts / ladders, and distinctly uninterested in fairies and baby rabbits wearing trousers. Look for books that foster existing interests and link with possible new ones. Why should your child read a book that he or she doesn't have any interest in? Do you ever do that, unless forced to by your work?

Bear in mind that while we all read for pleasure, we each find pleasure in different things. Some people get pleasure from books about quantum mechanics; others from poetry; or fantasy; or novels based within a realistic setting. Once you accept that pleasure is our overriding motive for choosing a particular book, you will probably agree that we should allow children the same freedom. Besides, if we don't give children freedom in the books they read, we'll turn them off reading altogether. Books are not medicine.

Rant over. There's inspiring non fiction out there, especially for the age range covered by this guide. The list below contains some of the best. I have not divided it by age because it really depends on the child. Just browse and have fun together! ●

Arts, Sport and Hobbies

I Spy: Shapes in Art by Lucy Micklethwait (***UFBG*** 118)

My Animal Art Class by Nellie Shepherd

Ballet School / Gymnastics School by Naia Bray-Moffatt

The Magnificent I Can Read Music Book by Kate Petty, illustrated by Jennie Maizels

Starting Soccer by Helen Edom

My Daddy is a Pretzel: Yoga for Parents and Kids by Baron Baptiste, illustrated by Sophie Fatus

The Gardening Book by Jane Bull

Kids' First Cook Book from Dorling Kindersley

Life Experiences

Mummy Laid an Egg by Babette Cole (having a baby)

Why, Charlie Brown, Why? by Charles M. Schultz (having a very ill friend)

When Dinosaurs Die: A Guide to Understanding Death by Laurie Krasny Brown and Marc Brown (death)

The World

A Is for Africa by Ifeoma Onyefulu (***UFBG*** 66)

I Is for India by Prodeepta Das

The World Came to My Place Today by Jo Readman, illustrated by Ley Honor Roberts (***UFBG*** 199)

If the World Were a Village by David J. Smith and Shelagh Armstrong

The Global Garden by Kate Petty, illustrated by Jennie Maizels

Why Should I Recycle? by Jen Green, illustrated by Mike Gordon

What Are Rainbows Made Of? **Stepping Stones** series

Science and Maths

Think of a Number by Johnny Ball

Senses by Jinny Johnson

The Super Science Book by Kate Petty, illustrated by Jennie Maizels

Poo: A Natural History of the Unmentionable by Nicola Davies, illustrated by Neal Layton

Hair by Sally Kindberg

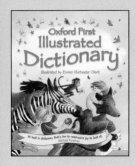

Animals

Big Blue Whale by Nicola Davies, illustrated by Nick Maland (*UFBG* 74)

Is a Blue Whale the Biggest Thing There Is? by Robert E. Wells (*UFBG* 248)

Think of an Eel by Karen Wallace, illustrated by Mike Bostock (*UFBG* 184)

Caterpillar Caterpillar, **Read and Wonder** series by Vivian French, illustrated by Charlotte Voake

All Pigs Are Beautiful by Dick King-Smith, illustrated by Anita Jeram

The Emperor's Egg by Martin Jenkins, illustrated by Jane Chapman

Surprising Sharks by Nicola Davies, illustrated by James Croft

General

First Thousand Words series by Heather Amery, illustrated by Stephen Cartwright (*UFBG* 234)

Oxford First Illustrated Dictionary

Oxford First Encyclopedia

How Things Work

Cars, Trucks and Things that Go by Richard Scarry (*UFBG* 80)

In Spectacular Cross-section by Stephen Biesty (*UFBG* 245)

What Is a Wall After All? by Judy Allen, illustrated by Alan Baron

Woolly Jumper: the Story of Wool by Meredith Hooper, illustrated by Katherine McEwen (*UFBG* 199)

History

Shakespeare / Nelson / The Beatles, etc. **Brilliant Brits** series by Richard Brassey

Knight / Pirate / Fighter Pilot, etc. **Tough Jobs** series by Helen Greathead, illustrated by Bob Dewar

Britannia: 100 Great Stories of British History by Geraldine McCaughrean, illustrated by Richard Brassey

Toys / Homes / Seaside Holidays, etc. **Start-up History** series by Stewart Ross

SPINDERELLA
Julia Donaldson, illustrated by Liz Pichon

Spinderella is a football-playing spider, but chaos reigns when her siblings try to play matches and their games disintegrate into brawling free-for-alls. The problem is that no one can count, and therefore cannot select teams of equal numbers. But Hairy Godmother is at hand to show Spinderella how to learn her numbers and sort everything out.

This slim, colourful book makes a great story for parent and child to read together, and later for the child to read alone. The numeracy theme extends into the back of the book with quizzes and games.

Sonia Benster

* * * * * * *

STANLEY BAGSHAW series Bob Wilson

'In Huddersgate (famed for its tramlines),
Up north where it's boring and slow,
Stanley Bagshaw resides with his Grandma
At number 4 Prince Albert Row'

Whether finding something huge in the canal, inadvertently saving Huddersgate Albion football team from defeat, foiling a robbery when shopping for pork pie and cheese, or unwittingly making an enormous wheel which floats over Huddersgate like an UFO, Stanley Bagshaw is a delightfully unaware anti-hero. The stories are told in rhyming couplets with colourful, witty, detailed pictures, occasional droll comments from the cat and comforting tea (featuring fish, peas and chips) from Grandma.

■ Look out for: *Stanley Bagshaw and the Fourteen-foot Wheel* and *Stanley Bagshaw and the Short-sighted Football Trainer*, among other titles.

Stanley Bagshaw and the fourteen-foot wheel
written and illustrated by BOB WILSON

These irresistible comic-strip stories, set in the flat-cap North, are great for reading aloud or for independent reading.

Caroline Pitcher

289

STINK: THE INCREDIBLE SHRINKING KID
Megan McDonald, illustrated by Peter Reynolds

This is a story about Judy Moody's younger brother James – or Stink, as he's affectionately known! He's the shortest kid in his year and is also shorter than his sister – something Judy enjoys pointing out. With sibling rivalry a major issue, a fluid story that's easy to follow, great illustrations – including short comic strips that tell Stink's fantasies – and lots of humour, especially puns, these stories are great for boys and girls who want chapter books that won't make them struggle too hard.

Leonie Flynn

> ■ There are two other **Stink** books so far: *Stink and the Incredible Super-Galactic Jawbreaker* and *Stink and the World's Worst Super-Stinky Sneaker.*

* * * * * * *

THE STINKY CHEESE MAN AND OTHER FAIRLY STUPID TALES
Jon Scieszka and Lane Smith

This book was a revelation when it was first published in 1992. Each story is a shameless inversion of a traditional fairy tale. 'The Ugly Duckling' is very short because she is ugly, and that's that; Jack forms a Faustian pact with the Giant, and the race between the tortoise and the hare continues to this day, because it isn't quite the race Aesop had envisaged.

In addition, the design of the book subverts all conventions – it's the Table of Contents that falls on Chicken Licken's head. Compulsively entertaining, it works best with children aware of the original stories – they'll revel in its ingenious wickedness.

Lindsey Fraser

THE STINKY CHEESE MAN *and other* FAIRLY STUPID TALES

- Chicken Licken
- The Really Ugly Duckling
- The Tortoise and the Hare
- Cinderumpelstiltskin
- Little Red Running Shorts
- Jack's Bean Problem
and much, much, more!

BY JON SCIESZKA & LANE SMITH

THE STORY OF EVERYTHING
Neal Layton

Bang! The universe expands – and so does this book, exploding in all directions! The momentum never stops, with flaps, moving parts, swirling letters and vibrant colours. Neal Layton brilliantly combines child-like illustration with sophisticated, quirky art and imaginative typography in a pop-up novelty book that is educational yet wonderfully irreverent and never patronising. Stars, sponges, swamps, mesopithecuses, mice, mammoths, humans, houses – there's plenty to enjoy with a child and to share with your friends... even if they're adults.

Sarah Manson

* * * * * * *

TAKING THE CAT'S WAY HOME
Jan Mark, illustrated by Paul Howard

William starts at Jane's school and begins bullying her. When he threatens to 'get' Jane and her friend, Andrea, they run away following the route that Jane's cat takes along the wall behind their houses. William follows but ends up lost and frightened. The girls' revenge is sweet as they watch a tearful William taken home by Jane's mum. This subtle and funny tale is written for small children bewildered by their first experience of bullying. It shows that bullies are cowards, and even the most timid of us can stand up to them if we are only brave and thoughtful enough.

Gill Vickery

THE THREE LITTLE WITCHES STORYBOOK
Georgie Adams, illustrated by Emily Bolam

The ideal bridge between picture books and short novels, this is a lively, funny, mischievous book, comprising eight mini-episodes, following the adventures of three little girl witches. Although the main characters are girls, other characters will enchant boy readers in equal measure, and everyone will love the puns, spells, rhymes and magic. The text and full-colour cartoon illustrations are beautifully integrated so that both leap around the pages. There are sound effects for young readers to join in with, making this the perfect shared experience.

Jon Appleton

* * * * * * *

THE THING IN THE BASEMENT
Michaela Morgan, illustrated by Doffy Weir

The first day at a new school is always a nail-biting time. But in Scott's case it is extraordinary and mysterious. Michaela Morgan has written a great story that gets right into the mind of a boy with an over-active imagination and a bad case of nerves. Late for assembly and soon lost in an echoing maze of unfamiliar corridors, Scott finds himself in a place that is hot, noisy and terrifying. Children will rejoice at the resolution of the story and delight in the final twist.

Karen Wallace

* * * * * * *

TIARA CLUB series Vivian French

The **Tiara Club** series is one of many developed recently for younger readers and the books serve an important purpose in exercising newly acquired reading skills through sympathetic characters and stories that resolve satisfactorily. The Royal Palace Academy for the 'eparation of Perfect Princesses provides the backdrop 'hese lively tales about a group of princesses 'ined to gain those all-important Tiara points.

Fraser

TILLY MINT TALES
Berlie Doherty, illustrated by Tony Ross

When Tilly Mint's mum goes out to work, she is minded by dotty yet oddly feisty Mrs Hardcastle. Once Mrs H begins to snore, magical things happen. Tilly meets Leaf Lords, learns to fly to Australia, rides a merry-go-round horse, travels on the white owl's back to send away the black bird of night, and has adventures with Dodo, Frog, Lizard and a Lion as gentle as milk.

These delightful stories, many of which include a poem or two, seamlessly mingle the real and imaginary worlds of the child, and have humorous and affectionate drawings by Tony Ross. They're also just the right length to be read at bedtime, but your audience may well want more than one. Berlie Doherty wrote these stories for Radio Sheffield, and they read aloud beautifully.

Caroline Pitcher

* * * * * * *

TITCHY WITCH AND THE STRAY DRAGON
Rose Impey, illustrated by Katharine McEwen

This engaging tale of a small, enthusiastic and occasionally accident-prone witch is one of a series of eight, written for very young readers. They are almost like small-format picture books so the choice of illustrator is crucial to the success of the story. Here we have a great team. The gentle tale of a child wanting a pet is given a twist by the house cat and witch's helper, Cat-a-bogus. Naturally, Cat-a-bogus is jealous of the baby dragon who turns up on the doorstep, in the same way an older child might be jealous of a new baby. In the end, a solution is found and everyone is happy, but not before the subjects of sibling rivalry, running away from home and finding compromises have all been addressed in a funny, charming way.

These books are difficult to write because the few words they contain have to work on many levels. Bravo, Titchy Witch!

Karen Wallace

■ There are many more titles in the series: *Titchy Witch and the Birthday Broomstick*; *Titchy Witch and the Bully Boggarts*; *Titchy Witch and the Disappearing Baby*; *Titchy Witch and the Frog Fiasco*; *Titchy Witch and the Get Better Spell* and *Titchy Witch and the Magic Party*.

THE TROUBLESOME TOOTH FAIRY
Sandi Toksvig, illustrated by Georgien Overwater

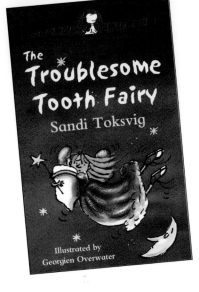

Jessica's granny is wonderfully batty. She goes line dancing, wears cowboy clothes and shares champagne with her grandaughter – though, of course, it's really lemonade poured into champagne glasses! When Jessica loses a tooth, Granny tells her a story about one of her own lost teeth, and the adventure she had with a trainee Tooth Fairy that ended up with her being taken to Tooth Fairy Land and almost never getting home again.

This has short chapters, easy vocabulary and a lovely, light-hearted story in which the tooth fairy might – or might not – be real.

Leonie Flynn

* * * * * *

THE TWITS see p.228.

* * * * * *

UG
Raymond Briggs

This is storytelling by comic strip, ideal for readers ready to move on from Briggs' *The Snowman* (*UFBG* 173) and *The Bear* (*UFBG* 210). Ug is an inventor and forward thinker, ridiculed for his outlandish ideas about cooking dead animals on the fire or skinning them to make soft trousers. Ug's dad Dug, mother Dugs and friend Ag cannot keep up with his energy and questioning spirit. The story has a rich seam of pathos as Ug's quest fails due to lack of technology. As well as the central joke of the Flintstones-style setting, there is the chance for children to empathise with Ug, an inquisitive child squashed by adults.

Geraldine Brennan

THE VELVETEEN RABBIT
Margery Williams, illustrated by William Nicholson

Williams' tale of the meaning of love was written soon after the First World War and is filled with a haunting sense of loss. It's a gentle and lovely book of a very English kind, with deftly written imagery of wildlife and the countryside. The little velveteen rabbit is loved so much by his boy that he becomes shapeless and balding. Eventually tossed aside by adults, the rabbit cries one real tear. In that instant a miracle takes place that children never fail to wonder at. It's no accident that the book has been a favourite for over 80 years.

Gill Vickery

VIOLET AND THE MEAN AND ROTTEN PIRATES
Richard Hamilton, illustrated by Sam Hearn

Violet is found abandoned as a baby by a bunch of the meanest and rottenest pirates that ever were. They take her in and teach her their piratical ways – and soon she is spitting, tying knots and scrambling through the rigging with the best of them. The one thing she is not allowed to do is join the pirates on a raid – or at least, not until she's eight years old…

This is a hilarious story for fluent readers – and a great book to be read in instalments to younger children. The pirates are scary and endearing in turns, throwing their victims overboard, then having a nice cup of tea.

Susan Reuben

Pink Books and Poo Books

It's true that many children do fall into the stereotype, with girls preferring books about princesses and ponies and fairies, and boys going for football and fart jokes. But however many of these sometimes formulaic books publishers may churn out, there really is a world beyond, says **Leonie Flynn**.

An alien walking into any large bookshop in this country would assume that once young children approach school age they are strictly regulated by gender as to the content of the books they're allowed to read. Actually, looking at most adult fiction shelves, they might even consider the same applies there. The prevalence of chick-lit and aga-sagas for women (all with pastel-coloured covers) and action-adventure and guns for men (all with grim-faced ex-SAS types in Noir-esque moody lighting) is overwhelming.

There may be fewer guns in the books for six-year-olds, but every other stereotype lives and breathes, with fart and poo-obsessed heroes, characters who relish being naughty or are budding secret agents. The girls' shelves are lined with pink, pretty, sparkly books, often about princesses, ponies, fairies, or some combination of all three. And all these books do have their place, just as in adult reading, where sometimes you want an undemanding book, or to wallow in gentle things one day and yet read about gang-crime in London's less salubrious suburbs the next. That's fine – of course it is.

If you've got a reluctant reader of either gender then quite often the key to their enjoyment of reading will be precisely these books – gender-specific series fiction. Quite why scatological books should be what boys want to read is something of a mystery to some parents, who find themselves distinctly uncomfortable with the content of many of these stories. The same applies to the pink, sparkly 'girly' ones. Do you really want your little girl just reading about make-up and finding the perfect pink pen? (Because fairies only write in pink, of course.)

My advice is to let the child in question work through what is usually just a phase in their reading, and then gently encourage an interest in less narrowly stereotypical stories...

So, you want something a little less production-line, yet you've still got a boy who wants jokes and a girl who loves pink. Quite often, specific authors are the best things to look out for. Ian Whybrow writes great books for boys, whether it's the **Little Wolf** series (*UFBG* 257) or his **Books for Boys** series. Jacqueline Wilson is famous for writing books that girls love, yet her stories for younger readers are equally accessible by both genders, and *Cliffhanger* (*UFBG* 218) is a particularly great story for boys. Steve Cole is another boy-oriented writer, his books full of jokes so bad that

The Beano would blush to include them! Ditto Tony Mitton, whose rhyming stories about knights and giants are brilliant for boys.

Girls, partially because they usually find their reading 'feet' earlier than boys, have more choice, and with Berlie Doherty's *Tilly Mint Tales* (*UFBG* 293), Dick King-Smith's animal stories, *Judy Moody* (*UFBG* 250), *My Naughty Little Sister* (*UFBG* 268), Magdalen Nabb's **Josie Smith** stories and many more, should always be able to find something of interest in any bookshop.

Lauren Child is loved by both boys and girls, but that's because she's a genius – her books seem to be very girly, until you sit a boy down to read one, then it's apparent that they're just good books. Which is the key. Once the reading habit is in place, the book world is your child's playground, and it will be the story that counts, not the free glittery wings, and not the amount of poo jokes per page. ●

Pink Books (sugar and spice and all things pink and sparkly)

Felicity Wishes series by Emma Thomson (*UFBG* 229)

Little Princesses series by Katie Chase (*UFBG* 256)

Magic Pony Carousel series by Poppy Shire (*UFBG* 259)

Secret Fairy series by Penny Dann (*UFBG* 166)

Princess Poppy series by Janey Jones (*UFBG* 159)

Rainbow Magic series by Daisy Meadows (*UFBG* 280)

Pony Mad Princess series by Diane Kimpton

Tiara Club series by Vivian French (*UFBG* 292)

Poo Books (snips and snails and not a fairy in sight)

Captain Underpants series by Dav Pilkey (*UFBG* 216)

The Adventures of Super Diaper Baby by Dav Pilkey

Dirty Bertie series by Alan MacDonald, illustrated by David Roberts (*UFBG* 225)

The Story of the Little Mole Who Knew It Was None of His Business by Werner Holzwarth (*UFBG* 176)

Horrid Henry series by Francesca Simon (*UFBG* 242)

The Giggler Treatment by Roddy Doyle (*UFBG* 238)

Fungus the Bogeyman by Raymond Briggs

Yuck series by Matt and Dave, illustrated by Nigel Baines

WHEN WE WERE VERY YOUNG
A.A. Milne, illustrated by E.H. Shepard

Before Dr Seuss there was A.A. Milne – and before *Winnie-the-Pooh* there were these charming collections of nonsense poems. Children will love the characters: Alice, who's marrying a guard at Buckingham Palace; the three little foxes who lost their soxes, and James James Morrison Morrison Weatherby George Dupree, who 'took great care of his mother though he was only three'. Adults will enjoy the invocation of a bygone age, one of milkmaids and lavender sellers, where nurses and nannies reign supreme – all brought to life in Ernest Shepard's wonderful drawings.

Laura Hutchings

* * * * * * *

WHERE'S WALLY? Martin Handford

If you want to keep a small child quiet, put him or her in front of a **Where's Wally?** book. The intricately detailed illustrations contain thousands of little figures, but only one of them is Wally. Sometimes he's easy to find, but sometimes he seems to be not there at all – especially in the pages that appear to be all little Wally figures (though there is only ever one real Wally). First published in 1987, the books have grown to become a global phenomenon, with Wally re-named in each country – in France as Charlie, in Germany as Walter and most successfully in America as Waldo, where he even had a TV series! The later books contain more-complex searches, for Wally's friends as well as for some objects. Most importantly, **Where's Wally?** books are full of visual puns and they encourage concentration as well as the visual interpretation of story.

Leonie Flynn

WHIZZIWIG
Malorie Blackman

Whizziwig is an alien. Her spaceship gets hit by some space debris and she makes an emergency landing on Earth. On Ben's roof, to be exact. Ben takes a little while to get used to Whizziwig – especially as she is a 'wish-giver', and the only way she can fix her ship is to grant wishes. Except you can only wish for things for other people – and you also have to be very careful exactly what you wish for. As Ben finds out when he ends up with a garden full of bicycles... Taking Whizziwig to school, though it seemed like a good idea, complicates things, and Ben has to do some fast thinking to save her from the school bully.

Malorie Blackman tells stories with wit and panache. Giggle-aloud funny, yet also thought-provoking, this is perfect for boys and girls eager to read something a little more challenging. There is a sequel, *Whizziwig Returns*, and the two books are available bound into one.

Leonie Flynn

* * * * * * *

WINDOW
Jeannie Baker

Don't be alarmed by books without text. Here, everything you need is in the pictures. Baker's collages use real elements from recognisable settings – this is Australia, but it could be anywhere – so we feel part of the world of the book. The view from each double-page spread is from the same window. Over time, characters stand and watch, as we do, the changes to the landscape outside. Bush gives way to houses, to shops, and so on. The characters grow up, too. Drawing on visual clues, we can make our own observations about the nature of change and the importance of conservation.

Jon Appleton

Everybody's Favourite...

WINNIE-THE-POOH
A.A. Milne, illustrated by E.H. Shepard

It's hard to imagine that anybody consulting the *UFBG* isn't already familiar with the wonderful, timeless, iconic Winnie-the-Pooh, and doesn't have their own affectionate feelings for and memories of him. But just in case there are still any Pooh-less readers out there, let me just say that these stories about a boy and his bear contain some of the most endearing and delightful characters ever put in a book, within stories that are as relevant, fresh, wise and gloriously funny today as when they were first written. Every child deserves to get to know Winnie-the-Pooh and his friends. So, for that matter, does every grown-up – this is a book to rediscover by reading it with your child.

Catherine Robinson

In our enthusiasm for the groundbreaking, the surprising, the new, we can forget the treasures that have surrounded us for years. One such is *Winnie-the-Pooh* and its companion volume *The House at Pooh Corner*. The Bear of Very Little Brain first appeared in 1926. Sadly, he is now known to many children only in the over-coloured and mawkish Disney version. It's time to Reclaim the Original, featuring the charm of E.H. Shepard's illustrations and the wit of A.A. Milne's text with its Many Capital Letters for Important Things.

What is very special about the **Winnie-the-Pooh** books is that both adults and children relish them. It's a real treat to read them aloud to a child, and then follow through with a visit to the verse collections *When We Were Very Young* (*UFBG* 298) and *Now We Are Six*. Many a grown-up is still chanting verses from these collections, still playing Poohsticks and still keeping a wary eye out for Heffalumps – and is ready to pass on these treasures to each new generation.

Michaela Morgan

THE WISHING CHAIR ADVENTURES
Enid Blyton

Two children wander into an antique shop one day and find an incredible chair that will take them wherever they wish to go. So they keep it in their playroom, and whisk off on adventures whenever they can. Of course, things don't always go according to plan, and they frequently meet nasty creatures who try to take the chair and cause all sorts of other trouble.

This is the first in a series of three books about the wishing chair, which have the trademark Blyton features of rollicking, adventurous storylines and a fast-paced, unchallenging text.

Susan Reuben

* * * * * * *

THE WOMAN WHO WON THINGS
Allan Ahlberg, illustrated by Katharine McEwen

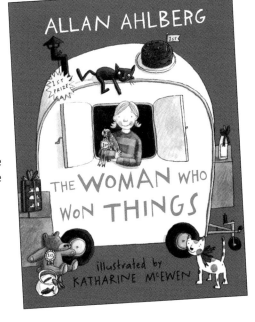

You haven't encountered the Gaskitt Family stories? Start right here. Ahlberg, that master of tales for young children, excels at capturing ordinary domesticity with a twist. Things go wrong, mysteries crop up, surprises startle, and words and pictures do amazing things from spread to spread. Short lines and short chapters make this easy to get into. Available in colour and small-format black-and-white, the books in this series look so incredibly enticing, and Katharine McEwen's illustrations have a totally contemporary but recognisable look that will have wide appeal.

Jon Appleton

Picture Books For Ever

Just because your child can read the words now, don't dismiss picture books! There are some great picture books for older children, says **Prue Goodwin**, and everything to be gained from keeping them in the habit of reading pictures as well as words.

I was sharing a picture book with an eager little group at an infant school the other day when one or two of them started quietly to weep. The book was *Don't Let Go!* by Jeanne Willis and Tony Ross: a simple tale of learning to ride a bike. At least, that's what it seemed to be about – but something in the book moved these listeners to tears. Perhaps the fact that this was a little group of *parents* at an infant school had something to do with it. A couple of dozen words and some typically amusing pictures had the power and effect usually associated with a beautifully crafted sonnet. And why should it not? All literature has the potential to engage readers emotionally, and 'picture book' is a genre of literature. Children's books in general are often referred to lightly, as though writing for children is easy or insignificant, and picture books are often treated as though they should be 'grown out of'. However, they should never be perceived as solely for young children; many picture books are way beyond their understanding.

The best picture books are multi-layered, with both words and pictures carrying a wealth of possible meanings. Despite this richness, children are sometimes discouraged from continuing to read picture books. Which is a great shame. So if you think picture books should be left behind when a child has learnt to read, think again. Some of the most enjoyable and challenging titles are intended for six- and seven-year-olds, and we would be doing our children a grave disservice if we encouraged them to abandon this splendid and satisfying genre of literature.

A picture book is a lot more than a lavishly illustrated story. To understand a picture book, readers are required to combine meanings revealed through both words and images. When there are several layers of meaning in a picture book, the same book can be enjoyed in different ways. Read, for example, *Zagazoo* by Quentin Blake (*UFBG* 201). The story is very entertaining for all readers, but only an adult could possibly fully appreciate the whole meaning. As children grow older, picture books can only enhance their development as readers, develop their visual literacy and speed their journey towards literary competence.

Children who learn to read quite quickly need to have their attention drawn to other aspects of narrative, such as setting, character and themes in the storyline. Many picture books provide visual examples of these literary devices that enable inexperienced readers to understand meanings created beyond the literal. For example, in Helen Cooper's *Pumpkin Soup* (*UFBG* 160), look how cleverly she depicts three individual characters, a variety of settings and the thematic threads of the plot. In her more-recent book, *Delicious*, she even has a sub-plot running parallel to the main story, making it a very sophisticated read for the under sevens.

I could go on – but where would I stop? To hinder children's access to their literary heritage would be criminal. Make sure, whatever their age or ability – and long after they have passed the age of seven – that children always have picture books in their reading diet. ●

Picture Books for Older Readers

The Wolves in the Walls by Neil Gaiman, illustrated by Dave McKean

The Day I Swapped My Dad for Two Goldfish by Neil Gaiman, illustrated by Dave McKean (*UFBG* 221)

In Spectacular Cross-section series by Stephen Biesty (*UFBG* 245)

Greek Myths by Marcia Williams

The Adventures of Robin Hood by Marcia Williams

How to Live Forever by Colin Thompson (*UFBG* 243)

Meerkat Mail by Emily Gravett (*UFBG* 261)

Zoo by Anthony Browne (*UFBG* 305)

Asterix books by René Goscinny, illustrated by A. Uderzo

Tintin books by Hergé

THE WORST WITCH series
Jill Murphy

A story set in a school for witches long before Harry Potter came on to the scene. Mildred Hubble is always in trouble; she's the worst witch at Miss Cackle's Academy for Witches. But Mildred turns out to be a hero when she bravely saves the school from disaster – and gains a half-day holiday for everyone for her pains.

Girls fight over this book, and want the sequels as soon as they can get their hands on them. Murphy writes and illustrates with great humour and without the sense of menace present in some of the **Harry Potter** stories; these are books that children know are not to be taken too seriously.

Wendy Cooling

> ■ Read them all! The books in the series are: *The Worst Witch*; *The Worst Witch Strikes Again*; *A Bad Spell for the Worst Witch*; *The Worst Witch All at Sea* and *The Worst Witch Saves the Day*.

* * * * * * *

YOUNG ROBIN HOOD
Ian Whybrow, illustrated by Tony Ross

Ever wondered what Robin Hood was like as a kid, when he was Robin Goodfellow and his band of skinny scapegrace mates consisted of Daniel Tucker (Friar Tuck), William Bartlett (called Scarlett because of his hot temper) and John Little – who wasn't so little? The short chapters include funny stories about each of the would-be Merry Men and a plot involving an archery contest, a lump of garlic and a lot of 'twang'.

Written as part of the **Books for Boys** series, from the first page this promises no kissing or cuddling and lots of gallop and, yes… even more twang!

Leonie Flynn

ZEUS ON THE LOOSE John Dougherty

Alex makes a temple of Zeus at school out of a cereal packet and loo rolls. Then one of his classmates accidentally says a prayer asking Zeus himself to turn up... and he does. The comedy potential of trying to hide a genuine, full-sized Greek god in an ordinary primary school is fully exploited. Zeus is quite determined to stick to the usual Greek god-like activities, including receiving sacrifices and starting wars. With the help of some roast-beef flavoured crisps and a vaulting horse from the gym, Alex manages to keep things under control... more or less.

This is a fantastically silly book that had me laughing out loud in the first 30 seconds, and repeatedly throughout the rest of the story. Adventures continue in *Zeus to the Rescue*.

Susan Reuben

* * * * * * *

ZOO Anthony Browne

Who are zoos really for? That's the question that lingers throughout this marvellous picture book, and which stings at the end. A family make a day visit to the zoo, but it isn't the happy diversion they are expecting. Miserable animals look out between bars. The family isn't amused – what about the animals? Browne is renowned for his dark, dry wit, that pokes fun at the ironies of modern life, and which incisively dissects family life. He delights in the surreal. Not to everyone's taste, his stunning picture books for older readers are nevertheless memorable and thought-provoking.

Jon Appleton

Pop-up Books for Older Children

The Wizard of Oz by Frank L. Baum and Robert Sabuda

The Night Before Christmas by Clement C. Moore and Robert Sabuda

Captain Scurvy's Most Dastardly Pop-up Pirate Ship by Nick Denchfield and Steve Cox

The Global Garden by Kate Petty and Jennie Maizels

Fungus the Bogeyman Plop-up Book by Raymond Briggs

NOTES ON CONTRIBUTORS

GILES ANDREAE has written many best-selling picture books including *Rumble in the Jungle*, *Giraffes Can't Dance* and *Pants*. However, he is possibly best known as the creator of the stickman poet, Purple Ronnie. Giles lives in London and Cornwall with his wife and four young children.

NOGA APPLEBAUM is completing a PhD in Children's Literature at Roehampton University. Her short stories have been short-listed for several awards, and in 2005 she won the London Writers' Competition in the Children's Literature category.

JON APPLETON has worked as a reviewer and editor of children's books for over ten years. He had lots of fun editing *The Ultimate Book Guide* for 8–12s when working at A & C Black, and just as much fun (though less stress) contributing to *The Ultimate Teen Book Guide* and this volume. He works as Senior Editor at Orion Children's Books.

EILEEN ARMSTRONG is a school librarian in Northumberland, a reviewer and feature writer for a variety of professional journals and author of *Fully Booked: Reader Development and the Secondary School LRC*. She is currently chair of the School Library Association.

LAURA ATKINS lives in Rottingdean and has edited children's books, done postgraduate research on children's publishing and taught many courses. A freelance children's book consultant, she also runs conferences at the NCRCL at Roehampton University.

LIZ ATTENBOROUGH was a children's book publisher for 24 years, including 12 years as Puffin Editor. She was Director of the National Year of Reading (1998–1999) and now manages Talk To Your Baby, the early language campaign of the National Literacy Trust.

IAN BECK has illustrated and written over 60 books for children including several nursery-rhyme collections. He published his first novel for children, *The Secret History of Tom Trueheart: Boy Adventurer*, in 2006.

SONIA BENSTER, proprietor for 31 years of the specialist Huddersfield Children's Bookshop, is a regular reviewer and has been the judge for several major children's book prizes.

MIKE BOSTOCK graduated with a degree in illustration from Bath Academy of Art, and has since illustrated and written a number of picture books for children. He is a winner of the Kurt Maschler award and lives in London.

TONY BRADMAN has been involved in children's books as a writer, editor of anthologies of short stories and poetry, and reviewer for over 25 years. He has written for all ages, and his books have been published all over the world.

GERALDINE BRENNAN is Books Editor of *The Times Educational Supplement* and has judged many children's book awards, including the 2006 Branford Boase Award and the 2006 Costa Children's Book of the Year.

MISHTI CHATTERJEE is the director of Mantra Lingua, a publisher of dual-language children's books and multimedia resources. Mantra publishes award-winning titles in over 40 dual-language editions and are the recent winners of the 2005 and 2006 WOW Awards.

JANE CHURCHILL is Director of BookIt!, the children's programme of the Cheltenham Literature Festival and is an editorial advisor and scout for a French publisher.

STEPHEN COLE grew up loving books, went to UEA to read more of them, and ended up writing and editing them for a living. In other walks of life he has been an editor

of BBC children's magazines and commissioner of Doctor Who novels, videos and audiobooks.

WENDY COOLING see p.7.

CHRIS D'LACEY has been writing children's fiction for approximately 12 years. He is probably best known for his series of fantasy books about dragons. In July 2002, he was awarded an honorary doctorate by the University of Leicester (where he worked for 28 years) for his services to children's fiction.

In the 15 years since her first book was published (*A Squash and a Squeeze*), **JULIA DONALDSON** has become one of the world's most acclaimed children's authors. Her most famous title is *The Gruffalo*, with illustrator Axel Scheffler. Although perhaps best known for her picture book texts, she has written lots of fiction for older children, too.

JANE DOONAN has been writing, reviewing, and lecturing on the aesthetics and dynamics of picture books for over 20 years. Her studies of the works of picture-book makers and illustrators appear in international journals, and she has contributed to major works of reference. She published *Looking at Pictures in Picture Books* in 1992.

MALACHY DOYLE is Irish, lives in Wales and is married to an Englishwoman. He writes teenage books, young fiction and picture books. *The Dancing Tiger* won the Nestlé Silver Award, and his most recent picture book is *When a Zeeder Met a Xyder*.

JULIA ECCLESHARE is Children's Books Editor of the *Guardian* and co-director of the Centre for Literacy in Primary Education. She is the author of *Treasure Islands: 'Woman's Hour' Guide to Children's Reading, Beatrix Potter to Harry Potter: Portraits of Children's*

Writers, and co-author with Nicholas Tucker of *The Rough Guide to Books for Teenagers*. In 2000, Julia was awarded the Eleanor Farjeon Award for her outstanding contribution to children's books.

PATRICIA ELLIOTT's novels for older children include *Murkmere* and *The Ice Boy*. Her latest is *The Night Walker*, a supernatural thriller set in contemporary London. Patricia teaches writing workshops and lives in West London with her husband, two sons and dog.

LINDSEY FRASER see p.7.

VIVIAN FRENCH is the author of over 200 books, ranging from stories for toddlers up to teenage novels. She likes non fiction just as much as fiction, and plays and poems as well... and when she's not writing she's usually reading. Or talking...

SARAH FROST MELLOR is the mother of a five-year-old tomboy who eats books for breakfast and had much to say about the reviews Sarah wrote for this guide. In her spare time, of which she hasn't nearly enough, Sarah is writing a crime novel.

NIKKI GAMBLE is Associate Consultant at the Institute of Education, the University of London and Director of Write Away. She is also a committee member on the British section of the International Board on Books for Young People (IBBY).

ADÈLE GERAS has written more than 90 books for young people, and three books for adults. She lives in Manchester, and has two daughters and two grandchildren.

PIPPA GOODHART is the author of over 50 books for children, including early readers, novels and picture books. *You Choose* was chosen by Bookstart as an ideal book for young children.

PRUE GOODWIN has been a teacher in primary and middle schools, an advisory teacher and a university lecturer in literacy education. She currently works as a freelance lecturer in literacy and a consultant on children's books, and works part time at the University of Reading.

DEBORAH HALLFORD is a freelance project consultant specialising in children's literature and arts projects, and co-editor of *Outside In: Children's Books in Translation* and *Universal Verse: Poetry for Children*.

ELIZABETH HAMMILL is a Founding Director of Seven Stories, the Centre for Children's Books, a project that she initiated and developed over ten years as Artistic Director. Currently establishing the Centre's collection, she brings her earlier experiences as a children's bookseller, literary festival programmer, critic and lecturer to all her work.

ANTONIA HONEYWELL is the proud originator of two unpublished novels and two small children. She cherishes hopes that the former will make her fortune, but suspects that she may have to rely on the latter for that, too.

LAURA HUTCHINGS is Head of English at a prep school in north London. Four nephews (Alex, Colin, Robert and David) and one niece (Emma) have been instrumental in acquainting her with many of the books recommended here.

KATIE JENNINGS is a children's fiction and non-fiction editor at a certain London publishing house (which just happens to publish *The UFBG*). Like most people in children's book publishing, she owns a cat.

ARIEL KAHN teaches creative writing at various universities, including courses in crafting picture books and comics. He has published several short stories and poems, and is currently working on his first novel.

PATRICIA LEGAN works in a prep school in London developing (teaching) reading. She loves reading to the younger boys and gains extra pleasure when they realise they can read back to her!

YZANNE MACKAY prepared for her contribution to this book by spending ten years editing publications on Bulgarian economics and Iraqi politics. She now writes murder-mystery games from home.

SARAH MANSON runs a literary agency specialising in fiction for children aged eight and above. She worked in publishing for ten years and as a chartered school librarian for eight years.

KELLY MCKAIN has written over 20 books for children and teens, including the **Mermaid Rock**, **Totally Lucy** and **Pony Camp Diaries** series. She loves being a full time author – the writing itself is such fun, the school visits are great, and it's a licence to be nosy!

MARGARET MEEK (SPENCER) is Reader Emeritus at the Institute of Education, the University of London. She was Reviews Editor of *The School Librarian* for two decades and recipient of the Eleanor Farjeon Award. Among her publications are *Learning to Read*, a book for parents and teachers, and *How Texts Teach What Readers Learn* (her favourite).

PHILIPPA MILNES-SMITH is a literary agent and children's specialist at LAW (Lucas Alexander Whitley). She has worked for many years in children's publishing and was previously Managing Director of Puffin.

TONY MITTON is a children's poet and picture book writer who also performs his work in schools, libraries and at festivals. He has written many collections of poems, humorous tales in verse and verse picture books.

MICHAELA MORGAN has written over 100 fiction, non-fiction, picture books and poetry books for children. Her work is published internationally and has been short-listed for the Children's Book Award and the Blue Peter Book Award.

NICOLA MORGAN see p.7.

HELEN NORRIS found her way into the world of children's book publishing by working for Philippa Milnes-Smith at LAW. She now works in the foreign rights department at Usborne Books.

JANETTA OTTER-BARRY is editorial director of Frances Lincoln Children's Books. The best-known books on her list are *Amazing Grace* by Mary Hoffman and *Black Ships Before Troy* by Rosemary Sutcliff. Janetta has two teenage daughters, on whom she tries out her publishing ideas.

CAROLINE PITCHER is a storymaker. Her books range from illustrated stories such as *The Winter Dragon* and *Lord of the Forest*, to novels such as *Mine*, *The Gods Are Watching* and *The Shaman Boy*.

Growing up on Sark gave **MARTIN REMPHRY** a fertile imagination, which helps when it comes to illustrating children's books. He has always drawn instead of writing as he's a terrible speller, but he keep promising one day to write the stories he started as a child.

CATHERINE ROBINSON's first book, *Lizzie Oliver*, was published in 1987. Recent titles include the teen novel *Tin Grin* and its sequel *Fat Chance*. Catherine lives in north Wales with her husband and teenage son.

MICHAEL ROSEN is one of Britain's best-loved childrens' poets. He is also a radio broadcaster and performer. His many titles include the poetry collections *Quick, Let's Get Out of Here* and *You Wait Till I'm Older Than You!* and the picture-book classic, *We're Going on a Bear Hunt*. In 2007 he was named the fifth Children's Laureate.

KATHRYN ROSS see p.7.

TONY ROSS Born in 1938 in London, just in time for the war. Art school in Liverpool, just in time for rock 'n' roll. Then advertising for four years, and when that went pear-shaped, taught graphic design at Manchester Poly. Earliest published work was cartoons in *Punch* and other mags, with the first of about 800 books being published around 1973. TV series worked on include *Towser*, *Dr Xargle*, *Horrid Henry*, and *The Little Princess*. Some awards and exhibitions, mainly overseas. I love Siamese cats.

NICK SHARRATT has illustrated all kinds of children's books, from board books for babies to teenage fiction. He has worked with lots of authors, most notably Jacqueline Wilson, and he writes his own picture books, too.

HELEN SIMMONS currently works in a small independent bookshop in Bath. She has been involved with children's books for most of her career, which has included driving a bus full of books and authors around Scotland and being a school librarian.

MADELYN TRAVIS is Website Features Editor for Booktrust and Associate Editor of *The Journal of Children's Literature Studies*. Madelyn and her three-year-old son Samuel read together every day, and the picture books she has reviewed in this guide are among his current favourites.

At age ten, **SIMON-PETER TRIMARCO** discovered reading and ran away to fantasyland whenever he could. He now works for The Kilburn Bookshop in London advising people what to read and what (really, they should know better) not to read.

KAYE UMANSKY has written over 100 books, including novels, plays and music books. She lives in London with her husband, daughter and two cats called Alfie and Heathcliff.

ELEANOR UPDALE is the author of the award-winning **Montmorency** series of historical novels for older children and adults. She is a patron of the Prince of Wales Arts & Kids Foundation, and a trustee of the charity Listening Books.

GILL VICKERY won The Fidler First Novel Award with her book *The Ivy Crown*. Her passion for Italian art is reflected in her story, 'Angelino's Snowman', and in the teenage collection *In the Frame*. Her current novel is also set in Italy.

KAREN WALLACE has published over 170 books and won a number of awards. Her work ranges from fiction to non fiction, from picture books to teenage novels. She also writes for children's television.

JEANNE WILLIS wrote her first book when she was five. She had her first picture book published when she was 21 by Andersen Press and has now written over 100 books for children including poetry and novels. She is married with two children and lives in north London with three cats in assorted colours.

EDGARDO ZAGHINI has an MA in Children's Literature, is a chartered librarian and author of *Pop-Ups: A Guide to Novelty Books*, *The Children's Book Handbook*, *Outside In: Children's Books in Translation* and *Universal Verse: Poetry for Children*. He has been a Committee member of IBBY and the CBHS (Children's Books History Society).

JONNY ZUCKER writes for children and teenagers. His work includes the **Festival Time** series and the **Venus Spring** series. Along the way, he has worked as a stand-up comedian and primary school teacher.

ACKNOWLEDGEMENTS

It will come as no surprise that this guide represents the hard work of a huge number of people, and the support of many others. Beginning, of course, with our 72 contributors. A rather smaller army worked on this than on previous volumes, but made up for it with massive talent and generosity. Needless to say, this is their book.

Then to the *UBG*s' most loyal friend, our agent Philippa Milnes-Smith, who has nursed the *UBG* project from the very first and – with her assistants Helen Mulligan, Helen Norris and Ayesha Mobin – has taken such good care of us in the lively years since.

At A & C Black, huge thanks to our editors Susila Baybars and Katie Jennings: they have given this guide – like its predecessor – vast amounts of their time and energy. Their good judgment has served us and these books tremendously well.

Also at A & C Black, special thanks to Rebecca Caine, who has got people talking about the guides, has taken us on the road to festivals, and generally reminded us that the books do have a life after publication.

The wonderful cover features artwork by Lydia Monks and the introduction is by Julia Donaldson – we're thrilled to have the work of people we so admire featuring prominently in the *UFBG*.

Thanks also to Michelle Canatella, who designed the inside pages. We think they look fantastic.

Many thanks to Anthony Reuben for his great forbearance at the growing piles of books in the house and to Isaac for being our top baby book tester.

To Laura, for help conventional (writing entries, reading many, many books) and unconventional (keeping Leonie in order, managing wayward plumbers, etc.). Basically for everything, as usual.

Also to the people at ICONS, for keeping Danny gainfully employed while work on this book was going

on. Likewise all at Arnold House – especially headmasters Nicholas Allen and Vivian Thomas – for keeping Leonie employed and providing the ideal setting for her to hone her book-recommending skills.

To all our friends and colleagues who have helped with this selection, thank you. To Chester, for not minding too much when the *UFBG* insisted on intruding in his holiday. And to The Kilburn Bookshop for supplying most of the books recommended herein – Simon and Sarah, you're stars!

We were in a position to compile the first two books entirely through our real passion for good children's books. After all, what better way could there be to express that passion than by assembling hundreds of people to rave noisily about their favourite reads, page after page? But for this volume we felt that, as well as having recommendations of books by people who loved them, we also needed to take into account the fact that the parents, teachers, librarians, etc. who would be reading the guide may be looking for answers to practical questions: What should I look for in a picture book? What's a good book for a child just starting to read? Why are nursery rhymes important?... And for this we needed a specialised panel of contributors, with expert knowledge of areas from baby books to early literacy. The features they've written in many ways provide the guide's backbone, and we thank them for this important work. (And in the case of Margaret Meek, for some wonderful correspondence, too.)

We've been especially fortunate to have worked with the people who agreed to take on the roles of the book's advisers: Wendy Cooling, Lindsey Fraser and Kathryn Ross, and Nicola Morgan. Their help has been generous and robust, their advice hugely wise, and more appreciated than we can say.

For permission to reproduce copyright material in *The Ultimate First Book Guide*, the publisher thanks:

ANDERSEN PRESS for permission to reproduce the illustration on p.65 by David McKee from *Elmer*. Additional thanks for permission to reproduce the following covers: on p.226, *The Dog in the Diamond Collar* by Rebecca Lisle; on p.302, *Don't Let Go* by Jeanne Willis and Tony Ross; on p.97, *Elmer* by David McKee; on p.38, *Elmer's Colours* by David McKee; on p.103, *Frog is Frog* and *Frog is Hero* by Max Velthuijs; on p.168, *Frog in Winter* by Max Velthuijs; on p.40, *From Acorn to Zoo* by Satoshi Kitamura; on p.110, *Halibut Jackson* by David Lucas; on p.116, *Hungry! Hungry! Hungry!* by Malachy Doyle, illustrated by Paul Hess; on p.48, *I Want My Potty* by Tony Ross; on p.151, *The Opposite* by Tom MacRae, illustrated by Elena Odrioza; on p.158, *The Polar Express* by Chris Van Allsburg; on p.193, *Who's in the Loo?* by Jeanne Willis, illustrated by Adrian Reynolds.

ANOVA BOOKS for permission to reproduce the following covers: on p.124, *Little Red* by Lynn Roberts, illustrated by David Roberts, © Pavilion Children's Books 2005; on p.176, *The Story of the Little Mole Who Knew it Was None of His Business* by Warner Holzwarth, illustrated by Wolf Erlbruch, © Pavilion Children's Books 1989.

BAREFOOT BOOKS for permission to reproduce the spread that appears on p.13 from *Bear in a Square* by Stella Blackstone. Text © 1998 by Stella Blackstone. Illustrations © 1998 by Debbie Harter. Additional thanks for permission to reproduce the following cover: on p.270, *The Gigantic Turnip* by Alexei Tolstoy. Illustrations © 1998 Niamh Sharkey.

BARN OWL BOOKS for permission to reproduce the cover of *Stanley Bagshaw and the Fourteen-foot Wheel* by Bob Wilson, on p.289.

BLOOMSBURY PUBLISHING PLC for permission to reproduce the following covers: on p.79, *Can You Hear the Sea?* by Judy Cumberbatch, illustrated by Ken Wilson-Max; on p.221, *The Day I Swapped My Dad For Two Goldfish* by Neil Gaiman, illustrated by Dave McKean; on p.169, *Leo's Dream* by Antonie Schneider, illustrated by Helga Bansch; on p.145, *No Matter What* by Debi Gliori; on p.277, *Polly's Running Away Book* by Frances Thomas, illustrated by Sally Gardner; on p.187, *Two Left Feet* by Adam Stower; on p.169, *The Wizard, the Ugly and the Book of Shame* by Pablo Bernasconi; on p.302, *The Wolves in the Walls* by Neil Gaiman, illustrated by Dave McKean.

DAVID HIGHAM for permission to reproduce the spread that appears on p.180 from *That Pesky Rat* © 2002 Lauren Child and the following covers: on p.82, *I Will Not Ever Never Eat a Tomato* © 2000 Lauren Child; on p.217, *Clarice Bean, That's Me* © 1999 Lauren Child. All titles published by Orchard Books.

EGMONT BOOKS for permission to reproduce the following covers: on p.66, *Aaaarrgghh, Spider!* by Lydia Monks; on p.231, *Dilly and the School Play* by Tony Bradman, illustrated by Susan Hellard; on p.235, *Flat Stanley* by Jeff Brown, illustrated by Scott Nash; on p.244, *How to Write Really Badly* by Anne Fine; on p.231, *Long Grey Norris* by Malachy Doyle, illustrated by Sholto Walker; on p.136, *Mr Tickle, Mr Bump, Mr Greedy* and *Mr Bounce* in the **Mr Men** series by Roger Hargreaves; on p.137, *Mr Wolf's Week* by Colin Hawkins; on p.42, *Muddlewitch Does Magic Tricks* by Nick Sharratt; on p.231, *My Brother Bernadette* by Jacqueline Wilson, illustrated by David Roberts; on p.268, *My Naughty Little Sister* by Dorothy Edwards, illustrated by Shirley Hughes; on p.275, *The Owl*

Who Was Afraid of the Dark by Jill Tomlinson, illustrated by Paul Howard; on p.281, *The Real Tilly Beany* by Annie Dalton, illustrated by Kate Sheppard; on p.303, *The Adventures of Tintin: The Black Island* by Hergé; on p.58, *Thomas Races to the Rescue: A Fold-out Track Book*; on p.185 and p.196, *Thomas the Tank Engine: The Complete Collection* by The Rev. W. Awdry; on p.185, *Thomas and Friends Activity Sticker Pad*; on p.295, *The Velveteen Rabbit* by Margery Williams, illustrated by William Nicholson; on p.300, *Winnie-the-Pooh* by A.A. Milne, illustrated by E.H. Shepard.

FRANCES LINCOLN CHILDREN'S BOOKS for permission to reproduce the illustration that appears on p.17 from *Chimp and Zee* by Laurence and Catherine Anholt, illustration copyright © Catherine Anholt 2001. Additional thanks for permission to reproduce the following covers: on p.126, *Amazing Grace* by Mary Hoffman and Caroline Binch; on p.39, *Chidi Only Likes Blue* by Ifeoma Onyefulu; on p.86, *The Colour of Home* by Mary Hoffman, illustrated by Karin Littlewood; on p.227, *Dogs' Night* by Meredith Hooper, illustrated by Allan Curless and Mark Burgess; on p.128, *I is for India* by Prodeepta Das; on p.118, *Jamela's Dress* by Niki Daly; on p.119, *Jinnie Ghost* by Berlie Doherty, illustrated by Jane Ray; on p.38, *Lemons Are Not Red* by Laura Vaccaro Seeger; on p.125, *Tim All Alone* and *Tim to the Lighthouse* in the **Little Tim** series by Edward Ardizzone; on p.128, *Long-Long's New Year* by Catherine Gower, illustrated by He Zhihong; on p.129, *Looking After Louis* by Lesley Ely, illustrated by Polly Dunbar; on p.128, *The Most Magnificent Mosque* by Ann Jungman and Shelley Fowles; on p.132, *Mariana and the Merchild* by Caroline Pitcher, illustrated by Jackie Morris; on p.143, *Next!*

by Christopher Inns; on p.40, *Out for the Count* by Kathryn Cave and Chris Riddell; on p.162, *Rainbow Bird* by Eric Maddern, illustrated by Adrienne Kennaway; on p.170, *Sing Me a Story* by Grace Hallworth, illustrated by John Clementson; on p.154, *Yuck!* by Mick Manning and Brita Granström.

FRANKLIN WATTS LTD for permission to reproduce the cover of *Is the Blue Whale the Biggest Thing There Is?* by Robert E. Wells, on p.248.

GULLANE CHILDREN'S BOOKS for permission to reproduce the cover of *Sometimes I Like to Curl Up in a Ball* by Vicki Churchill, illustrated by Charles Fuge, which appears on p.174.

HARPERCOLLINS PUBLISHERS LTD for permission to reproduce the illustration on p.138 from *Mog the Forgetful Cat* by Judith Kerr © 1970 Judith Kerr and on p.203 from *Paddington Bear* by Michael Bond © 1998, 2005 Michael Bond. Additional thanks for permission to reproduce the following covers: on p.198, *The Brambly Hedge Collection* by Jill Barklem © 2005; on p.77, *Busiest People Ever* by Richard Scarry © 1976, 2005 Richard Scarry; on p.80, *Cars, Trucks and Things That Go* by Richard Scarry © 1974, 2001 Richard Scarry; on p.81, *The Cat in the Hat* Dr Seuss Properties™ © 1957, Dr Seuss Enterprises, L.P. All rights reserved; on p.220, *The Dancing Bear* by Michael Morpurgo, illustrated by Christian Birmingham © 2003 Michael Morpurgo, Christian Birmingham; on p.114, *How to Catch a Star* by Oliver Jeffers © 2004 Oliver Jeffers; on p.117, *I Love You, Blue Kangaroo!* by Emma Chichester Clark © 1998 Emma Chicester Clark; on p.47, *In Wibbly Pig's Garden* by Mick Inkpen; on p.297, *Josie Smith at the Seaside* by Magdalen Nabb, illustrated by Pirkko Vanio © 2000 Magdalen Nabb, Pirkko Vanio; on p.257,

Little Wolf's Book of Badness in the **Little Wolf** series by Ian Whybrow, illustrated by Tony Ross © 1996 Ian Whybrow, Tony Ross; on p.129, Lost and Found by Oliver Jeffers © 2005 Oliver Jeffers; on p.37, Melrose and Croc by Emma Chichester Clark © 2005 Emma Chichester Clark; on p.149, On a Tall, Tall Cliff by Andrew Murray, illustrated by Alan Snow © 2004, 2005 Andrew Murray, Alan Snow; on p.142, My Grandmother's Clock by Geraldine McCaughrean, illustrated by Stephen Lambert © 2002, 2003 Geraldine McCaughrean, Stephen Lambert; on p.276, Paddington Bear by Michael Bond © 1998, 2005 Michael Bond; on p.157, Everybody's Friend Percy and Percy's Friends the Rabbits in the **Percy the Park Keeper** series by Nick Butterworth © 2001, 2002 Nick Butterworth; on p.165, Russell the Sheep by Rob Scotton © 2005 Rob Scotton; on p.54, Tiger by Nick Butterworth © 2006 Nick Butterworth; on p.186, The Tiger Who Came to Tea by Judith Kerr © 1968 Judith Kerr; on p.192, The Whisperer by Nick Butterworth © 2004 Nick Butterworth; on p.200, Yertle the Turtle and Other Stories Dr Seuss Properties™ © 1950, 1951, 1958, renewed 1977, 1979, 1986 CAT - © 1957, Dr Seuss Enterprises, L.P. All rights reserved.

HODDER AND STOUGHTON LIMITED for permission to reproduce the spread that appears on p.291 from The Story of Everything by Neal Layton, and the illustration from Kipper by Mick Inkpen that appears on p.9. Additional thanks for permission to reproduce the following covers: on p.72, Bear by Mick Inkpen; on p.58, Felicity Wishes Pop-up Fairy House by Emma Thomson; on p.229, Perfect Polly in the **Felicity Wishes** series by Emma Thomson; on p.115, The Huge Bag of Worries by Virginia Ironside, illustrated by Frank Rodgers; on p.99 and p.121,

Kipper's A to Z by Mick Inkpen; on p.150, One More Sheep by Mij Kelly, illustrated by Russell Ayto.

JACKIE MORRIS for permission to reproduce the cover of How the Whale Became and Other Stories by Ted Hughes, illustrated by Jackie Morris, which appears on p.243.

JANE NISSEN BOOKS for permission to reproduce the cover of Clever Polly and the Stupid Wolf by Catherine Storr, illustrated by Marjorie Ann Watts, which appears on p.218.

KINGFISHER for permission to reproduce the following covers: on p.155, Amazing Machines: Cool Cars; on p.204, Adventures of the Little Wooden Horse. Both published by Kingfisher Publications Plc, all rights reserved.

LITTLE, BROWN AND COMPANY for permission to reproduce the cover of When Dinosaurs Die by Laurie Kransy Brown and Marc Brown, which appears on p.287.

LITTLE TIGER PRESS for permission to reproduce the inside spread that appears on p.101 from The Fantastic Mr Wani by Kanako Usui. Additional thanks for permission to reproduce the following covers: on p.68, Augustus and His Smile by Catherine Rayner; on p.29, Happy Dog Sad Dog and Whose Tail? by Sam Lloyd; on p.35, Little Fish by Guido van Genechten; on p.53, Ten Wriggly Wiggly Caterpillars by Debbie Tarbett; on p.144, Nobody Laughs at a Lion by Paul Bright, illustrated by Matt Buckingham.

MACMILLAN CHILDREN'S BOOKS for permission to reproduce the inside spread that appears on p.108 from The Gruffalo by Julia Donaldson, illustrated by Axel Scheffler, and the inside spread that appears on p.200 from The Emperor of Absurdia by Chris Riddell. Additional thanks for permission to reproduce the following covers: on p.213, Blobheads and Blobheads Go

Boing! in the **Blobheads** series by Paul Stewart, illustrated by Chris Riddell; on p.18, Fish and Ladybird and on p.18 and p.57, Butterfly in the **Clackety-Clacks** series by Luana Rinaldo; on p.219, Cosmo and the Magic Sneeze by Gwyneth Rees; on p.20 and p.57, Dear Zoo by Rod Campbell; on p.28, Goodnight Moon by Margaret Wise Brown, illustrated by Clement Hurd; on p.108, The Gruffalo by Julia Donaldson, illustrated by Axel Scheffler; on p.261, Meerkat Mail by Emily Gravett; on p.41, Mother Goose's Nursery Rhymes illustrated by Axel Scheffler, with additional stories by Alison Green; on p.44, Orange Pear Apple Bear by Emily Gravett; on p.156, Peace at Last by Jill Murphy; on p.46, Poppy Cat's Happy Day by Lara Jones; on p.163, Room on the Broom by Julia Donaldson, illustrated by Axel Scheffler; on p.85, The Smartest Giant in Town by Julia Donaldson, illustrated by Axel Scheffler; on p.195, Wolves by Emily Gravett.

MANTRA LINGUA for permission to reproduce the following covers: on p.182, The Elves and the Shoemaker by Henriette Barkow, illustrated by Jago; on p.182, Little Red Hen and the Grains of Wheat by Leign Ann Hill; on p.183, Journey Through Islamic Art by Na'ima Bint Robert, illustrated by Diana Mayo.

MERCIS PUBLISHING for permission to reproduce the illustration from Miffy by Dick Bruna, on p.37.

MIKE JUBB for permission to reproduce 'Ho Ho Ho: A Tonic for the Chronically Phonic', which appears on p.209.

MILET for permission to reproduce the following covers: on p.183, Chameleon Races (English-Chinese), written and illustrated by Laura Hambleton, Chinese translation by Hong Dai, © Laura Hambleton 2005 © Milet Publishing 2005; on p.168, Pink Lemon, written and illustrated by Hervé

PENGUIN GROUP (USA) INC for permission to reproduce the following covers: on p.130, *Madeline* and *Madeline in London* by Ludwig Bemelmans; on p.190, *The Whales' Song* by Dyan Sheldon, illustrated by Gary Blythe.

PHAIDON PRESS LTD for permission to reproduce the cover of *Nicholas* by René Goscinny, illustrated by Jean-Jacques Sempé, on p.273.

THE RANDOM HOUSE GROUP LTD for permission to reproduce the following inside spreads: on p.84, from *Mr Magnolia* by Quentin Blake; on p.50, from *Rosie's Walk* by Pat Hutchins; on p.62, from *Where the Wild Things Are* by Maurice Sendak. Additional thanks for permission to reproduce the following covers: on p.98, *Alfie Gets in First* by Shirley Hughes; on p.15, *Bing: Get Dressed* by Ted Dewan; on p.75, *Bob Robber and Dancing Jane* by Andrew Matthews, illustrated by Bee Willey; on p.83 and p.223 *Clown* by Quentin Blake; on p.93, *Dogger* by Shirley Hughes; on p.95, *Edwardo, The Horriblest Boy in the Whole Wide World* by John Burningham; on p.104, *George and the Dragon* by Chris Wormell; on p.197, *The Hutchinson Treasury of Children's Poetry*, collected by Alison Sage; on p.249, *Jack Stalwart: The Escape of the Deadly Dinosaur* by Elizabeth Singer Hunt; on p.256, *The Whispering Princess* in the **Little Princess** series by Katie Chase; on p.232, *Magic Mr Edison* by Andrew Melrose, illustrated by Katja Bandlow; on p.135, *Mr Magnolia* by Quentin Blake; on p.146, *Not Now, Bernard* by David McKee; on p.147, *Old Bear and Friends* and *Ruff* in the **Old Bear** series by Jane Hissey; on p.113, *Pass the Jam, Jim* by Kaye Umansky, illustrated by Margaret Chamberlain; on p.159, *The Fair Day Ball* and *Friends Together* in the **Princess Poppy** series by Janey Louise Jones; on p.160, *Pumpkin Soup* by Helen Cooper; on p.50

and p.85, *Rosie's Walk* by Pat Hutchins; on p.164, *The Runaway Train* by Benedict Blathwayt; on p.171, *Slow Loris* by Alexis Deacon; on p.177, *Susan Laughs* by Jeanne Willis, illustrated by Tony Ross; on p.179, *Tanka Tanka Skunk!* by Steve Webb; on p.294, *The Troublesome Tooth Fairy* by Sandi Toksvig, illustrated by Georgina Overwater; on p.188, *The Very Small* by Joyce Dunbar, illustrated by Debi Gliori; on p.113, *Traction Man* by Mini Grey; on p.191, *When Sheep Cannot Sleep: The Counting Book* by Satoshi Kitamura; on p.22 and p.62, *Where the Wild Things Are* by Maurice Sendak; on p.299, *Whizziwig* by Malorie Blackman.

ROUTLEDGE CLASSICS for permission to reproduce Edward Lear's *A Book of Nonsense*, which appears on p.279. Published by Routledge. Designer: Keenan at Keenan Design.

SCHOLASTIC LIMITED for permission to reproduce the following covers: on p.216, *The Adventures of Captain Underpants* by Dav Pilkey © 1999 Dav Pilkey; on p.205, *Airy Fairy: Magic Mix Up!* by Margaret Ryan, illustrated by Teresa Murfin © 2005 Teresa Murfin; on p.11, *Baby Einstein: Neighbourhood Animals* by The Baby Einstein Company, LCC © 2003; on p.11, *Baby Einstein: See and Spy Counting* by The Baby Einstein Company, LCC © 2001; on p.232, *Creepy Crawlies: The Talent Contest* by Damon Burnard © 2004 Damon Burnard.

SIMON AND SCHUSTER CHILDREN'S BOOKS for permission to reproduce the following covers: on p.207, *Alice's Adventures in Wonderland* by Lewis Carroll and Robert Sabuda; on p.90, *The Dancing Tiger* by Malachy Doyle, illustrated by Steve Johnson and Lou Fancher; on p.106, *Gilbert the Great* by Jane Clarke, illustrated by Charles Fuge; on p.253, *Littlenose the Hunter* by John Grant, illustrated by Ross

Collins; on p.148, *Olivia* by Ian Falconer; *Yuck's Fart Club* in the **Yuck** series by Matt and Dave, which appears on p.297.

STRIPES PUBLISHING for permission to reproduce the following covers: on p.240, *Chloe and Cracker* in the **Pony Camp Diaries** series by Kelly McKain; on p.225, *Fleas!* and *Pants!* in the **Dirty Bertie** series by Alan MacDonald, illustrated by David Roberts. All titles published by Stripes Publishing, an imprint of Magi Publications.

TAMARIND LIMITED for permission to reproduce the following covers: on p.126, *Baby Goes* by Verna Wilkins, illustrated by Derek Brazell; on p.91, *Dave and the Tooth Fairy* by Verna Wilkins, illustrated by Paul Hunt.

TEMPLAR PUBLISHING for permission to reproduce the following covers: on p.10, **Amazing Baby**®: *Hide and Seek!*; on p.131, *Man on the Moon* by Simon Bartram; on p.190, *What Pet to Get?* by Emma Dodd.

TREEHOUSE CHILDREN'S BOOKS for permission to reproduce the following covers: *Miaow!* and *Grrrr!* by Steve Cox and Richard Powell, which appear on p.56. Reproduced courtesy of Treehouse Children's Books.

USBORNE PUBLISHING LTD for permission to reproduce the following covers: on p.233, *The Amazing Adventures of Hercules* Copyright © 1982, 2004, 2007 Usborne Publishing Ltd; on p.71, *First Thousand Words in English* Copyright © 1996, 2003 Usborne Publishing Ltd; on p.71, *First Thousand Words in French* Copyright © 1979, 1995, 2002 Usborne Publishing Ltd; on p.140, **Usborne First Experiences** series: *Going on a Plane* Copyright © 2005 Usborne Publishing Ltd; on p.140, **Usborne First Experiences** series: *Going to the Hospital* Copyright © 2005 Usborne Publishing Ltd; on p.140, **Usborne First Experiences** series: *Going to School* Copyright © 2005 Usborne Publishing Ltd; on p.297, *Princess Ellie to the Rescue* Copyright © 2004 Usborne Publishing Ltd; on p.233, *Stories of Giants* Copyright © 2003 Usborne Publishing Ltd. All titles published by permission of Usborne Publishing, 83–85 Saffron Hill, London, EC1N 8RT, UK. www.usborne.com.

WALKER BOOKS LTD for permission to reproduce the following spreads: on p.33, illustration © 2000 Jez Alborough from *Hug* by Jez Alborough; on p.298, illustration © 1988, 1994, 1997 Martin Handford from *Where's Wally Now?* by Martin Handford. Additional thanks for permission to reproduce the following covers: on p.196, cover illustration © 1999 Helen Oxenbury from *Alice in Wonderland* by Lewis Carroll, illustrated by Helen Oxenbury; on p.69, cover illustration © 2004 Simon James from *Baby Brains* by Simon James; on p.73, cover illustration © 2004 Clare Jarrett from *The Best Picnic Ever* by Clare Jarrett; on p.76, cover illustration © 2004 Bruce Ingman from *Boing!* by Sean Taylor, illustrated by Bruce Ingman; on p.74, cover illustration © 1997 Nick Maland from *Big Blue Whale* by Nicola Davies, illustrated by Nick Maland; on p.78, cover illustration © 1988, 2005 Barbara Firth from *Can't You Sleep, Little Bear?* by Martin Waddell, illustrated by Barbara Firth; on p.88, cover illustration © 1998 Katharine McEwen from *Cows in the Kitchen* by June Crebbin, illustrated by Katharine McEwen; on p.89, cover illustration © 2003 Houghton Mifflin Company from *Curious George Visits a Toy Shop* by Margret and H.A. Rey; on p.89, cover illustration © 2002 Houghton Mifflin Company from *Curious George and the Birthday Surprise* by Margret and H.A. Rey; on p.198, cover illustration © 2007 Robert Sabuda

and Matthew Reinhart from *Encyclopedia Prehistorica: Mega Beasts* by Robert Sabuda and Matthew Reinhart; on p.271, cover illustration © 2000 Jane Ray from *Fairy Tales* by Berlie Doherty and Jane Ray; on p.112, cover illustration © 1986 Jill Murphy from *Five Minutes' Peace* by Jill Murphy; on p.32, cover illustration © 2005 Petr Horáček from *Flutter By, Butterfly* by Petr Horáček; on p.109, cover illustration © 1994 Anita Jeram from *Guess How Much I Love You* by Sam McBratney, illustrated by Anita Jeram; on p.56, cover illustration © Jan Pieńkowski from *Haunted House* by Jan Pieńkowski; on p.250, cover illustration and Judy Moody font © 2000 Peter Reynolds from *Judy Moody* by Megan McDonald, illustrated by Peter Reynolds; on p.122, cover illustration © Sarah Fox-Davies from *Little Beaver and the Echo* by Amy MacDonald, illustrated by Sarah Fox-Davies; on p.36, cover illustration and Lucy Cousins font © 1999 Lucy Cousins from *Where is Maisy?* by Lucy Cousins; on p.260, cover illustration © 2000 Marcia Williams from *Marcia Williams' Comic Strips: Bravo, Mr. William Shakespeare!* by Marcia Williams; on p.30, cover illustration © Michael Foreman 1991 from *Mother Goose* illustrated by Michael Foreman; on p.274, cover illustration © 2003 Terry Milne from *The Night of the Unicorn* by Jenny Nimmo, illustrated by Terry Milne; on p.43, cover illustration © 1998 Jane Chapman from *One Duck Stuck* by Phyllis Root, illustrated by Jane Chapman; on p.274, cover illustration © 1997, 2007 Anthony Lewis from *The Owl Tree* by Jenny Nimmo, illustrated by Anthony Lewis; on p.158, cover illustration © 2005 Colin McNaughton from *Potty Poo-Poo Wee-Wee!* by Colin McNaughton; on p.32, cover illustration © 2005 Petr Horáček from *Run, Mouse, Run!* by Petr

Horáček; on p.51, cover illustration © 2006 Petr Horáček from *Silly Suzy Goose* by Petr Horáček; on p.175, cover illustration © 1994 Helen Oxenbury from *So Much* by Trish Cooke, illustrated by Helen Oxenbury; on p.52, cover illustration © 2003 Jez Alborough from *Some Dogs Do* by Jez Alborough, on p.39, cover illustration © 1998, 2005 Penny Dale from *Ten in the Bed* by Penny Dale; on p.154, cover illustration © 1993 Mike Bostock from *Think of an Eel* by Karen Wallace; on p.184, cover illustration © 1986 Helen Craig from *This is the Bear* by Sarah Hayes, illustrated by Helen Craig; on p.223, cover illustration © 2002 Cathie Felstead from *Under the Moon and Over the Sea* edited by John Agard and Grace Nichols, illustrated by Cathie Felstead; on p.60, cover illustration © 1993 Julie Lacome from *Walking Through the Jungle* by Julie Lacome; on p.23 and p.189, cover illustration © 1989 Helen Oxenbury from *We're Going on a Bear Hunt* by Michael Rosen, illustrated by Helen Oxenbury; on p.61, cover illustration © 2003 Petr Horáček from *What is Black and White?* by Petr Horáček; on p.199, cover illustration © 2003 Katharine McEwen from *Woolly Jumper* by Meredith Hooper, illustrated by Katharine McEwen; on p.233 and p.301, cover illustration © 2002 Katharine McEwen from *The Woman Who Won Things* by Allan Ahlberg, illustrated by Katharine McEwen; on p.201, cover illustration © 1994, 1999 Axel Scheffler from *You're a Hero Daley B!* by Jon Blake, illustrated by Axel Scheffler.

All efforts have been made to seek permission for copyright material, but in the event of any omissioins, the publisher would be pleased to hear from copyright holders and to amend these acknowledgements in subsequent editions of *The Ultimate First Book Guide*.

INDEX